Dr Daniel Baldino is the Head of Politics and International Relations at the University of Notre Dame, Fremantle. He is a political scientist, specialising in Critical Security Studies, US National Security Strategy, Australian Foreign Policy and Terrorism/Counter-Terrorism. His latest book is the co-edited *Contemporary Challenges to Australian Security* (2012). Previously he has been a Research Associate at the Library of Congress, Washington, DC and a visiting scholar at the Security and Governance Program, East-West Center, Hawaii.

The truth about intelligence in Australia

SPOOKED

EDITED BY
DANIEL BALDINO

NEWSOUTH

A NewSouth book

Published by
NewSouth Publishing
University of New South Wales Press Ltd
University of New South Wales
Sydney NSW 2052
AUSTRALIA
newsouthpublishing.com

© University of New South Wales Press Ltd 2013
First published 2013

10 9 8 7 6 5 4 3 2 1

National Library of Australia Cataloguing-in-Publication entry
Title: Spooked: The truth about intelligence in Australia/edited by
Daniel Baldino.
ISBN: 9781742233888 (paperback)
      9781742241630 (ePub/Kindle)
      9781742246642 (ePDF)
Subjects: Australian Security Intelligence Organisation.
      War on Terrorism, 2001–2009.
      Intelligence service – Australia.
      Secret service – Australia.
      National security – Australia.
      Espionage – Australia.
      Spies – Australia.
Dewey Number: 327.1294

Design Josephine Pajor-Markus
Cover design Xou Creative
Cover images Thinkstock
Printer Griffin

CONTENTS

CONTRIBUTORS

DR ANNE ALY is an Early Career Research Fellow at Curtin University. She has a professional background in policy, having worked as a Senior Policy Officer and Manager within the Western Australian Government. Anne has published widely on diverse issues including Muslim identity, Muslim media activism, terrorism and the Internet, the terrorism discourse, and counter-terrorism responses. She is the author of *Terrorism and Global Security: Historical and Contemporary Approaches* (2011).

DR DANIEL BALDINO is the Head of Politics and International Relations at the University of Notre Dame, Fremantle. He is a political scientist, specialising in Critical Security Studies, US National Security Strategy, Australian Foreign Policy and Terrorism/Counter-Terrorism. His latest book is the co-edited *Contemporary Challenges to Australian Security* (2012). Previously he has been a Research Associate at the Library of Congress, Washington, DC and a visiting scholar at the Security and Governance Program, East-West Center, Hawaii.

DR JESSIE BLACKBOURN is a Postdoctoral Research Fellow on the Australian Research Council Laureate Fellowship 'Anti-Terror Laws and the Democratic Challenge' in the Gilbert + Tobin Centre of Public Law at the University of New South Wales. She has published articles in a number of journals including *Parliamentary Affairs*, *Statute Law Review*, *Journal of Commonwealth*

Criminal Law and *Terrorism and Political Violence*. Her current research focuses on the post-enactment review of anti-terrorism laws in Australia, Canada and the United Kingdom.

DR CINDY DAVIDS is Associate Professor in the School of Law at Deakin University, Melbourne. She is the author of *Conflict of Interest in Policing: Problems, Practices, and Principles* (2008). Her current research focuses on financial crime, bribery of foreign officials, and international policing and law enforcement, particularly in the Pacific region.

DR ROBERT IMRE is a Senior Lecturer at the University of Newcastle. He has an interdisciplinary background in a number of academic fields. Connecting his research is a concern with the manner in which people interact with their governments. This includes studies of and research into diverse areas such as terrorist movements, comparative education systems, and the use of social media by governments, both in election campaigns and in policy controversies.

PROFESSOR PETER LEAHY is the Director of the National Security Institute at the University of Canberra. He was Chief of the Australian Army from 2002 to 2008 and was a high-level consumer of intelligence from 1997, when he commanded Australia's Ready Deployment Force, until his retirement from the Army in 2008 at the rank of Lieutenant General in the appointment of Chief of Army.

PROFESSOR JUDE MCCULLOCH is Professor of Criminology at Monash University. Her research focuses on state terror, state violence and state crime. She has published more than fifty chapters and journal articles and three books, edited special editions of journals and written for major newspapers and magazines. Her research and publishing spans police shootings, counter-terrorism laws and policing, deaths in custody, (in)security, pre-crime, and the violence of incarceration. Her major contribution has been to describe, analyse and theorise the growing integration of national security and the police and military under conditions of neo-liberal globalisation. Her latest books are *State Crime and Resistance* (Elizabeth Stanely and Jude McCulloch, eds) and *Borders and Crime* (Jude McCulloch and Sharon Pickering, eds).

DR CHRISTOPHER MICHAELSEN is a Senior Lecturer at the Faculty of Law at the University of New South Wales, and a member of the Australian Human Rights Centre. He teaches and specialises in public international law, human rights and international security. Prior to joining UNSW, he served as a Human Rights Officer (Anti-Terrorism) at the Office for Democratic Institutions and Human Rights (ODIHR) of the Organization for Security and Cooperation in Europe (OSCE) in Warsaw, Poland.

MICHAEL MORI is a retired Lieutenant Colonel in the US Marine Corps, in which he has served as a prosecutor, defence counsel and military judge. He is a Senior Fellow with the Melbourne School of Law Masters Program. Michael is the author of a book with the working title 'In the Company of Cowards', a forthcoming non-fiction work covering his time as defence counsel for a Guantanamo Bay detainee before the US Department of Defense's military commissions.

Dr Mark Rix is a Senior Lecturer in the University of Wollongong's Sydney Business School, where he teaches corporate governance and human resource management. His research interests include the role of public interest litigation in bringing about progressive social change, human rights and the rule of law, and counter-terrorism in liberal democracies like Australia.

Dr Ben Saul is Professor of International Law at the Sydney Centre for International Law at The University of Sydney, and a barrister. Ben is internationally recognised for his work on terrorism, human rights, the law of armed conflict and international criminal law, and his research has been cited in various international and national courts. He has published nine books, over seventy refereed journal articles and book chapters, and over 150 other publications, and delivered hundreds of public seminars.

Dilan Thampapillai is a Lecturer in the School of Law at Deakin University. He researches on free speech, international law and intellectual property law.

David Vakalis is a Masters candidate in Monash University's Department of Criminology. His thesis is on moral panic and South Australia's 2008 'anti-bikie' laws. David's other research interests include state and corporate crime, deviance, social control, transnational organised crime, 'counter-terrorism' policing, and social movements.

ACRONYMS

ADF	Australian Defence Force
AFP	Australian Federal Police
AIC	Australian intelligence community
ALRC	Australian Law Reform Commission
ASIO	Australian Security Intelligence Organisation
ASIS	Australian Secret Intelligence Service
ASTJIC	Australian Theatre Joint Intelligence Centre (Note: now JOIC)
BW	Biological warfare
CDF	Chief of the Defence Force
CIA	Central Intelligence Agency
COAG	Council of Australian Governments
CW	Chemical warfare
DFAT	Department of Foreign Affairs and Trade
DIGO	Defence Imagery and Geospatial Organisation
DIO	Defence Intelligence Organisation
DSD	Defence Signals Directorate
FOI Act	*Freedom of Information Act* 1982
Humint	Human intelligence
IGIS	Inspector-General of Intelligence and Security
IRA	Irish Republican Army
JI	Jemaah Islamiyah
JOIC	Joint Operations Intelligence Centre

NSA (US)	National Security Agency
NATO	North Atlantic Treaty Organisation
NSC	National Security Committee of Cabinet
ONA	Office of National Assessments
PJCAAD	Parliamentary Joint Committee on ASIO, ASIS and DSD
PJCIS	Parliamentary Joint Committee on Intelligence and Security
Sigint	Signals intelligence
UKUSA	Agreement governing Sigint relationship between the UK, US, Australia, Canada and New Zealand
UNMOVIC	United Nations Monitoring, Verification and Inspection Commission
UNSCOM	United Nations Special Commission
WMD	Weapons of mass destruction

INTRODUCTION: THE OTHER WORLD

Daniel Baldino

> One who knows the enemy and knows
> himself will not be endangered in a
> hundred engagements. One who does
> not know the enemy but knows himself
> will sometimes be victorious, sometimes
> meet with defeat. One who knows neither
> the enemy nor himself will invariably be
> defeated in every engagement.
>
> *Sun Tzu, 'The Art of War'*

Successfully managing threats like terrorism not only requires knowing your enemy. As renowned Chinese military strategist Sun Tzu emphasises, it also demands an understanding of the motivations for one's own behaviour.

Direct, truthful self-assessment requires, in part, brutal honesty, a degree of self-discipline, critical reflection and a preparedness to acknowledge uncomfortable facts. It might entail questioning popular ideas about dark-skinned, bearded terrorists and their way of thinking. Or querying Australia's track record of blind loyalty to the hegemonic power of the US. It

1

might recognise that some vulnerabilities are inevitable; that intelligence officers are not seers and that intelligence estimates must help inform political decisions – and not vice versa. It might caution that we need to resist the hyperbole about a boundless 'global war on terror' created by self-interested parties. It might acknowledge that the political guarantee of complete security is unattainable. Terrorism is a tactic, and cannot be 'defeated' – although terrorist threats can certainly be mitigated and intelligence collection and analysis should always strive for improvement. And while specific groups like Al-Qaeda can be tracked and dismantled, diminishing the appeal of their extremist ideas will move into a longer-term 'winning hearts and minds' strategy.

In addition, we need to talk more candidly about resilience and recovery – how societies will, or should, maintain social normality and a lucid rationale in response to whatever fallout might be the consequence of contemporary security challenges. Compounding such complexities, the world of terrorism, security and counter-intelligence tests ethical boundaries, can fall prey to mistruths and exaggeration and does generate widespread rumour, scepticism and paranoia. So in reallocating resources and remodelling capabilities in the search for safety from newfangled monsters, are we reliant on repeated, demonstrable truths and common sense solutions, or are we disoriented by fear and seduced by propaganda, political stage shows, bar-room gossip, science fiction premises, conspiracy theories and Hollywood movie scripts?

The latest James Bond film *Skyfall* is a case in point. *Skyfall* was about assaults on computer systems and the manipulation of technology to endanger human lives. A former British operative, Raoul Silva, had turned into a demented cyber-terrorist. He sets out to exploit existing system weaknesses by hacking intelligence systems, stealing data and blowing up MI6 headquarters. He aims to command and disrupt critical infrastructure and sensitive information flows in the United Kingdom and beyond. The 21st-century redefinition of a cutting-edge global threat is neatly repackaged as an avalanche of dangerous cyber-attacks and destabilising cyber-intrusions. But while this is a frightening scenario, how likely is this type of event to materialise beyond the silver screen? Similarly, in the popular television drama *24*, torture ('enhanced interrogation') to fight terrorism is repeatedly shown to be more effective than other methods in extracting valuable information. But how does this relate to, or translate into, valid actions to deal with real-life terrorism?

Or, switching to recent national security dramas, incidents like 9/11, the Bali bombings and the attacks at the Boston Marathon have all sparked recriminations about how intelligence and investigation have failed to meet the onslaught of well-planned terror threats. As a result, we witness renewed calls for expanded state secrecy, boosted executive powers and full-blown security escalations that usually sit alongside the erosion of traditional legal and political rights – a perennial means-justifies-ends philosophy. Media explanations of tragic events tend towards state-of-emergency speculations that highlight the many potential pathways to death, decay and harm. Thugs, misfits and criminals are elevated into insane holy warriors with a supervillain status, who pose an existential threat. Other ideas that tend to recirculate and hold popular sway include the assumption that asylum seekers arriving by boat might be terrorists; that we are facing an inevitable 'clash of civilisations', with the West against the rest; that secrecy and behind-the-scenes exchanges remain critical to ensure victory; that long-distance drone attacks are efficient and a basic step in maintaining the upper hand against hostile enemies; that organisations like ASIO are out of control; that Julian Assange is a digital devil (or hero); and that every bored 15-year-old nerd with a laptop is a budding national security hazard.

But again, do such propositions or characterisations bear any resemblance to present-day reality? Are contemporary controversies represented and assessed in an upfront, nuanced and level-headed manner? Or do we lend our energies to 'quick-fix' solutions that may actually create more harm than good? It is critical that we base our opinions and projections on analysis and evidence rather than anxiety and unsubstantiated assertions. Of course, increased levels of secrecy, misinformation and dubious leadership activities in the name of security will continue to generate inaccurate reports, erode trust and create mixed messages. In turn, policymakers and other self-interested parties are capable of both driving and exploiting public ignorance and uncertainty about unknown or imminent dangers.

Human imagination is a fertile but misleading tool in assessing real-life dangers and judging the likelihood of impending risks. The 9/11 commission once famously stated that the tragedy was due, in part, to 'a failure of imagination'. But historical experience also warns of blind spots and shortfalls based on an over-fixation on rhetorical rather than real threats. Part of the problem is that we base the metrics for 'success' on films and fiction. We overstep in dealing with tragedy. We are prone to fits of panic. We try to fight fleas with sledgehammers. We tend to embrace a siege mentality. We are seduced by conspiracy theories. We are entirely reactionary in efforts to prevent the last threat rather than taking positive steps to mitigate or contain existing threats. We have a tendency to focus on improbable, far-removed or hypothetical – albeit spectacular – hazards, like 'cyber-9/11s', while underplaying or ignoring the consequences of immediate and steady challenges to human security like climate change, disease, poverty and energy shortages.

In 2013, the program *Q&A* had Microsoft founder Bill Gates as a guest. The host, Tony Jones, asked Gates if he was concerned about a gloomy future based on technology-generated forms of peril that will endanger people's lives.

> TONY JONES: Including warfare … and indeed we have drones already, these robots flying over different countries, assassinating people. The future, according to futurologists who look at robotics, could be of tiny swarms, insect-size drones, able to infiltrate people's houses and kill them. And do you think about the future? Do you think about these kind of things, how it might look?

> BILL GATES: Well, today we have real insects invading people's homes. It's called malaria and it actually does kill people. So I have a strange obsession with the present.

The above exchange neatly captures a multifaceted psychological and cultural phenomenon – that fears about unknown or random threats and imaginary nightmare conditions appear to easily swamp other types of dangers that are rooted in present realities and remain more likely risks.

Group-think is a factor in the production of fears that distort our perception. The pull towards an ugly nationalism might be another. So might the direct consequences of political scare-mongering coupled with glib media coverage about the changing nature of security, power and identity. Adding to the mix is the fact that terrorism and intelligence are entrenched in official secrecy. Traditionally, spy agencies have been inclined to operate behind closed doors. Many security operations remain covert. Discussion is classified. The instinct is a straightforward need-to-know positioning. Although it is acknowledged that some level of secrecy might be required (intelligence, for example, can be grounded in highly confidential sources), the inherent trade-off is the breeding of public mistrust, confusion, frustration and suspicion when people attempt to evaluate the next generation of real and serious threats.

So beyond debate over the identification and prioritisation of threats, the closed nature of security management translates into indistinct commentary about holes in our defences – life-and-death situations that 'might or will happen'. This list of multiple, ambiguous threats can be very difficult for the average citizen to keep in perspective. Instead, we seem to be stuck with a mechanical state of striking out in a militarised manner and then hoping hard-line antidotes will obliterate our problems. And in regard to resolutions like torture or detention, the more out of mind and out of sight the better. Simultaneously, it is rare that a leader appears willing to stick their neck out to declare that something is broken, or perhaps foolish, in the defence and security realm. The go-to position is a Hulk-like smash – to talk in heroic terms, champion tough-minded offensive engagement and advocate better surveillance and related measures until all dangers are evaporated and our foes lie blue and lifeless at our feet.

Certainly, after the tragic events of 9/11 the Western world, including Australia, has found itself increasingly worried and vulnerable to indistinct threats, including rogue agents, rogue scientists, failed states, cyber-warriors, mad mullahs, fugitive whistle-blowers and so-called 'boat people' ('plane people' are apparently okay). Again, fear and loathing appear to have played a significant role in shaping the urgent collective need for a more active and vigilant defence. We've talked about unconstrained military confrontation – a so-called 'war on terror', with no end in sight. As proof of our commitment and patriotism, we joined America's moral crusade against an incoming 'axis of evil' and were covered in blood and dust in locations like Afghanistan and Iraq while turning a blind eye to the use of CIA killer drones to act as judge, jury and executioner in places like Pakistan and Yemen.

Without doubt, the security community has a tough gig – 'Victory has a thousand fathers, but defeat is an orphan.' And unquestionably, the security sector was suddenly propelled back into the spotlight after 9/11. A well-executed (but extremely lucky) series of co-ordinated terrorist attacks destroyed the twin towers in New York, severely dented the Pentagon and murdered almost 3000 people. A group of 19 single-minded men – who had arrived in the United States primarily on tourist or business visas – had successfully hijacked four commercial jets and instantly transformed American, and global, threat perceptions and security preoccupations. Valid questions bubbled to the surface: were the terror attacks an intelligence failure? How did the US giant get blindsided by a small group of 'evildoers'?

At the very least, the terrorists responsible for the 9/11 attacks, and those who supported them, would not be able to run and hide from the United States and its allies. 'I don't care what the international lawyers say, we are going to kick some ass.' This quote is attributed to former US President George W. Bush. The world was divided into stark black and white – you were either 'with us or against us'. Led by Osama bin Laden, these violent enemies belonged to a loosely organised inter-national organisation called Al-Qaeda, which in Arabic means 'The Base'.

Bush wanted bin Laden, 'dead or alive'. A US$50 million bounty was placed on bin Laden's head. The United States would not be intimidated, nor would it be deterred. The White House promised the American people a pattern of relentless, sustained pressure on Al-Qaeda and its affiliates. Such policy imperatives and security initiatives were coloured by the poli-tics of protection and an instinct for retribution. A CIA official stated that 'I want bin Laden's head shipped back in a box filled with dry ice. I want to be able to show bin Laden's head to the president.' Bin Laden was shot in the head and killed in 2011 in a compound near Islamabad, Pakistan through a daring raid by US special forces.

This latest terror group has been elevated as a dire threat; an existential peril. The struggle was now seen as being between freedom and fanaticism; the terrorist agenda as born out of a blind hatred of the West. Inevitably, future targets would involve the slaughter of innocent civilian bystanders. By this reasoning, the launch of a 'war on terror' is justified as basic self-defence. New levels of warfare – coloured with jingoistic window-dress-ing – and spy craft insist that 'the gloves come off': the intro-duction of 'enhanced interrogation techniques'; the extension of executive branch powers; the expansion of secrecy provisions; the acceleration of government data-gathering efforts and the launch of 'preventative' wars to deal with 'rogue' regimes. US military strength would be pre-emptively applied in an increas-ingly borderless world. Concurrently, at a domestic level, citi-zens in democratic societies displayed a willingness to sacrifice age-old civil and political liberties and traditional safeguards for optimum protection, ironically, to preserve 'who we are' – a 'we had to destroy the village in order to save it' logic.

The classic folk story of Chicken Little – a hen who believes the sky is falling when something falls on its head – offers an important cautionary insight into today's culture of pervasive fear, reaction, illusion, negative stereotypes and secrets.

Open, democratic societies will always remain vulnerable to threats like asymmetric terrorism. The need for smart and cool-headed defence planning is obvious. But to what extent do modern-day citizens, politicians and the media play the role of Chicken Little? For instance, while the word 'terrorism' triggers a range of strong emotional reactions, and despite the horrors of 9/11, a lot more people will die annually from traffic accidents and lung disease than of terrorism. Maybe we should declare a bonus war on cars and cancer (although sending a drone after smokers might be unwarranted overkill).

The aim of this book is to encourage clear-eyed strategic thinking and provide some sound backdrop to multitudinous security challenges. Each chapter is evidence-based and committed to critical and investigative analysis – all contributors wish to shine a torch in murky corners and address ways of avoiding future missteps and mishaps. It is worth asking if the post-9/11 obsession with absolute security has gone too far. Many recent events – from state-sponsored assassination to Wikileaks to revelations about citizen monitoring via government spy programs – have raised peoples' awareness and doubts. At the very least, the reduction of fear, and some careful reflection on fashionable assumptions – such as the one that terror attacks might destroy our society – are central in managing complex security problems.

Inattention, half-truths and conjecture about terrorism and intelligence have serious costs, such as the feeding of public panic, the wasting of critical resources, the production of unrealistic expectations, and the creation of harmful, unworkable policy frameworks. Better appreciating the psychological, not just physical, dimensions of the 'war on terror' will remain crucial. Of course, some hope remains that political leaders are beginning to genuinely contemplate whether the security pendulum has swung too far. In mid-2013, US President Barack Obama declared in regard to fighting terrorism that 'unless we discipline our thinking, our definitions, our actions, we may be drawn into more wars we don't need to fight, or continue to grant Presidents unbound powers more suited for traditional armed conflicts between nation states.' But we still have a long way to go to reorient national security frameworks and detoxify an ingrained 'what if' threat narrative.

This book will explore some of the prevalent myths, misunderstandings and controversies about the intricate world of intelligence, security and threat perceptions: in order to defeat terrorism, we must no longer misstate or ignore facts and allow ourselves to be terrorised. It is hoped a look behind the curtains will allow people to think more laterally, rationally and analytically about future cultural and political choices. At the very least, any discussion of new or evolving threats must avoid inaccurate, panic-stricken and counterproductive tendencies to respond like Chicken Little and agonise that the sky is about to fall. Each chapter will highlight a popular idea, speculative report or fashionable assumption about modern-day security problems and the engagement of related 'spy games', and then act to provide a reality check.

Christopher Michaelsen, a specialist in the field of international security, asks how real and dangerous is the modern day threat of terrorism in Australia and how terrorism has been depicted by the Australian government, as well as examining the search to balance national security with democratic governance. The Australian government's account of the threat of terrorism has in many ways replicated the alarmist narrative created by the US White House, particular that under former US President George W. Bush. While 9/11 was an extreme event, Michaelsen concludes that although terrorism is portrayed as an unprecedented security crisis, Islamist terrorism does not constitute a threat of significant concern for Australia.

Anne Aly, one of Australia's foremost academics dealing with counter-terrorism, explores the reasoning behind the notion that Australia is a target for terrorists. She presents some of the most common theories explaining the root causes of terrorist violence, and why terrorists might target democratic nations like Australia. She points out that the notion that terrorists will target Australia because of a blind hatred of Western values is a highly unhelpful assertion – a myth – that has contributed to social divisions and misunderstandings about the root causes of terrorism, and leads to ineffective responses to the problem of terrorism.

Cindy Davids has worked extensively with police and the Office of the Ombudsman, exploring issues of professional ethics, regulation and accountability. Dilan Thampapillai, prior to becoming an academic, was a lawyer with the Attorney-General's Department and the Australian Government Solicitor. Together, Davids and Thampapillai debunk the myth of asylum seekers as a threat to the security of the nation. They argue that, for far too long, Australian politicians and elements of the media have played up the idea that asylum seekers represent a clear and present danger. This idea has found fertile ground in parts of the populace and has seeped into our national security laws. The 'threat' is a construction that has little basis in fact, but it has served to bolster the electoral stocks of politicians as they play on human fears about holes in security and a wariness of 'the other'. It becomes clear that a rethink of how asylum seekers are assessed from a security perspective, and how they are perceived in the general community, can provide a revival of the humanitarian concern that underlies the 1951 Refugee Convention.

I am a political scientist specialising in critical security studies, Australian foreign policy and counter-terrorism. In my chapter, I argue that the threat of cyber-terrorism is over-hyped. It can be argued that, despite alarmist predictions, many cyber-terrorism and other cyber-threat related stories are manageable and do not constitute a national security crisis. Political or media beat-ups about an emerging cyber-terror pandemic will lead to persistent public confusion, unnecessary economic burdens and heavy-handed legislative reactions which could end up damaging the very thing we are fighting for: our democratic way of life, including the protection of privacy rights, access to information and online freedom.

Former US military lawyer and human rights advocate Lieutenant Colonel Michael Mori, USMC (Ret) is the lawyer who defended Guantanamo detainee David Hicks. He explores a poorly kept secret – the use of routine drone strikes to kill terrorists or people believed to fit the patterns of terrorist behaviour. He addresses topics such as the ethics of assassination, the role of international law and the risk of civilian deaths – all central to the US drone strike program in far away locations like Pakistan, Yemen and Somalia. He argues that drone strikes are not only morally troubling but have a highly questionable legality and sharp political costs, and remain a grossly ineffective military option. The US track record in targeted killing is spotty, yet the executive branch of the US government continues to overreach. Worryingly, rules and guidelines for this shadow war remain unspecified and indistinct. Leaders and citizens need to make a better attempt to understand the risks, costs and strategic limitations of armed drone strikes.

The search for better security does not come cheap. Peter Leahy – who retired from the army in July 2008 year after a 37-year career as a soldier, having concluded his career with a six-year appointment as Chief of Army – explores whether bigger budgets equate to better intelligence. Since 9/11, a plethora of reviews and inquiries into who was responsible has catapulted the management and performance of the security sector into the forefront of public debate. So are Australian taxpayers today getting quality control and bang for their buck? Despite substantial and rapid increases in budgets for Australia's intelligence community since 9/11, many of which can be seen as justifiable, many challenges remain. And not all intelligence failings are due to basic resourcing issues.

Prior to working in universities, Professor Jude McCulloch worked as a lawyer for sixteen years, providing legal services to disadvantaged members of the community and developing legal policy at all levels. David Vakalis is currently a research assistant at Monash, and has been involved social justice movements for a number of years. Their chapter begins with a basic international law definition of torture and details of its prohibition under international law, then goes on to debunk the intelligence-related rationale for torture. They address a number of key myths central to contemporary arguments in favour of torture, relating to the extent of torture, the common victims of torture, the nature of torture and, finally and crucially, its effectiveness in generating meaningful intelligence. They argue that the idea of torture as a means to elicit timely, reliable information is a myth.

Mark Rix is an academic with a significant background in the fields of counter-terrorism, citizenship and human rights. His chapter investigates the use of secrecy as a weapon in the 'war on terror'. Rix questions whether preventing the public and the media from knowing much, if anything, about how ASIO fights this war actually protects Australia and makes Australians more secure from the threat of terrorism. By considering the legislation giving ASIO the 'special powers' of questioning and detention even of persons not suspected of having committed a terrorism offence, and which enables it to refuse disclosure of any information about its activities or of the nature and level of the terrorism threat faced by this country, the chapter seeks to provide an answer to the very serious question of whether and how much security there is in secrecy.

Ben Saul, who is a Professor of International Law at the University of Sydney and a barrister (including in the International Criminal Tribunal for the former Yugoslavia), interrogates some of the frequent legal claims circulating about WikiLeaks. His chapter first examines claims that WikiLeaks has broken the law, endangered security and risked lives, and in doing so shows how the law both goes too far and does too little in the name of security. The chapter also queries whether WikiLeaks has acted in the interests of human rights and freedom of information, and whether Assange is so threatened that he deserves asylum, or should face justice for abusing women. It concludes that the cases for and against WikiLeaks and Assange are both exaggerated, and that truth gets in the way of fantastic stories.

Jessie Blackbourn is a Postdoctoral Research Fellow on the Australian Research Council Laureate Fellowship whose areas of expertise include international terrorism and counter-terrorism legislation. She questions the notion that there has been no valid scrutiny of Australia's anti-terrorism laws, and shows that, while the process has not been perfect, Australia's anti-terrorism laws have been subjected to a number of different review processes, including by parliamentary committees, judge-led inquiries and panels of commissioners. The chapter assesses the successes and failures of those reviews against three criteria: whether the reviews have been comprehensive; whether they have been independent; and whether they have managed to shape the government's anti-terrorism agenda. Using the same criteria, the chapter then questions whether the establishment of an office of independent scrutiny in 2010, dedicated to the review of Australia's national security and anti-terrorism laws, has further increased accountability and the level of scrutiny that those laws receive.

Robert Imre has an interdisciplinary background in a number of academic fields. His research and teaching experience includes global terrorism and genocide studies. His chapter explores the build-up to the invasion of Iraq in 2003, and its aftermath, which has costs tens of thousands of lives. In particular, he addresses whether intelligence shaped policy or policy shaped intelligence – or both. Certainly, in the botched hunt for Iraq's alleged weapons of mass destruction stockpiles, the use of intelligence reports to support the war rationale led to the corrosion of public confidence in political leadership, democratic principles and the mission of intelligence. The WMD fiasco has engendered hostility around the world regarding the role of spies and the professionalism of intelligence analysts and agencies. The chapter highlights the fact that the interaction between the intelligence community and political decision-makers is too often oversimplified and is far from one-dimensional.

The manner in which the Australian community chooses to perceive and address each of the above issues, controversies and challenges has the potential to reduce future security breakdown, panic, mismanagement, misconduct and disappointment. These are not simple problems, straightforward dilemmas or easily digestible topics. But honest, evidence-based investigations of complexities – such as notions that the threat of Islamic terrorism is a central security concern for Australia – remain essential to delineate fact from fiction, to filter disinformation and to construct creditable, sustainable and effective national security platforms.

1

'ISLAMO-FASCISM' – THE SHAPE OF FUTURE CONFLICT?

Christopher Michaelsen

'Islamist Terrorism is one of our biggest security threats.'

HARDLY. The notion that Islamist terrorism constitutes one of the biggest security threats to Australia has been advanced by various Australian governments in the post-9/11 era. We have been told to prepare for a decades-long fight against ruthless, invisible enemies who hate our way of life and seek to destroy our society. As then Prime Minister John Howard said, '[T]hat attack of eleventh of September was as much an attack on Australia as it was on America. It not only killed Australians in the World Trade Centre, but it also assaulted the very values on which this nation is built.'[1] These and other views have been repeatedly advanced by Australian leaders. They can also be found in various policy documents such as the two counter-terrorism White Papers of 2004 and 2010 as well as in several reports to Parliament by Australia's domestic security agency, the Australian Security Intelligence Organisation (ASIO). As of June 2013, the government's official threat level in Australia remained at 'medium' – a terrorist attack could well occur.[2]

In light of heavily publicised campaigns to promote public awareness on terrorism and national security, it is perhaps not surprising that Australians indeed believed that a terrorist attack in Australia was only a matter of time. According to an opinion poll published by the *Sydney Morning Herald* in late April 2004, 68 per cent expected that terrorists would strike Australia before too long.[3] In late 2007, 66 per cent were 'concerned' that a 'major terrorist attack on Australian soil' was going to take place in the 'near future'.[4] Figures from opinion polls conducted on behalf of the Lowy Institute for International Policy tell a similar story. In 2006, 73 per cent of respondents considered 'international terrorism' a 'critical' threat.[5] In the 2008 poll, this number was slightly down, at 66 per cent.[6] At the tenth anniversary of the 9/11 attacks in 2011, 60 per cent of Australians considered the ability of terrorists to launch a major attack against Australians as 'the same' as at the time of the 2002 Bali bombings, with another 19 per cent saying it was now 'greater'.[7]

So, are those public sentiments justified? How real and dangerous is the threat of terrorism in Australia? How has it been portrayed by the Australian government? Who is actually threatening us? And what is actually being threatened?

The terrorism rhetoric of the Australian government

When four hijacked planes crashed into the World Trade Center in New York City, the Pentagon in Washington DC, and into a remote field in Pennsylvania on the morning of 11 September 2001, most Australians were about to go to bed or asleep already. Not so their Prime Minister, John Howard, who had flown into Washington on 8 September 2001 for an extensive working visit that included the first face-to-face meetings with President George W. Bush and key members of his administration. Three days later, however, Howard found himself at the epicentre of the emotional firestorm that engulfed the United States in the aftermath of the unprecedented terrorist attacks. Howard's presence in Washington and his first-hand experience of the surreal and dramatic events that unfolded on 9/11 not only forged his close personal relationship with President Bush but also had a lasting impact on his approach to the challenges associated with the evaluation of the threat of international terrorism back home.[8]

On 11 September 2001, Howard was scheduled to open a business forum at the US Chamber of Commerce to build momentum for a free-trade agreement between Australia and the United States. The Prime Minister was in his hotel room preparing for an informal press conference with Australian journalists before his departure to the business forum when his press secretary, Tony O'Leary, knocked on the door and informed him that a plane had struck the World Trade Center. A few minutes later, Howard's personal protection details from the Australian Federal Police and the US Secret Service decided that there was an urgent need to get the Prime Minister somewhere safer. Howard and his staff were rushed to the Australian Embassy, nine blocks away, where they spent the rest of the day in the second sub-basement, a windowless maintenance area below street level with a makeshift kitchen, dusty tables and broken chairs. Having witnessed the Pentagon burning a few hundred metres away and having watched the World Trade Center's twin towers collapse live on television, Howard experienced the events of 9/11 in a direct way that no other foreign leader did.

After consulting with Australian officials assembled in the Embassy's sub-basement and with key Cabinet members in Canberra in the middle of the night, the Prime Minister personally drafted a short letter to President Bush expressing horror at the loss of life and pledging 'Australia's resolute solidarity with the American people at this most tragic time'.[9] Two days later, the Prime Minister returned to Canberra and invoked Article IV of the ANZUS Pact, the first Australian prime minister to do so since the treaty was concluded in 1951.[10] At a press conference on 14 September 2001 he declared it was the 'unanimous view' of the Cabinet that Australia stood ready to 'cooperate within the limits of its capability concerning any response that the United States may regard as necessary in consultation with her allies'. The Prime Minister made clear, moreover, that 'at no stage should any Australian regard this as something that is just confined to the United States. It is an attack upon the way of life we hold dear in common with the Americans.'[11]

In the following years, the Australian government's description of the threat of terrorism perfectly replicated the narrative offered by the Bush administration in Washington. The replications not only contained the same metaphors and analogies but, at times, the very same wording President Bush used in his speeches following the 9/11 attacks. From the first, the President had made it clear that the United States had been attacked for its virtuous qualities rather than its policy choices. According to the President, the reasons for the assault were to be found in the identity and nature of the terrorists and not in any concrete political grievances. America was targeted simply because the attackers were primitive, barbarian, intolerant and envious. The terrorists' motivations were rooted in their hatred of democracy and freedom as well as in anti-globalisation and anti-modernism.[12]

By explaining the attacks with reference to the alleged character of the perpetrators, Bush sought to suppress any alternative interpretations of 9/11. In doing so, the President implicitly dismissed any possibility that the attacks could have been read in connection with American foreign policy. The 9/11 attacks were rather portrayed as being directed against the United States' longstanding traditions of freedom and democracy. As a consequence, all nations that shared the United States's democratic traditions and principles were under threat. Developing the notion of the civilised world under attack also enabled the Bush administration to portray the fight against terrorism as a generational challenge of historic proportions. As Richard Jackson has pointed out, one of the consequences of these constructions, and most likely part of their intended function, was to de-historicise the 9/11 attacks from the recent past, while simultaneously imposing a radically different set of interpretations.[13]

In Australia, Prime Minister Howard adopted this different set of interpretations as his own. Speaking on national television in 2005, he declared that 'we are dealing with a group of fanatics who have no tolerance for our way of life, who will not be happy unless they have brought down our way of life and imposed their own.' Indeed, the terrorists' objective was 'the destruction of our kind of society'.[14] The Prime Minister employed similar language in his Australia Day address to the National Press Club in Canberra on 25 January 2006. He pointed out that terrorism remained the 'defining element in Australia's security environment' as we knew 'what our enemies think and what they are capable of'. According to Howard, these enemies 'hate our freedoms and our way of life'. Indeed, they 'despise our democratic values' and have 'nothing but contempt for a diverse society which practices tolerance and respect'.[15]

The then Foreign Minister, Alexander Downer, portrayed the threat of terrorism to Australia in similarly misconceived terms. Launching the 2004 White Paper on International Terrorism, he claimed that Al-Qaeda and other terrorists pursued a 'terrorist project of limitless ambition'. Australia was therefore engaged in a 'struggle to the death over values'. Islamic terrorist organisations, Downer pointed out, remained 'convinced that their destiny [was] to overshadow the democratic West'. Indeed, the terrorists had embarked on a ruthless mission to 'destroy our society by waging a version of total war'. The 'islamo-fascists', continued Downer, 'cannot achieve their aims through persuasion – only through fear and chaos … Their precise goals and ideologies are so extreme – and their methods are so evil – that it is difficult for us to understand them.' Al-Qaeda's intent was 'genocidal and utterly uncoloured by reason, restraint, compassion or a notion of shared humanity'.[16]

The Rudd government largely refrained from employing such colourful rhetoric. Nonetheless, its underlying message remained much the same: the terrorist threat had become a 'persistent and permanent feature of Australia's security environment' and terrorism 'continues to pose a serious security challenge to Australia'. Moreover, Australia now faced 'an increased terrorist threat from people born or raised in Australia who take inspiration from international Jihadist narratives'.[17] This assessment was also shared by Rudd's successor. The Gillard government's National Security Strategy, launched in January 2013, continued to consider terrorism and violent extremism as a 'key national security risk'.[18] Similarly, ASIO, in its latest report to Parliament, refers to the 'unfortunate reality' that the threat of terrorism remained 'real and persistent' and therefore represented the 'greatest focus' of ASIO's attention.[19]

As Anne Aly points out (see chapter 2), the 'values/our way of life' narrative offered by the Australian government, in particular during the Howard years, was both simplistic and misleading. What's more, as Aly has noted, this narrative prevented 'any expanded, nuanced and insightful analysis of why terrorists use violence or the threat of violence and how we might best act to mitigate or prevent it'.[20] In fact, none of the government pronouncements offered any detailed insights on who was actually threatening us. The statements by government representatives simply referred to 'Al-Qaeda', 'a group of fanatics', 'terrorists' or simply 'enemies'. Yet such broad classifications did little to assist in identifying the source of the threat – a key first step in any threat analysis.

Who is threatening us?

Contemporary terrorism is commonly associated with so-called Islamist or Jihadi terrorism, although the usage of both terms is controversial.[21] Indeed, the federal government's 2010 Counterterrorism White Paper stated that 'the main source of international terrorism and the primary terrorist threat to Australia and Australian interests today comes from people who follow a distorted and militant interpretation of Islam that calls for violence as the answer to perceived grievances.'[22]

A key exponent of Islamist terrorism is Al-Qaeda, which was reportedly founded in the late 1980s by fighters of the Mujahideen campaign against Soviet forces in Afghanistan.[23] Most commentators agree that Al-Qaeda is not a traditional terrorist group with control and command structures but is best described as a decentralised network.[24] Other authors go further and even question the accuracy of portraying Al-Qaeda as a network.[25] They argue that the term 'network' is misleading, as it still implies that a well-organised core leadership in charge of the organisation or network continues to exist.[26] These scholars prefer to refer to Al-Qaeda as an ideology.[27]

While Al-Qaeda may be most accurately described as an 'ideology' rather than an 'organisation' or 'network', such classification is hardly constructive for the purposes of identifying the source of the contemporary threat. In order to escape these analytical difficulties, Philippe Errera, a senior analyst of the French government, proposed using the image of 'three circles' to describe different threat dimensions.[28] According to Errera, the first circle consists of the 'traditional' Al-Qaeda leadership – that is, Osama bin Laden and other individuals who planned the 1998 US Embassy bombings in East Africa, or the attack on the USS *Cole* and 9/11.[29] Significant progress has been made in disrupting the activities of this first circle, including killing bin Laden himself. Many commentators thus doubt that Al-Qaeda is capable of carrying out another mass-casualty attack of the scale of 9/11.[30]

In the second circle are terrorist groups that may share some of the transnational ideology of the traditional Al-Qaeda leadership, but which were born out of local conflicts. The groups of this circle mainly feed off localised grievances and define their objectives mostly in reference to local political conditions. Oliver Roy, for instance, has characterised these groups as 'territorialised'.[31] Although these assertions may elicit debate from specialists, and criticism from political leaders in whose interest it is to portray 'their' terrorists exclusively as Al-Qaeda affiliates or 'franchisees', one could place in this category groups like the Kashmiri Lashkar-e-Taiba. In Southeast Asia, organisations belonging to the second circle would include Jemaah Islamiyah, the Abu Sayyaf Group, the Moro Islamic Liberation Front, the Misuari Renegade/Breakaway Group and the Philippine Rajah Sulaiman movement.

The boundaries of the second circle are not fixed and there are no universal metrics to measure and characterise relations between the groups or networks of the first and second circles. This means that operational and financial links may exist between the two circles. These links, however, are unlikely to be of fundamental importance to the operation of the respective organisation or group. As Errera has put it, this second circle is 'still composed of groups and individuals whose primary objective is not that of Osama Bin Laden; ridding the world of Jews, infidels and apostates would be nice, but in the meantime they will probably settle for less.'[32]

The third circle consists of individuals or groups of individuals who profess to act in the name of Al-Qaeda but who may not have any connections to the first and second circles. It is these individuals or groups that are commonly referred to as 'home-grown' terrorists or 'Jihadists'. In 2010, for instance, three Melbourne men were found guilty of a home-grown terror plot to launch a suicide attack on the Holsworthy army base in Sydney.[33] As with the second circle, the exact outline of the third circle cannot be drawn, partly because individuals belonging to this circle tend to operate autonomously and for a range of different reasons. As George Tenet, a former CIA director, has observed, 'these far-flung groups increasingly set the agenda, and are redefining the threat we face. They are not all creatures of Bin Laden, and so their fate is not tied to his. They have autonomous leadership, they pick their own targets, they plan their own attacks.'[34]

The potential size of the third circle is uncertain, as future recruits may currently have no visible violent, 'terrorist' or radical tendency. In fact, the processes of radicalisation, including the psychological and social dynamics that lead from alienation to action, are complex, obscure and subject to change over time. Research into this multifaceted issue suggests that violent extremism is always engendered by a range factors which include not only religious aspects but also personality, nationalism, separatism and discrimination.[35] Scholars commonly agree that no single root cause is instrumental.[36]

How, then, do these three circles of threat apply in the Australian context?

A central argument put forward by the Howard government as to why Australia was a target for terrorist attacks was that Al-Qaeda had referred to Australia in a number of public statements. Specifically, the Howard government's assumption that Australia was a terrorist target was mainly based on a number of statements allegedly made by bin Laden. In these statements, bin Laden referred to Australia in the context of the separation of East Timor from Indonesia, the military operations in Afghanistan, the Bali bombings of 2002, the situation in Palestine, and the 2003 invasion of Iraq.

The significance of the public statements of bin Laden and Al-Qaeda has been controversial. It is certainly prudent for a government to take such statements seriously. On the other hand, one must not overestimate the importance of these communiqués and internet warnings. In many cases is nearly impossible to establish with any degree of certainty whether or not these statements are in fact authentic. Even in cases where statements are believed to be authentic, it is still essential to recognise the divide between intent and capability of terrorist organisations or militants. Just because a terrorist organisation indicates that it is willing to launch attacks does not automatically mean that it is also capable to do so. Indeed, statements may be issued for various reasons or purposes. Terrorist organisations may deliberately issue warnings as a tactical measure to provoke public discomfort. They may issue statements to pressure governments politically, perhaps even with a view to influencing foreign policy decisions.

The threat that Al-Qaeda posed to Australia seemed rather low for a number of reasons. To begin with, Australia appeared to be a poor strategic choice and an unlikely target for an Al-Qaeda–organised attack. Indeed, an attack on Australia's homeland appeared to be of very little value to either Al-Qaeda or the regionally-based Jemaah Islamiyah (JI). As Jason Burke and others have pointed out, a primary goal of Al-Qaeda has traditionally been to beat back what it perceived as the West's aggressive project of denigrating, dividing and humiliating Islam – a project supposedly begun during the medieval Crusades and later periods of colonial rule.[37] Ultimately, Al-Qaeda envisaged the establishment of a single Islamic state, or 'caliphate', in the lands roughly corresponding to the furthest extent of the historic Islamic empire. While geostrategic objectives form part of the Al-Qaeda ideology, Islamist militancy is also notably driven by local grievances.

Bin Laden's primary focus has always been to topple the regime in Saudi Arabia.[38] However, when Islamist militants grew increasingly frustrated by their failure to change the domestic status quo in countries like Egypt, Saudi Arabia and Algeria, they turned their attention to striking at the Arab regimes' Western sponsors. Although Australia qualified as a Western country, it was rather improbable that it represented one of these sponsors. Indeed, in contrast to the United States and other key Western powers like the United Kingdom, France and Germany, Australia's political leverage in the Arab world remains very limited. Given that Al-Qaeda's planning and operational capabilities were relatively constrained, it was thus unlikely that the network would 'waste' its limited resources on planning an attack on a rather low-profile target like Australia. A decade after 9/11, with bin Laden and key figures at the core of the traditional Al-Qaeda killed or captured, the first circle of threat seems to have further lost relevance for Australia, at least as a direct threat.

In the Southeast Asian region, JI represents one of the groups that would classify as belonging to the second circle of threat. JI is commonly considered to be responsible for the attacks against two nightclubs on the Indonesian resort island of Bali on 12 October 2002. This attack confirmed terrorism's place at the centre of contemporary Australian politics, as it was Australia's first (and only) experience with mass-casualty terrorism. Despite testimony from the ring-leaders of the terrorist attacks that they were targeting Americans and Westerners in general, a popular misperception in Australia was that the attacks were a deliberate strike against Australians.[39] And, as David Wright-Neville has noted, the Australian government did not work to 'disabuse Australians of this perception'.[40] As a result, the Bali bombings triggered an important psychological reappraisal in Australia of national security threats and, as Carl Ungerer has observed, Australians have been 'more willing to accept the proposition that terrorism shifted from a nuisance criminal behaviour that predominantly affected parts of the Middle East, to an immediate security problem on Australia's doorstep'.[41]

This proposition was actively advanced by the Howard government, which repeatedly referred to the Bali bombings as evidence that the threat of terrorism had reached Australia. Similar assessments were made by think tanks and scholars. A 2004 report by the Australian Strategic Policy Institute, for instance, concluded that Australia faced 'an unprecedented risk from terrorism'. While the report acknowledged that the Bali bombings 'were not specifically directed against Australia, but rather were an attack against the West more generally', it nonetheless found that 'JI would undoubtedly attack targets in Australia if it had the means and could find a suitable point of weakness.'[42] This assessment encapsulated a widely held belief that Australia was at direct threat from JI as Al-Qaeda's 'local branch office' in Southeast Asia. It followed a general trend that described JI as an Al-Qaeda affiliate, or some variation thereof.

Nevertheless, the assumption that JI represented Al-Qaeda in Indonesia, or in the Southeast Asian region more generally, was both inaccurate and misleading. As Indonesia specialist Sidney Jones has pointed out, 'JI was never an al-Qaeda franchise; there were always parts of JI that objected to the bin Laden interpretation of jihad, at least as it applied to Southeast Asia.'[43] In an earlier publication, Jones described the relationship between Al-Qaeda and JI as comparable to that of a non-governmental organisation with a funding agency.[44] However, even this characterisation may suggest links between JI and Al-Qaeda that did not necessarily exist in practice. Imam Samudra, one of the JI operatives responsible for the Bali bombings, for instance, was interviewed by the *London Times* newspaper journalist Michael Sheridan in 2008. Asked whether there were any financial links between his group and Al-Qaeda, Samudra stated:

> It's not correct. The money was not from Osama [bin Laden], it was from other people. This is an important

point. Maybe some try to make a link between Al-Qaeda and us. Now I don't know about this. We are not linking. The only link is *iman* (faith), the only link is *aqida* (creed) because Osama's God is Allah and my God is the almighty Allah. His mission is similar to my mission to help Muslims around the world. You get the point? Right.[45]

Likewise, it is highly questionable whether JI posed a direct threat to Australia (as opposed to a threat to Australian interests in Indonesia or Southeast Asia). For example, an attack by JI on Australian soil seemed unlikely because it would hardly have fit the group's political agenda. JI's principal objective has always been the establishment of a fundamentalist Islamic government in Indonesia, a goal that has been described as the 'one constant of the organisation since the beginning'.[46]

It has also been suggested that the establishment of fundamentalist Islamic government in Indonesia would ultimately be followed by the formation of a unified Islamic state in the Southeast Asian region. This state, or 'caliphate', would stretch from southern Thailand, through the Malay Peninsula (including Singapore), across the Indonesian archipelago and into the southern Philippines.[47] However, such claims are problematic. As Jones has pointed out:

The assumption that JI's main objective was an Islamic state in archipelagic Southeast Asia (Daulah Islamiyah Nusantara) comes from looking at the organisation at a particular time and place: Singapore and Malaysia in 2001. In June 2001, the Malaysian government accused Abu Jibril, a close associate of Abu Bakar Ba'asyir, of working for the creation of such a state, and some of the

Singaporean detainees arrested in late 2001 told their
interrogators that this indeed was the organisation's goal.
This information was then published in the Singapore
White Paper in early 2003, a widely used source for
everyone writing on terrorism in Southeast Asia, and so
became an established 'fact'.[48]

Even if one accepted that the establishment of a unified Islamic
state in the Southeast Asian region formed part of JI's objectives,
it remains unclear whether this would include parts of Northern
Australia. Furthermore, it remains questionable how attacks on
Australian soil would further any of these aims. While attacks
on Australian interests in Indonesia and elsewhere in Southeast
Asia may appear 'beneficial', for they could be regarded as chas-
ing Western 'infidels' from 'Islamic land', it is difficult to see
how an attack inside Australia would yield similar profits. These
strategic and theoretical considerations notwithstanding, there
is also little evidence to suggest that JI set up operations in Australia in practice. In particular, available information indicates
that even modest attempts to raise funds in Australia for activities in Indonesia were unsuccessful.[49]

The third circle of threat is considered to consist of
individuals commonly referred to as 'home-grown' terrorists.
In Australia, too, there is concern that individuals professing
to act in the name of Al-Qaeda could launch attacks. Some
commentators have raised alarm and warned that home-
grown terrorism constitutes an unprecedented threat. Rohan
Gunaratna, for instance, speaking on Australian television in
2007, claimed that home-grown terrorists presented 'the biggest
security challenge to Australian law enforcement and to security
and intelligence services'.[50] ASIO's Deputy Director-General,

in September 2008, also warned that 'terrorism-related activity continues to take place in Australia' and that the agency was 'aware of Australians who hold extremist views, including some who have trained overseas with terrorist groups, or engaged in jihad activities'.[51] A similar assessment can be found in ASIO's 2011–12 Report to Parliament, which confirms that the 'threat of home-grown terrorism remains a principal concern'.[52]

To date, 23 individuals have been convicted of terrorism offences. Yet, while these cases confirm that there is a small number of Australians who hold extremist Islamist views, it is important to keep things in perspective. For example, the situation in Australia is hardly comparable to the conditions and dynamics in the United Kingdom, France and other parts of Europe. The Australian cases also demonstrate that extremist views do not necessarily lead to violent action. None of the penalised actions of the prosecuted individuals amounted to immediate preparatory action for a terrorist act. Moreover, none had progressed to a stage where possible targets for attacks had been properly identified. This does not mean, of course, that the penalised actions or certain individuals did not pose any threat whatsoever. After all, it only takes a few determined individuals to launch an attack. It remains questionable, however, whether the small number of 'extremists' who are ready to employ violence can be considered an unprecedented threat to Australia's national security.

What is the threat?

Having identified a possible source of the threat, it is equally important to clarify who or what is actually threatened by terrorist violence. Terrorism unquestionably threatens the safety and physical integrity of individuals as well as property. Recent terrorist attacks resulted in substantial loss of life and considerable damage to property. The 2002 Bali attacks, for instance, killed 202 people and injured 200. The 2004 Madrid bombing resulted in the deaths of 192 and left 2050 injured. The 2005 London bombings killed 56 people and resulted in around 700 people being injured. The 9/11 attacks in New York and Washington were by far the most destructive. The attacks claimed the lives of 3017 people and injured over 6300. Nonetheless, it should be kept in mind that 9/11 was an extreme event: it was – and remains – the only occasion on which more than a few hundred people have been killed in a single terrorist attack by a non-state actor.

It is important to recognise, then, that conventional forms of violence such as traditional and civil wars have almost always been more deadly. For example, the Costs of War Project has estimated that, at minimum, between 123 000 and 134 000 civilians were killed in Iraq from 2003 to 2013.[53] As of May 2013, the death toll in the civil war in Syria had reached an estimated 80 000.[54] The objective significance of terrorism as a threat to safety and individual physical integrity further diminishes when one compares terrorism-related fatalities to fatalities totally unrelated to political or armed violence. In the United States, for example, terrorism poses a far lesser statistical threat to life than most other activities. In 2001, three times as many people in the United States died of malnutrition, and almost 40 times as many people died in car accidents during the same year,[55] not to mention the significant number of people who die in the United States every year from gun-related violence.[56] Even with the 9/11 attacks included in the count, the number of Americans killed by international terrorism since the late 1960s is about the same as the number killed over the same period by severe allergic reaction to peanuts, lightning, or accident-causing deer.[57]

At the global level, the statistics are equally revealing. Anthony Cordesman and Brian Jenkins have independently provided lists of violence committed by Islamist extremists outside of such war zones as Iraq, Israel, Chechnya, Sudan, Kashmir and Afghanistan, whether that violence be perpetrated by domestic terrorists or by ones with substantial international connections.[58] The total number of people killed in the five years after 9/11 in such incidents comes to some 200 to 300 per year. By comparison, over the same period far more people have perished in the United States alone in bathtub drownings.[59] Perhaps even more significantly, the annual deaths from terrorism pale into insignificance next to the 40 000 people who die every day from hunger, the 500 000 people who are killed every year by the use of small arms and light weapons, and the number of people who die annually from diseases like influenza (3.9 million), HIV-AIDS (2.9 million), diarrhoeal illnesses (2.1 million) and tuberculosis (1.7 million).[60]

Terrorism has also been portrayed as a significant threat to the economy, with considerable implications for the national interest of countries affected. The economic destruction of 9/11 was indeed unprecedented (in terms of terrorist attacks). Nevertheless, even the extreme events of 9/11 have not had an enduring impact on the world's most powerful economy. A 2002 report prepared for the US Congress, for example, analysed the economic effects of 9/11 and concluded that 'the loss of lives and property on 9/11 was not large enough to have had a measurable effect on the productive capacity of the United States.'[61] A study focusing exclusively on the New York area reached similar conclusions. In the aftermath of the 9/11 attacks, New York City's economy contracted briefly but sharply. Many businesses were forced to shut down, mostly temporarily, and tens of thousands of workers were either dislocated for a short time or lost their jobs. However, the study also found that although the attacks caused a sharp temporary disruption in the economy, an advantageous industry mix – one weighted towards high-paying, rapidly expanding industries – kept the city well positioned for growth over the medium term.[62] Similar conclusions were reached by a number of other studies.[63]

The terrorist attacks in Madrid and London also did not have any lasting negative economic impacts in Spain and the United Kingdom respectively, nor on the European economy more generally.[64] For instance, the S&P 500 Index dropped 1.5 per cent on the day of the Madrid attacks.[65] However, it recovered most of that loss the next day.

Similarly, there were limited immediate reactions to the 2005 London bombings in the world economy as measured by financial market and exchange rate activity. The pound fell 0.89 cents to a 19-month low against the US dollar. The FTSE 100 Index fell by about 200 points in the two hours after the first attack. While this was its biggest fall since the start of the 2003 Iraq war, by the time the market closed, the index had recovered to only 71.3 points (1.36 per cent) down on the previous day's three-year closing high.[66] Markets in France, Germany, the Netherlands and Spain also closed about 1 per cent down on the day. US market indexes rose slightly, in part because the dollar index rose sharply against the pound and the euro. The Dow Jones Industrial Average gained 31.61 to 10 302.29. The Nasdaq Composite Index rose 7.01 to 2075.66. The S&P 500 rose 2.93 points to 1197.87 after declining up to 1 per cent.

Every benchmark gained 0.3 per cent.[67] The markets picked up again on 8 July 2005 as it became clear that the damage caused by the bombings was not as great as initially thought. By close of trading the market had fully recovered to above its level at start of trading on 7 July 2005, the day of the attacks. These developments led the chief investment strategist at Prudential Equity Group LLC in New York, Edward Keon, to observe that 'the markets reacted the way they often do under periods of great stress, initially dropping and then recovering.'[68]

The examples of recent terrorist attacks suggest that terrorism does not have a significant *direct* effect on Western economies. However, the attacks did have considerable *indirect* effects. Gail Makinen, for instance, has pointed out that over the longer run 9/11 adversely affected US productivity growth because resources were being used to ensure the security of production, distribution, finance and communication.[69] The yearly budget for the Office of Homeland Security, for instance, continues to be set at around $50 billion.[70] More generally, unprecedented amounts of money have been spent on improving infrastructural security at airports, highways, seaports and electric and nuclear power facilities. Nevertheless, while the increased spending on 'security'-related issues may have had a considerable economic impact, it is important to recognise that this impact is *indirect* in nature.

Finally, some commentators have argued that terrorism represented a threat to the democratic state. The new wave of terrorism, so the argument ran, challenged the legitimacy of the state itself: if governments were unable to safeguard the physical safety and integrity of their own citizens, then citizens could have little faith in the protective function of the state.[71] Yet, this is unconvincing. Western values and the political and economic structures that express them are far too robust to be susceptible to destabilisation by terrorist attacks, however horrific and genuinely tragic they may be. Even 9/11, the most audacious and single largest terrorist attack in history, did not compromise the essential workings of government.

Similar observations can be made regarding other terrorist attacks, both past and present. Historically, non-state terrorist activity has neither significantly undermined nor damaged the national cohesiveness or integrity of liberal democracies.[72] Germany, Italy, the United Kingdom and many other countries – including Israel – have lived with terrorist activity for many years without such activity seriously threatening their very existence. In fact, previous experiences of political violence posed a somewhat greater threat to the stability of these states. In particular, left-wing and separatist terrorism campaigns in Europe enjoyed a certain degree of popular support or sympathy, at least as far as key political objectives were concerned. This meant that these campaigns had a form of legitimacy to them which was far more threatening to the stability of Western democracies than contemporary Islamist terrorism.

Conclusion

Although portrayed as an unprecedented security issue, Islamist terrorism hardly constitutes a threat of significant concern for Australia. There is little evidence to suggest that Al-Qaeda or Jemaah Islamiyah had (and have) the capacity to undermine our national security. The terrorism prosecutions in Australia to date indicate that a small number of locally based individuals are prepared to engage in violence in pursuit of international 'jihad'. It is prudent to monitor this development and consider strategies to manage it. However, this threat must be kept in perspective. It is neither comparable to the threat of home-grown terrorism faced by other Western countries, nor does it have the capacity to destabilise Australia politically and/or economically. To this day, not a single person has been killed in a terrorist attack on Australian soil in the post-9/11 era. In fact, a calculation of annual fatality risks for the period 1970–2013 reveals that the risk of getting killed in a terrorist attack in Australia is about 1 in 38 300 000. This figure alone should prompt a comprehensive re-evaluation of our perception of the contemporary terrorist threat and how to respond to it.

1   John Howard, National Press Club Address, 8 November 2001. See also the Hon John Howard, MP, 'Address at the National Remembrance Service honouring the victims of the terrorist attacks in Bali', 16 October 2003; 'Govt argues against increased terror threat', *ABC News (Online)*, 16 March 2004, last accessed 7 June 2013 <www.abc.net.au/worldtoday/content/2004/s1066853.htm>.

2   National Terrorism Public Alert System (online), last accessed 7 June 2013 <www.nationalsecurity.gov.au/>.

3   'Australians expect terrorist strike', *Sydney Morning Herald*, 21 April 2004.

4   'Terrorism still seen as a threat by Aussies', *Australian*, 19 August 2008.

5   Ivan Cook (2006) *Australia, Indonesia and the World – The Lowy Institute Poll 2006*, Lowy Institute for International Policy, Sydney, pp. 9–11.

6   Fergus Hanson (2008) *Australia, Indonesia and the World – The Lowy Institute Poll 2008*, Lowy Institute for International Policy, Sydney, p. 5.

7   Fergus Hanson (2011) *Australia and the World – The Lowy Institute Poll 2011*, Lowy Institute for International Policy, Sydney, p. 12.

8   The description of Prime Minister Howard's visit in Washington DC in the days surrounding 11 September 2001 draws largely on Donald Debats, Tim McDonald and Margaret-Ann Williams (2007) 'Mr Howard Goes to Washington: September 11, the Australian–American Relationship and Attributes of Leadership', *Australian*

Journal of Political Science, vol. 42, no. 2, pp. 231–51. This article is based on several interviews with John Howard and other members of his staff at the time.

9   Cited in Debats, McDonald and Williams (2007), 'Mr Howard Goes to Washington', p. 239.

10 For the history of the ANZUS Pact see, e.g., Joseph M. Siracusa and David G. Coleman (2006) *Australia Looks to America: Australian–American Relations since Pearl Harbor*, Regina Books, Claremont, CA, pp. 33–50.

11 'Government Invokes ANZUS Treaty', Prime Minister's Press Conference, 14 September 2001, last accessed 7 June 2013 <australianpolitics.com/foreign/anzus/01-09-14anzus-invoked. shtml>.

12 President George W. Bush, 'Address to Joint Session of Congress', 20 September 2001; President George W. Bush, 'U.S. Attorneys on Front Line in War', Remarks by the President to U.S. Attorneys Conference, Presidential Hall, Dwight David Eisenhower Office Building, 29 November 2001.

13 Richard Jackson (2005) *Writing the War on Terrorism*, Manchester University Press, Manchester, p. 58; see also Anne Aly's chapter in this book.

14 Transcript of interview with Prime Minister John Howard, Channel Nine, 24 April 2005 (on file with author).

15 The Hon John Howard, MP, 'Australia Day Address to the National Press Club', Canberra, 25 January 2006, last accessed 7 June 2013 <australianpolitics.com/news/2006/01/06-01-25_howard.shtml>.

16 The Hon Alexander Downer, MP, 'Transnational Terrorism: The Threat to Australia', Speech to launch the White Paper on International Terrorism, National Press Club, Canberra, 15 July 2004, last accessed 7 June 2013 <www.foreignminister.gov.au/speeches/2004/040715_tt.html>.

17 Australian Government Department of the Prime Minister and Cabinet (2010) *Counter-Terrorism White Paper: Securing Australia/Protecting our Community*, DPMC, Canberra, pp. i, ii.

18 Australian Government Department of the Prime Minister and Cabinet (2013) *Strong and Secure: A Strategy for Australia's National Security*, DPMC, Canberra, p. 11.

19 ASIO Report to Parliament 2011–12, p. vii, last accessed 7 June 2013 <www.asio.gov.au/img/files/ASIO-Annual-Report-2011-12_full.pdf>.

20 Aly, chapter 2 in this book.

21 Karen Armstrong, 'The label of Catholic terror was never used about the IRA', *Guardian*, 11 July 2005; Jamal Nassar (2004) *Globalization and Terrorism: The Migration of Dreams and Nightmares*, Rowman & Littlefield, Lanham, MD, second edition.

22 DPMC (2010) *White Paper*, p. 8.

23 Peter L. Bergen (2006) *The Osama bin Laden I Know: An Oral History of Al-Qaeda's Leader*, Free Press, New York, pp. 74–80.

24 Paul Wilkinson (2007) 'The Threat from the Al-Qaeda Network' in Paul Wilkinson (ed.), *Homeland Security in the UK: Future Preparedness for Terrorist Attacks since 9/11*, Routledge, London, p. 25.

25 Marc Sageman (2008) *Leaderless Jihad: Terror Networks in the Twenty-first Century*, University of Pennsylvania Press, Philadelphia.

26 Bruce Hoffman (2004) 'The Changing Face of Al-Qaeda and the Global War on Terrorism', *Studies in Conflict and Terrorism*, vol. 27, no. 6, pp. 549–60.

27 Jason Burke (2004) 'Think Again: Al-Qaeda', *Foreign Policy*, no. 142 (May/June), pp. 18–26.

28 Philippe Errera (2005) 'Three Circles of Threat', *Survival*, vol. 47, no. 1, pp. 71–88.

29 Errera (2005) 'Three Circles of Threat', p. 73.

30 Mark Hosenball (2012) 'Al-Qaeda incapable of new mass-casualty attack, US officials say', *Huffington Post*, 27 April, last accessed 7 June 2013 <www.huffingtonpost.com/2012/04/27/al-qaeda-new-attack_n_1460463.html>.

31 Olivier Roy (2004) *Globalized Islam*, Columbia University Press, New York, p. 43.

32 Errera (2005) 'Three Circles of Threat', p. 74.

33 C. Le Garnd, 'Prosecutors apply to increase jail terms for three in Holsworthy plot', *The Australian*, 17 June 2013.

34 Jim Garamone (2004) 'Tenet briefs Senate on terror threats', US Department of Defense, 24 February, last accessed 5 July 2013 <www.defense.gov/News/NewsArticle.aspx?ID=27261>.

35 Jon Colen and Benjamin Cole (2009) *Martyrdom: Radicalisation and Terrorist Violence among British Muslims*, Pennant Books, London.

36 Robert S. Leiken (2005) 'Europe's Angry Muslims', *Foreign Affairs*, vol. 84, no. 4, pp. 120–35.

37 Burke (2004) 'Think Again: Al-Qaeda', pp. 18–26. For in-depth analysis see also Jason Burke (2003) *Al-Qaeda: Casting a Shadow of Terror*, I.B. Tauris, New York.

38 Burke (2004), 'Think Again: Al-Qaeda', p. 19.

39 Sonny Inbaraj, 'Bali attack directed at West, not Australia', *Asia Times (Online)*, 17 October 2002, last accessed 7 June 2013 <www.atimes.com/atimes/Southeast_Asia/DJ17Ae05.html>. Amrozi, the first of the Bali bombers to be arrested, has even told police that he was 'surprised' that so many Australians were killed in the attack, as he thought the target was Americans.

40 David Wright-Neville, *Fear and Loathing: Australia and Counter-Terrorism*, Real Instituto Elcano, 21 December 2005, p. 3.

41 Carl Ungerer (2006) 'Australia's Policy Responses to Terrorism in Southeast Asia', *Global Change, Peace & Security*, vol. 18, no. 3, p. 196.

42 Australian Strategic Policy Institute (2004) *Beyond Baghdad: ASPI's Strategic Assessment 2004*, ASPI, Canberra, p. 10.

43 Sidney Jones (2005) 'The Changing Nature of Jemaah Islamiyah', *Australian Journal of International Affairs*, vol. 59, no. 2, p. 172.

44 International Crisis Group (2003) *Jemaah Islamiyah in South East Asia: Damaged but Still Dangerous*, Asia Report No. 63 (26 August), p. 30.

45 'Extracts: Michael Sheridan interview with Bali bomber Imam Samudra', *Sunday Times* (London), 2 March 2008.

46 Jones (2005) 'The Changing Nature of Jemaah Islamiyah', p. 174.

47 Brek Batley (2003) *The Complexities of Dealing with Radical Islam in Southeast Asia: A Case Study of Jemaah Islamiyah*, Canberra Papers on Strategy and Defence No. 149, ANU, Canberra.

48 Jones, 'The Changing Nature of Jemaah Islamiyah', pp. 170–71.

49 Christopher Michaelsen (2005) 'Anti-Terrorism Legislation in Australia: A Proportionate Response to the Terrorist Threat?', *Studies in Conflict & Terrorism*, vol. 28, no. 4, pp. 321–39.

50 Rohan Gunaratna (2007) 'Homegrown terrorism', ABC, *The Drum*, 5 June, last accessed 7 June 2013 <www.abc.net.au/news/2007-06-05/homegrown-terrorism/60582>.

51 Deputy Director of ASIO, 'Australia's Security Outlook', Security in Government Conference, 16 September 2008.

52 ASIO Report to Parliament 2011–12, p. vii.

53 Costs of War Project, last accessed 7 June 2013 <costsofwar.org/article/iraqi-civilians>.

54 'Syria death toll at least 80,000, says U.N. General Assembly president', Reuters, 15 May 2013, last accessed 7 June 2013 <in.reuters.com/article/2013/05/15/syria-crisis-un-deaths-idINDEE94E0CJ20130515>.

55 Sarah Stephen (2004) 'Terrorism: Governments Fuel Fear,' in Justin

Healey (ed.), *Terrorism*, Spinney Press, Sydney, p. 39.

56 M. Cohen, 2013, 'Why does America lose its head over "terror" but ignore its daily gun deaths?', *Guardian*, 21 April 2013, last accessed 22 July 2013 <www.guardian.co.uk/commentisfree/2013/apr/21/boston-marathon-bombs-us-gun-law/print>.

57 John E. Mueller (2007) 'Terrorism, overreaction and globalization' in Richard N. Rosecrance and Arthur A. Stein (eds), *No More States? Globalization, National Self-determination, and Terrorism*, Rowman & Littlefield, Lanham, MD, p. 48. The 3572 people who died in terrorist attacks in 2001 were three times more likely to die from being hit by lightning.

58 Brian Michael Jenkins (2006) *Unconquerable Nation: Knowing Our Enemy and Strengthening Ourselves*, RAND Corporation, Santa Monica, CA, pp. 179–84; Anthony H. Cordesman (2005) *The Challenge of Biological Weapons*, Center for Strategic and International Studies, Washington, DC, pp. 29–31.

59 John Stossel (2004) *Give Me a Break*, HarperCollins, New York, p. 77.

60 Jackson (2005) *Writing the War on Terror*, p. 93.

61 Gail Makinen (2002) *The Economic Effects of 9/11: A Retrospective Assessment*, Report for Congress, 27 September, Library of Congress, Washington, DC, p. 2.

62 Jason Bram, Andrew Haughwout and James Orr (2002) 'Has September 11 Affected New York City's Growth Potential?', *Economic Policy Review*, vol. 8, no. 2, last accessed 7 June 2013 <www.newyorkfed.org/research/epr/02v08n2/0211bram/0211bram.html>.

63 See, e.g., Howard Chernick (ed.) (2005) *Resilient City: The Economic Impact of 9/11*, Russell Sage Foundation, New York; Harry W. Richardson, Peter Gordon and James E. Moore II (eds.) (2005) *The Economic Impacts of Terrorist Attacks*, Edward Elgar, Cheltenham.

64 R. Barry Johnston and Oana M. Nedelescu (2005) 'The Impact of Terrorism on Financial Markets', International Monetary Fund, Working Paper WP/05/60 (March), last accessed 22 July 2013 <www.imf.org/external/pubs/ft/wp/2005/wp0560.pdf>.

65 Dune Lawrence, 'U.S. stocks rise, erasing losses on London bombings, gap rises' *Bloomberg News (Online)*, 7 July 2005, last accessed 7 June 2013 <www.bloomberg.com/apps/news?pid=10000103&sid=aflPCIrU37Ns&refer=us>.

66 Juan Sanchez (2007) *Terrorism and Its Effects*, Global Media (electronic document), p. 14.

67 Cited in Lawrence, 'U.S. stocks rise, erasing losses on London
    bombings, gap rises'.

68 Cited in Lawrence, 'U.S. stocks rise, erasing losses on London
    bombings, gap rises'.

69 Makinen (2002) *The Economic Effects of 9/11*, p. 2.

70 US Department of Homeland Security, *Budget-in-Brief, Fiscal
    Year 2014*, last accessed 7 June 2013, <www.dhs.gov/sites/default/
    files/publications/MGMT/FY 2014 BIB - FINAL -508 Formatted
    %284%29.pdf>.

71 Audrey Kurth Cronin (2002) 'Rethinking Sovereignty: American
    Strategy in the Age of Terrorism', *Survival*, vol. 44, no. 2, p. 134.

72 Adam Roberts (2005) 'The "War on Terror" in Historical
    Perspective', *Survival*, vol. 47, no. 2, pp. 101–30. It is essential to
    differentiate between stable democracies and fragile states. While
    terrorist attacks may have the potential to destabilise fragile states
    and states experiencing civil strife, the same cannot be said in
    relation to stable Western democracies.

2

BECAUSE THEY HATE US

Anne Aly

'Terrorists will continue to attack Australia primarily because of "who we are", our freedoms and our culture.'

NO. BUT IT IS UNDERSTANDABLE TO THINK SO. It is relatively easy to dismiss terrorism as the conduct of mentally unstable individuals who are hell-bent on killing us – 'the West' – because of our values, our freedoms and our way of life. Frequently, terrorists are deciphered as psychopathic and filled with hatred. Or, as depicted by former Prime Minister John Howard, in addressing whether Australia's ongoing involvement in the Iraq war had created a larger risk of future terrorist attacks: 'we are a target because of who we are, rather than what we have done.'[1] However, isolating terrorism as a straightforward act of blind hatred against freedom does have a negative side-effect: it can prevent any expanded, nuanced and insightful analysis of why terrorists use violence or the threat of violence and how we might best act to mitigate or prevent it.

The Bali bombings

The 12th of October 2002 was a Friday night like any other in the bustling nightclub district of Kuta in central Bali. The streets and bars were packed with tourists and locals enjoying all that Kuta had to offer: music, night life and cheap alcohol. At around 11.05, a man known only as Iqbal strolled into the popular Paddy's Pub on Legian Street. He made his way through the crowd towards the centre of the pub, flicked a switch and detonated the suicide vest he was wearing. In the pandemonium that followed, patrons fled to the street, injured and confused. Some headed towards the shelter of the nearby Sari Club, just across from Paddy's. Nobody noticed the white Mitsubishi van parked outside the Sari Club, where Jimmi was waiting to detonate the second, vehicle-borne suicide bomb. The van exploded seconds after the first suicide attack. It was a much more powerful and devastating bomb that demolished the Sari Club, killed 202 victims (including 88 Australians) and left many more injured.[2]

The Indonesian arm of Jemaah Islamiyah (JI), a transnational militant Islamist group with links to Al-Qaeda, was found responsible for the attack. At midnight on 9 November 2008, three JI members convicted of planning and carrying out the 2002 Bali bombings – Imam Samudra, Amrozi Nurhasyim and Ali Ghufron – were executed by firing squad.

Just five days after the 2002 terrorist bombings in Bali, conservative columnist Greg Sheridan wrote 'Just as we love Australia, the evil men who murdered our people and others in Bali, they surely hate Australia. And why do they hate us? They hate us not for our wickedness, which is occasional and undeniable. They hate us for our oddly persistent goodness.'[3] A decade later, on the tenth anniversary of the Bali bombings, the *Telegraph*'s

Brendan O'Neill echoed Sheridan's summation of the attacks, stating that the attacks 'were clearly an expression of disgust against such nightlife, an attack on those who have the temerity to be hedonistic'. According to O'Neill's analysis of the tragic events, '[t]he most striking thing about the Bali attack was its naked loathing of what the terrorists no doubt considered to be "Western decadence" but which most of us would think of as "having a good time".'[4]

Without a doubt, understanding terrorism as impulsive rage or the heinous actions of murderous psychopaths who only want to kill us because of our 'persistent goodness' may appear a reasonable assumption in the immediate emotional aftermath of a terrorist attack – but the big picture is that terrorism is more than just a clear-cut *crime passionnel*.

The philosopher Socrates once said that from the deepest desires often comes the deadliest hate. Many accept that acts of violence are repeatedly committed by individuals who are driven to murderous rage by unbridled passions, passions with no constraints, like jealousy, lust, greed, vengeance, anger, love and hate. But dismissing terrorism as an act of wild, unlimited emotion has an important and counterproductive side-effect: the illustration of blind hatred, for example, has no moral and political context; it is merely inexplicable, unreasonable and irrational. And you cannot reason with uncontrolled hatred. As a consequence, such levels of loathing and detestation exonerate us from any sense of responsibility and, in turn, makes us all hapless victims of an irreconcilable, ideologically driven foe who cannot be appeased or reasoned with. By trying to explain terrorism as just the violent action of insane men and women who hate us, we not only exempt ourselves from any requirement for responsibility or accountability, but also renounce our power and ability to respond with anything but equal acts of violence and fear.

A clash of civilisations?

The United States's 'war on terror' response to the attacks of 9/11 marked the beginning of a new way of talking about terrorism that transformed the attack from a specific event to a broader range of local and global events and issues, all deemed to be a composite of the 'war on terror'. The framing of 9/11 attacks as a global battle between good and evil established the primary framework through which subsequent news reports on the 'war on terror' could be presented and understood. The 'war on terror' was depicted as a clash between the civilised world and those who engage in terrorism, making the religious ideology of terrorism inconsequent and unexplainable, except insofar as all the world's religions are constructed as part of the civilised world attacked by Al-Qaeda.

In 1993, Samuel Huntington advanced the theory of the 'clash of civilisations'. According to Huntington, the main source of international conflict after the Cold War will be cultural, not political. Samuel Huntington's 'clash of civilisations' thesis emphasised the persistence of cultural boundaries and the re-emergence of civilisational identity. Huntington's opinion is based on his perceived configuration of the newly emerging global pattern, situated in a period of shifting power structures and a diffusion of military and economic power, creating 'cultural fault lines'.[5] Further, the resurgence of religion throughout the world, claims Huntington, underlines the philosophical assumptions, values, ideologies and customs that separate different civilisations and that cause conflict. In this regard, Islam is a threat to Western liberal norms, states Huntington, who is emphatic that 'the underlying problem for the West is not Islamic fundamentalism. It is Islam, a different civilisation whose people are convinced of the superiority of their culture and are obsessed with the inferiority of their power.'[6]

Huntington's theory, advanced over a decade before 9/11, has gained some ground, due in part to the fact that the perpetrators of the terrorist attacks in New York, Bali, Madrid and London invoked Islam as justification for their actions, and fuelled by the kind of rhetoric in the public and media discourse on terrorism. In general, however, Huntington's theory has been dismissed because it transports terrorism from the realm of politics into the realm of cultural conflict, making it difficult, if not impossible, to retaliate with any reasoned, diplomatic response.[7]

Other significant problems with a 'clash of civilisations' world view also exist. It can produce negative stereotypes and gross oversimplifications – for example, there is in reality no single profile of a terrorist. It fails to fully recognise that Islamic (as well as 'Western') practice and beliefs are diverse, containing many internal differences, debates and developments.[8] And it can also be argued that any nationalist and fundamentalist assertions of identity need to be more closely examined as a part of a response or reaction to US hegemony, imbalances in a global free market system, a loss of economic sovereignty, social dislocation and/or the struggle for political self-determination – context is very important.[9]

All terrorists are Muslim ... except the 99.6 per cent that aren't

The question of what drives people to commit extreme acts of violence continues to dominate the field of terrorism studies. It is a question that has drawn comment and driven research in fields as varied as psychology, political science, criminology, history, international relations, strategic studies, sociology, anthropology, law and even economics. Attempts to come up with a useful and consistent personality profile of a terrorist have generally failed. This is because terrorists are diverse in terms of national origin, culture, religion, socioeconomic status, education and professional background and, importantly, in their motivations. For example, early profiles in the 1970s describe terrorists as middle- to upper-class university graduates with Anarchist or Marxist–Leninist ideological leanings.[10] More broadly, a wide range of scholars have rejected the prospect of a unique terrorist personality altogether. As captured by Paul Wilkinson: 'We already know enough about terrorist behavior to discount the crude hypothesis of a "terrorist personality" or "phenotype".'[11]

A number of attempts at the psychological profiling of terrorists have been based on the assumption that terrorists exhibited abnormal personality traits – either lacking sensitivity or being overly receptive and aggressive. As the myth of terrorists as one-dimensional psychologically disturbed individuals was debunked, researchers turned their attention to identifying terrorist traits based on the terrorist organisation or the kinds of terrorism engaged in. Again, these profiles have been criticised for being too static, and either too broad or too narrow to be of any value. As Marc Sageman says, 'It is easy to view terrorists as alien creatures who exist outside normal patterns of social interaction. But the sobering reality is that they don't. Socio-paths do not make capable terrorists – they seldom take orders and are rarely willing to sacrifice their lives for a larger goal.'[12]

One interesting endeavour to profile the individual dynam-ics of Lebanese Shi'a religious terrorists identified no less than thirty-two different character traits.[13] Alternatively, profiles of Palestinian suicide terrorists in the 1990s had described the average terrorist as a male aged between 18 and 27, unmarried and high school educated. Yet this profile transformed over time when expanded research established that almost half of Palestin-ian suicide bombers were actually aged 18 to 23, with a univer-sity or college education.[14] Interestingly, after the 9/11 attacks, the profile of Palestinian suicide bombers was no longer consid-ered relevant to identifying Al-Qaeda and other non-Palestinian religious terrorists.

Other current research on the life trajectories of Indo-nesian terrorists indicates that most have at least a high school education, if not a university or college degree. Only some individuals had a basic religious training, while others became radicalised while attending Madrasah (Islamic religious school) – radicalisation is the process by which an individual or group can become willing to perpetrate acts of violence, including ter-rorism. Further, all individuals believed, at one time or another, that violence was a justifiable means to achieving the political and ideological goals of a particular terrorist organisation.[15]

Taken as a whole, attempts to develop a profile of the indi-vidual terrorist mindset are essentially flawed because they assume that terrorists are somehow different from the rest of us, that there must be some kind of ingrained psychological explanation for what they do. Critically, the assumption that a unique terrorist personality exists implies that terrorists are individuals who are born with a predisposition to violence – but it fails to offer any meaningful explanation as to why terrorism exists in the first place, or to explore the social, political or economic conditions in which terrorism emerges and thrives. Marc Sageman delivers a concise and accurate analysis of why terrorist profiling does not work:

1   It sheds no light on the extent of terrorism and offers no answers about the threat of terrorism.
2   It assumes that a terrorist personality does exist.
3   It ignores the broader context in which terrorism occurs and focuses instead on the individual.
4   It assumes that terrorists are aware of their reasons for becoming terrorists and are able to verbalise their motivations in interview situations.
5   It offers no explanation of the distinction between those who become terrorists and those with similar backgrounds who do not.[16]

Sageman has also argued that the 9/11 leaders themselves were not on the whole religious when they became radicalised.[17]

That is not to say that there aren't some general personality and demographic traits that might be shared by terrorists or would-be terrorists. For instance, a report by the United States Federal Research Division suggests that terrorists exhibit some general personality traits such as alienation from society and a victim identity, devotion to a political or religious cause, loyalty to members of their cell or organisation, and high levels of intelligence, initiative and skill combined with a lack of remorse.[18] Demographically, terrorists tend to be male, aged between 18 and 26, and unmarried.

Yet despite these consistencies, the differences and disparity between terrorists far outweigh any similarities. The report by the Federal Research Division concluded that:

> unfortunately for profiling purposes, there does not appear to be a single terrorist personality ... The personalities of terrorists may be as diverse as the personalities of people in any lawful profession. There do not appear to be any visibly detectable personality traits that would allow authorities to identify a terrorist.[19]

In short, a terrorist will look, dress and act like any other person in any other lawful (or unlawful) profession.

The strategic terrorist

So what makes a terrorist tick? Since acts of terrorism cannot be entirely explained as an outcome of individual psychology or a propensity to violence, other researchers and scholars have turned their attention to the individual triggers to terrorism and applied theories of individual and group behaviour. There are many reasons why a person might join a terrorist group or cause. Various popular explanations attempt to explain terrorism as a calculated, tactical action by actors (terrorists) who are driven to violence (sometimes as a last resort) to achieve strategic goals.

Four of the more popular psychological theories applied to terrorist behaviour are Rational Choice Theory; Frustration–Aggression Hypothesis; Relative Deprivation Theory; and Oppression Theory. As their names suggest, these theories offer a framework for understanding how and why terrorism might occur in particular social, political or economic environments. Rational Choice Theory explains terrorism as a rational and strategic action taken by individuals who view violence as an effective means for achieving their goals. Frustration–Aggression Hypothesis argues that individuals will use terrorism as a violent response to their frustration and oppression. Similarly, Relative Deprivation Theory and Oppression Theory both see terrorism as an action taken by individuals in repressive environments, brought about by economic and class disparities (relative deprivation) or treatment that deprives them of their identity and dignity (oppression).[20]

One of the most well-known contributors to the debate is Robert Pape, who identified three levels of analysis for understanding the causal logic of suicide terrorists: strategic logic, social logic and individual logic.

He argues that the strategic goals of suicide terrorist groups are political and that even religious terrorist groups will use suicide bombing as a form of coercion to obtain their political goals:

> Terrorist suicide has not been well understood primarily because there was a tendency to view these terrorist as very similar to people who commit suicide due to depression or hopelessness. Unfortunately, this assumption misses the important facts because suicide terrorists are not seeking to end their lives, they are seeking to end something else. If foreign hands didn't control their country, they would not choose to die.[21]

Terrorism is a deliberate tactic employed by weak actors against a stronger, more militarily capable adversary. Suicide terrorism is particularly effective at influencing foreign military policy because its impact is magnified. In my own analysis of the five most common terrorist tactics, I determined that person-borne and vehicle-borne suicide attacks had the lowest frequency but highest fatalities of all terrorist tactics used between 2000 and 2009. Suicide attacks averaged 8 deaths for every suicide bomb, compared to 1.7 deaths for every bombing or explosion, 1.5 deaths for every arson or firebombing, 1.3 deaths for every armed attack and 0.7 deaths for every hostage or kidnapping.[22]

The social logic of suicide terrorism, according to Pape, refers to the level of social support for terrorism in its place of operation.[23] Suicide terrorism is most likely to be used as a strategy by groups in occupied territories who have nationalistic or self-governance goals. Sympathetic public support for the terrorists' objectives can act to sanction suicide attacks as martyr operations performed by altruistic individuals, people who are seen to be sacrificing their lives for community or country. In other words, those who we might refer to as terrorists are seen as freedom fighters, are repeatedly praised for their bravery and sacrifice, and can attract financial support.

On the whole, the individual logic of committed suicide attacks argues that suicide bombers are often well integrated in their communities and can enjoy substantial public support for their actions. Unlike other forms of suicide, suicide terrorism is not committed by individuals who are depressed, isolated or disenfranchised. Rather, suicide terrorists will see themselves as altruistic individuals and rationalise their violent actions as a legitimate form of self-sacrifice in the name of a greater cause.

Nonetheless, accepting that terrorism is a strategic choice of weak actors does have some potential pitfalls and relies on two important conditions. The first is that terrorists only use violence as a last resort because they are not able to achieve their political or social goals through other, non-violent, means. The second requirement is that terrorists actually want to achieve political or social change. This condition can be difficult to determine when acts of terrorism are perpetrated without any specific demands or when terrorists commit acts of violence anonymously.

The vengeful terrorist

From another angle, can terrorism be primarily motivated by the need for revenge for either real or perceived trauma or persecution?

The forensic psychologist Raymond H. Hamden has coined the term 'retributional terrorist' to describe terrorists who are motivated by the need to revenge past traumas. 'These are individuals who had no medical or psychological history of psychopathology. They may not have belonged to or favor any particular religious or political group or groups.'[24] The idea that terrorism can be motivated by a psychological need for revenge by means of retaliation appears in several psychological explanations of terrorism. These analyses maintain that terrorism is essentially an act of revenge fuelled by severe physical or mental trauma – like deep-rooted anger about persecution, oppression or humiliation. In some cases, and to some extent, this may be true.

For example, on 29 November 2001 a young Chechen woman named Elza Gazuyeva approached a Russian general and his officers. As she detonated several hand grenades killing the general, his officers and herself, she reportedly asked 'Do you recognise me?' With that, Gazuyeva became the second 'black widow' – the name given to female Chechen suicide bombers. Though reports differ in their details, it is believed that Gazuyeva committed an act of revenge against the general who had killed her husband, and the Russian troops who had shot dead her brother. One particularly gruesome account maintains that the

Russian general forced Gazuyeva to watch as he fatally stabbed her husband.[25]

Similarly, in one of the few studies on female suicide bombers, Mia Bloom has extensively researched the backgrounds of female suicide bombers in the Middle East, Sri Lanka, Chechnya and Columbia.[26] The research established that many of the women had been tortured, beaten and raped or sexually abused by the regimes they targeted. Bloom reported allegations that Tamil women in Sri Lanka who had been abused and humiliated by the Sinhalese security services later became part of the 'Birds of Paradise' – the name given to the unit of female suicide bombers of the Liberation Tigers of Tamil Eelam (LTTE).

Both of these cases – the female suicide bombers such as Chechnya's black widows and the Tamil Birds of Paradise – do fit the profile of the retributional terrorist. These women all survived an atrocity and/or were traumatised by the loss of their husbands, sons, brothers, fathers or cousins to a long, embittered conflict, or by their own personal experiences of rape, torture or abuse at the hands of the regimes they oppose.[27]

Marc Sageman's study of Islamist terrorists in 2008 paints a different picture. He concluded that very few had suffered trauma of any kind. However, the idea and importance of vengeance does feature in several explanations of terrorism and violent extremism – although not necessarily in response to any personally experienced trauma or repression.[28] At the very least, it can be argued that revenge is a powerful emotional path to violence but also one of humanity's most tragic vices. For centuries, revenge and violence have been central themes in literary tradition, from the early Greek notions of vengeance expressed in Homer's epic *The Odyssey* to Shakespeare's *Hamlet* and the story of the ill-fated *Romeo and Juliet*. Revenge and retribution for perceived wrongs appeal to our innate sense of justice and are often used to lend legitimacy to acts of violence that would otherwise be constructed as irrational and unjustified. It is no wonder, then, that some of Osama bin Laden's most well-known communications as the chief of Al-Qaeda represent an attempt to justify violent acts of terrorism as legitimate and equal revenge for past suffering. In his book *Knights under the Banner of the Prophet*, Ayman al-Zawahiri, Osama bin Laden's right-hand man, makes extensive reference to the humiliating 1967 defeat of the Egyptian army by the Israelis as a galvanising force for the radical Islamist movement in Egypt. The defeat saw a massive rise in the number of individuals joining the extremist movement.

In a video recording first released on 10 January 2006, entitled 'Letter to the Americans: why do we fight and resist you?', al-Zawahiri repeatedly justified the use of terrorism by Al-Qaeda as revenge for acts of aggression against Muslim nations by the United States:

> Why are we fighting and opposing you? The answer is very
> simple: Because you attacked us and continue to attack
> us … The blood pouring out of Palestine must be equally
> revenged. You must know that the Palestinians do not
> cry alone; their sons are not orphaned alone … Allah, the
> Almighty, legislated the permission and the option to take
> revenge. Thus, if we are attacked, then we have the right
> to attack back. Whoever has destroyed our villages and
> towns, then we have the right to destroy their villages and
> towns. Whoever has stolen our wealth, then we have the
> right to destroy their economy. And whoever has killed our
> civilians, then we have the right to kill theirs.[29]

Psychological theories of individual and group behaviour that are applied to acts of terrorism do provide some valuable insight into why terrorism occurs in some contexts, particularly where terrorism can be described as an act of revolt or retaliation against aggressive, hostile regimes. However, none of these theories offer any insight into why certain individuals who are oppressed, deprived and frustrated will turn to violence as a means of achieving their goals while the vast majority of those who are also oppressed, deprived and frustrated do not. They also fail to explain why terrorism can attract individuals from stable democracies who, presumably, have access to other (non-violent) forms of protest and political participation, or why international terrorists will attack foreign democratic states, killing innocent civilians.

We might easily apply Frustration–Aggression or Oppression Theory to situations like Chechnya, where the Chechens have fought a long, bitter battle for independence from the Russian Federation. Or the plight of the ethnic Kachin, who have been waging a war for independence in Northern Myanmar. It is also relatively easy to see how Pape's strategic logic can be applied in an analysis of terrorism in the occupied territories of Palestine, or in Iraq, where sectarian divisions between Sunni and Shiite groups have spiralled into the use of suicide bombings against political rivals. But can we apply such assessments to the 9/11 terrorist attacks, the London bombings in 2005 or the Bali bombings? Pondering the question of why terrorists target 'us', it is understandable that some people would assume it is 'because they hate us'.

West vs the rest

Popular analyses of the 9/11 attacks, the London bombings and the Bali bombings attribute these acts of terrorist violence to a deep-seated hatred of Western democratic values and culture. This analysis has been a staple of the popular media discourse on terrorism since the attacks on the Twin Towers in 2001.

Critically, the media plays a significant role in shaping how the public comprehends the visual images of international acts of terrorism that confront us on our television screens and in our newspapers. There are very few people who would not be able to recall exactly where they were or what they were doing when they first encountered the horrific images of a lone plane crashing into New York's Twin Towers on 9/11. Through the magic of television, events far away in space and time were brought into our homes and transformed us all into witnesses of one of the most horrific acts of terrorism in modern history. But photographs and images are only part of the story and the media is often called upon to make sense of these images for a confused audience.

After the 9/11 attacks the media discourse began to take shape around a number of prominent themes: good versus evil; the evil 'other' is Islamic terrorism; Osama bin Laden personifies this evil; the West must battle evil and protect freedom and democracy. In the United States, calls to patriotism and an appeal to collective identity to protect Western freedoms mobilised support for the US administration's response to the 9/11 attacks but also stifled any kind of debate or discussion on the possible motivations or cause for the attacks. Instead, the attacks were constructed as a vile act of a hateful and irrational foe whose only grievance was their abhorrence of Western democracy and its values of freedom and liberty. David Altheide asserts that media coverage of 9/11 demonstrated 'simply the enemy's dislike of the United States of America, its freedom and lifestyle. Indeed, anyone who suggested that the "cause" of the attacks was more complex and that the United States had angered many political groups by previous actions (e.g., support for Israel) was denounced.'[30] Australian scholar Lelia Green agrees with Altheide's assessment and suggests that it was the case that any critical analysis of the September 11 events was deemed 'not only un-American, but potentially anti-American'.[31]

A comprehensive analysis of the range of media coverage in *Time* and *Newsweek* magazines in the five weeks following the September 11 attacks identified five elements which were evident in both the official communication strategies of the US government and the media coverage of the attacks: the endorsement of American values and ideals; endorsement of the US as a world super-power; emphasis on a shared identity and national unity; shifting blame for the attacks and the notion of international support and sympathy for the United States, and; demonisation of the enemy and positioning of the United States as a noble leader in the fight against terrorism.

While the 9/11 attacks happened thousands of miles away, their impact and the impact of the US-constructed response did not escape Australians. Like much of the world, Australian audiences participated in watching the events of 9/11 unfold live on their television stations and over an extended period of coverage in both broadcast and print media. Australian newspapers recorded massive increases in circulation of up to 45 per cent in the immediate aftermath of the attacks, while the television news audience peaked at 5.87 million on the evening of 12 September 2001.[32] The most widely used graphic in Australian newspapers was the now familiar image of the World Trade Center towers engulfed in smoke moments before the second aircraft crashed into one of the towers.

The theme of war featured prominently in Australian press reports about the attacks, as did the theme of terrorism, with headlines such as 'America attacked', 'Terror war on America', 'It's war: America under attack' and 'Act of war'. Two, three and even four days later, newspapers were still producing special spreads on the attacks, including editorials and opinion pieces. One week after the events, for example, the *Gold Coast Bulletin* produced a 32-page advertisement-free full-colour liftout, as well as a further six pages of news, and the Sydney *Telegraph* produced three 16-page full-colour liftouts consecutively from 12 September.

In the first few hours after the 9/11 attacks it was already evident that the attacks would be presented as an act of war, setting the scene for the construction of a discourse that conceptualised reality as a world of opposing forces: the inherently good West and the inherently evil other. Several analyses by Australian researchers confirm that the Australian media's representation of the 9/11 attacks replicated those of the United States. Australians were invited to identify with the virtuous and moral West, under attack because it values democracy and liberalism. Australians became members of a shared Western democratic identity: this was no longer the US's fight, this was a fight for all Western nations, who would continue to be targets for terrorists wishing to undermine the cultural identity of the West. As shareholders in a Western cultural world view, Australians were urged to renew their commitment to the values of democracy and freedom and to view the terrorist attacks as an assault, not on the United States, but on Western civilisation in general.

Soft targets

The image of the radicalised, bearded suicide bomber making his way among the throngs of scantily clad, intoxicated Westerners and shouting 'Allah is great' before detonating his bomb is not entirely unfamiliar to many of us. This image represents everything about the popular construction of terrorism – an individual or group radicalised through a distorted interpretation of religion to kill Westerners because of their hedonistic lifestyle and liberal values; a clash of civilisations where violence is perpetrated against those who do not have the same cultural values; an inexplicable foe whose only desire is to rid the world of Western influence and inflict its own brand of Islamic Shariah.

When citizens are confronted with such stark images, one of the first things highlighted is the absolute contrast between the ominous figure of the suicide bomber and their victims. This thought pattern has repeatedly and automatically (and naturally) assumed that the terrorist is targeting potential victims because of who they are, where they are and what they are doing. But why do some (apparently Muslim) terrorists especially target buildings, clubs, hotels, sporting events and busy marketplaces filled with Westerners? The seeds of the 2002 Bali bombings were sown in a meeting in Thailand between JI operatives and its operational leader, Hambali (who was captured in 2005). At the meeting, Hambali declared that JI should focus its future attacks on soft targets that were frequented by Americans and their allies. In other words, the terrorists planned to hit targets – a busy bar, say, on a popular nightclub strip – that did not have much security.

Soft targets are those that are seen as easy to penetrate due to the lack of a strong security presence – crowded marketplaces, public transport facilities, hotels and clubs might all be seen as usually having relatively low security, alongside a high people flow.[33] In such environments, it is easier for a terrorist wearing a suicide bomb or a car packed with explosives to enter without being detected. In contrast, hard targets such as embassies, government buildings, ports and military facilities can be seen as too risky or too difficult because of higher levels of security.

It is also worth highlighting that terrorists will choose target locations that are likely to draw the most media attention possible. To do this, the terrorist attack hopes to be 'spectacular', in the damage to buildings and infrastructure it causes and/or in the number of casualties it produces. For example, in the 1960s and 1970s, terrorism took to the international stage. The most common tactic used at that time was international airline hijackings.[34] The hijackings, often of US aircraft, guaranteed terrorists the international media exposure they craved and provided them with an open forum to air their demands and influence foreign governments. As international protocols for dealing with airline hijackings were introduced and tightened, the number of hijackings fell dramatically. Yet the urge for terrorism to impact on an international stage had taken hold.

And as more probable targets have been made more difficult, with increased security measures designed to deter potential terrorist attacks, terrorists have simply changed tactics and sought new soft targets that can ensure 'success' – worldwide media exposure, high casualties and maximum destruction. From a strategic and tactical perspective, terrorists will maintain the search for soft targets that do not require a high level of sophistication or expense to penetrate – the most 'bang for their buck'. Indeed, consider the level of destruction caused by the 2005 London bombings, carried out by a small cell of four young men for a total cost of around A$16 000, or the Boston Marathon bombings, in which crude homemade explosive devices were made from pressure cookers packed with nails and ball bearings and transported in backpacks.[35]

Overall, many modern terrorist organisations are organised around small cells of operatives, in part to maintain secrecy and avoid detection. International protocols and national laws have clamped down on terrorist financing as a way of stopping major international acts of terrorism that require large amounts of funding. Localised attacks on discriminate targets such as assassinations of political figures are unlikely to draw the kind of media attention that terrorists favour. Mass attacks that cause maximum disruption and maximum casualties are much more likely to draw attention and to enable terrorists to incite fear in a wider population and coerce governments into complying with their demands. It is for these practical and tactical reasons that bombings and explosions, including suicide bombings, continue to be among the most common methods used by modern terrorists.

Much has been written about the Twin Towers in New York as a symbol of American capitalism and the Pentagon as a symbol of America's military might. In selecting the Twin Towers, the terrorists who perpetrated 9/11 were no doubt fully aware of the significance and connotation of their target choice. Additionally, the attack on the Towers was launched on a busy morning, just as the new work day was starting, ensuring that the buildings would be fully occupied. The destruction of the Twin Towers has altered the New York skyline forever. It is an enduring reminder of the frailty and vulnerability of Western power and wealth.

In choosing the Twin Towers as an attack target, the 9/11

terrorists aimed to reach several audiences. The terrorist act itself would send ripples of fear around the US (and the entire Western world). But the destruction of America's greatest symbol of its wealth and economic superiority also reached out to a different audience, inspiring those who felt aggrieved by globalisation, Western dominance and US economic policy. The destruction of the Twin Towers sent a powerful message about the capacity for a non-state group to resist, challenge and destroy US imperialism and capitalism.[36]

So in considering the symbolic value of terrorist targets, it can be argued that terrorism is not simply indiscriminate acts of violence by crazy madmen. Rather, the choice of target is carefully defined by a number of practical considerations (capacity, expense, security) as well as the message the terrorists wish to convey and the specific audience they wish to communicate to. The 2002 Bali bombers may well have chosen to attack Paddy's Bar and the Sari Club to send a message to a Western audience about their disdain for Australian values, freedoms and culture. But JI could just as well have chosen those attack sites because they were seen as soft targets and because they knew that both the sites were popular with Western tourists and service people.

The next step

How Western societies respond to terrorist attacks will remain a central feature of, and a defining challenge to, the symbolism that will endure after an attack. In the aftermath of 9/11 and related actions like the Bali bombings, popular but misguided reactions acted to reinforce Australian national identity and pitted the West – the coalition of the willing – against the other: an axis of evil. At the heart of the axis of evil was

Islam – a religion seen to be at odds with the cultural values of the West. Complex, dramatic events were quickly oversimplified and condensed into a narrow framework that highlighted attacks on our cultural values by an ideologically driven (and crazy) foe. The immediate answer to the question 'Why do they attack us?' simply becomes 'Because they hate us'. In turn, this can reinforce and even vindicate counterproductive 'clash of civilisations' mindsets, while ignoring or dismissing some of the underlying root causes that might motivate individuals to use violence, or the threat of violence.

1   J. Howard, cited in M. Seccombe and T. Allard, 'A world still stalked by terrorism', *Sydney Morning Herald*, 20 March 2004.

2   See T. Allard and M. Baker, 'PM's vow: we'll get the bastards', *Sydney Morning Herald*, 21 October 2002.

3   G. Sheridan, 'This nation we love must face the threat, and fight,' *The Australian*, 17 October 2002.

4   B. O'Neill, 'The Bali bombings revealed that Islamist thinking isn't that different from modern-day liberal miserabilism', *Telegraph*, 12 October 2012.

5   S. Huntington (1993) 'The Clash of Civilizations', *Foreign Affairs*, p. 72.

6   S. Huntington (1996) *The Clash of Civilizations and the Remaking of World Order*, Simon & Schuster, New York, p. 217.

7   L. Hader (1993) 'Islam: Contrived Threat', *Foreign Affairs*, vol. 72, no. 2.

8   M. Ahrari (1997) 'The Clash of Civilizations: An Old Story or New Truth?', *New Perspectives Quarterly*, vol. 14, no. 2, p. 57.

9   R. Falk (1997) 'False Universalism and the Geopolitics of Exclusion: The Case of Islam', *Third World Quarterly*, vol. 18, no. 1, pp. 14–19.

10 See E. Moxon-Browne (ed.) (1994) *European Terrorism*, G.K. Hall, New York.

11 P. Wilkinson (1986) *Terrorism and the Liberal State*, New York University Press, New York, p. 193.

12 M. Sageman (2008) *Leaderless Jihad: Terror Networks in the Twenty-First Century*, University of Pennsylvania Press, Philadelphia, PA.

13 A. Schbley (2003) 'Defining Religious Terrorism: A Causal and

Anthrological Profile', *Studies in Conflict and Terrorism*, vol. 26, pp. 105–34.

14 See C. Prestowitz (2003) *Rogue Nation: American Unilateralism and the Failure of Good Intentions*, Basic Books, New York.

15 C. Ungerer (2011) *Jihadists in Jail: Radicalisation and the Indonesian Prison Experience*, ASPI–RSIS Joint Report, Issue 40, May.

16 Sageman (2008) *Leaderless Jihad: Terror Networks in the Twenty-First Century*, pp. 16–20.

17 M. Sageman (2006) 'Islam and Al Qaeda' in A. Pedahzur (ed.), *Root Causes of Suicide Terrorism: The Globalization of Martyrdom*, Routledge, London, p. 126

18 Federal Research Division (1999) *The Sociology and Psychology of Terrorism: Who Becomes a Terrorist and Why?*, Library of Congress, Washington, DC.

19 Federal Research Division (1999) *The Sociology and Psychology of Terrorism: Who Becomes a Terrorist and Why?*, p. 60.

20 J. Victoroff (2005) 'The Mind of the Terrorist: A Review and Critique of Psychological Approaches', *Journal of Conflict Resolution*, vol. 49, no. 1, pp. 3–42.

21 R. Pape (2006) *Dying to Win: Why Suicide Terrorists Do It*, Gibson Square, London.

22 A. Aly (2011) *Terrorism and Global Security: Historical and Contemporary Perspectives*, Palgrave Macmillan, Melbourne.

23 Pape (2006) *Dying to Win: Why Suicide Terrorists Do It*.

24 R. Hamden (1986) *The Retributional Terrorist: Type 4*, Research at Center for International Development and Conflict Management, University of Maryland, College Park.

25 See also R. Pape, 'What makes Chechen women so dangerous?', *New York Times*, 30 March 2010.

26 M. Bloom (2007) 'Female Suicide Bombers: A Global Trend', *Daedalus*, vol. 136, no. 1, pp. 94–102.

27 M. Bloom, 2007, 'Female Suicide Bombers: A Global Trend'.

28 M. Sageman (2008) *Leaderless Jihad: Terror Networks in the Twenty-First Century*, p. 65.

29 A. Al-Zawahiri (2006) 'Knights under the Prophet's Banner' in L. Mansfield (trans.), *His Own Words: A Translation of the Writings of Dr Ayman al Zawahiri*, TLG Publications, New Jersey.

30 D. Altheide (2004) 'Consuming Terrorism', *Symbolic Interaction*, vol. 27, no. 3, p. 291.

31 L. Green (2002) 'Did the World Really Change on 9/11', *Australian Journal of Communication*, vol. 30, no. 2, p. 3.

32   M. Bromley (2003) 'A Sham Renaissance? 9/11 and the Authority of Newspaper Journalism', *Australian Journalism Review*, vol. 25, no. 1, pp. 5–31, and Peter Willcox (2001) 'Newspapers and the Terrorism War: News Priorities, Public Duty, and the Bottom Line', *Australian Journalism Review*, vol. 23, no. 2, pp. 7–20.

33   M. Sageman (2004) *Understanding Terror Networks*, University of Pennsylvania Press, Philadelphia, PA.

34   See also W. Landes (1978) 'An Economic Study of U.S. Aircraft Hijackings 1961–1976', *Journal of Law and Economics*, vol. 21, no. 1, pp. 1–31.

35   T. Witcher, 'Boston bombs packed in "pressure cookers"', *The Australian*, 17 April 2013.

36   For further reading, see B. Barber (1995) *Jihad vs. McWorld*, Ballantine Books, New York; A. Ahmed (2003) *Islam Under Siege*, Polity Press, Cambridge, UK; N. Chomsky (2001) *9-11*, Seven Seals Press, New York.

3

FEAR AND LOATHING: THE THREAT OF ASYLUM SEEKERS AND TERRORISM

Cindy Davids and Dilan Thampapillai

'You don't know who's coming, and you don't know whether they do have terrorist links or not.'[1]

PERHAPS – BUT THINK ABOUT IT! You probably don't know who's living down the street from you, or whether they have terrorist links or not. As human beings, asylum seekers are pretty much the same as existing citizens and residents of the country. Refugees arriving by boat are not much different from other refugees – such as those who arrive by plane – but the statement by former Prime Minister John Howard was only directed at so-called 'boat people'.[2] Evidence suggests that the idea that asylum seekers arriving by boat might be terrorists is no more likely than that the person down the street might be a terrorist. Yet John Howard's line implies that particular classes of refugees are inherently dangerous, and that there are definite links between refugees and terrorists.

Worries about security continue to linger in Australia's

collective thinking on asylum seekers. In the final days of the 2001 election campaign, John Howard uttered a simple, yet layered statement; the apparent intent and/or effect – then and now – is to suggest that asylum seekers may be a real threat. It insinuates that we do not and cannot know who or what types of people come here to seek refuge, and that we therefore should fear this group of people.

Since 2001, the link between so-called 'boat people' and terrorism has come to take on a broader meaning within Australian political discourse. The imperative to 'stop the boats' continues as a constant in the political arena, almost a decade after Howard first spoke the words quoted above. In the 2010 federal election, Opposition Leader Tony Abbott's line was 'We'll stand up for Australia. We'll stand up for real action. We'll end the waste, repay the debt, stop the new taxes and stop the boats.'[3] It continues to be implied that we must stop the boats for our own safety. Although direct references to 'terrorists' seem to have disappeared, continuing rhetoric against asylum seekers, from both the government and the opposition, presents a thin veneer over the continuing undercurrent of claims about threats to security and community safety.[4]

The phony 'threat'

This chapter will debunk the myth that asylum seekers represent a particular kind of threat to national security, and that harsh measures are required to discourage them from travelling to Australia in order to reduce the threat of terrorism. The truth is that Australia already has in place a robust set of laws to deal with any asylum seeker who might turn out to represent a threat to the community. It is also the case that Australia's legal and administrative actions against asylum seekers since 2001 are, at best, questionable with relation to our obligations under the 1951 Refugee Convention[5] and other international laws.[6] In short, the alleged threat to national security has been overstated and owes more to political imperatives than to a careful analysis of the facts – even though the latter is said to form the foundation of good intelligence work. At the same time, the 'tough on refugees' policies promulgated by both sides of the political spectrum have effectively denied and negated the humanitarian principles that underlie the Refugee Convention.

Threat or no threat?

The overwhelming majority of asylum seekers represent no threat at all. And in the rare instances in which Australia's security agency ASIO has deemed an asylum seeker to warrant an 'adverse' security assessment,[7] genuine concerns remain about legality and procedural fairness.[8] This relates to the manner in which decisions are made and the inability of the person concerned to either know or to challenge the evidence against them. Many of those who are detained, either as security threats or in the ordinary course of processing and admission, experience anxiety and depression in detention.[9] Prolonged detention is part and parcel of the harsh treatment meted out by government. Yet it is evident that detention only adds to the mental distress and health problems faced by asylum seekers. It undermines a person's ability to fit in and to integrate into the community when they are eventually released from detention.

Yet the threat narrative has a recognised political value. Recent political history has shown that the Howard government used it to great effect. By and large, the Coalition has carried on this approach in opposition. In early 2013, the Shadow Minister for Immigration, Scott Morrison, responded to an incident in which a man on a protection visa allegedly indecently assaulted a female student in her dormitory. Morrison suggested that local residents should be informed when asylum seekers moved into their area.[10] This was a response out of all proportion to the alleged act, when placed in context. Since November 2011 there have been 12 100 asylum seekers released into the community, of whom fewer than five have been accused of a serious offence[11] – a rate of criminality that is 45 times less than that of the general Australian population.[12]

Justifying harsh treatment

The viability of the threat narrative depends upon the existence of a cultural undercurrent of hostility to migrants and a lack of understanding in the community as to drivers of the asylum seeker phenomenon. Since 2008, approximately 30 000 asylum seekers have arrived in Australia seeking protection. The obvious question is: what could drive so many people to flee their home countries, to transit through other countries and to arrive in a place like Australia in order to seek long-term protection? The answer to that question lies within the debate over 'push' and 'pull' factors in asylum seeker policy. When the Howard government left office in November 2007 the number of boat arrivals coming into Australia had fallen to negligible levels. There were in fact just 110 boat arrivals in 2007.[13]

Yet the spectre of boat arrivals between 2008 and 2012 has raised a perception in some quarters of the community that the Rudd and Gillard governments have been weak on border protection.[14] Boat arrivals, officially referred to as 'irregular maritime arrivals', surged after late 2008.[15] Many of the new arrivals have come from Afghanistan, Iraq, Sri Lanka and Iran.[16] The acceptance rates for asylum seekers who enter Australia as irregular maritime arrivals are overwhelmingly high. For example, the Department of Immigration and Citizenship (DIAC) reported that in the 2010–2011 financial year some 90 per cent of Sri Lankan asylum seekers were granted protection visas.[17] Similarly, 92 per cent of Iraqi and 94 per cent of Afghan asylum seekers were successful in gaining a visa. Asylum seekers also arrive in Australia by plane; this mode of entry has historically accounted for between 96 and 99 per cent of asylum applications, and even under the present circumstances, where boat arrivals have increased dramatically, only about half of all onshore asylum applications come from people who have arrived by boat.[18] The acceptance rate for visa applicants who arrive by plane and seek protection is significantly lower than for those who arrive by boat.[19]

Taken at face value, it is a logical proposition that lax immigration laws will act as an enticement to asylum seekers in an environment where the movement of people is globalised and where smuggling networks exist. That said, as the number of asylum seekers rose in 2009 the Rudd government responded with increasingly harsh measures. In early 2010 the Rudd government announced a processing freeze on Tamil and Afghan refugees. Similarly, more people were placed in immigration detention under Australia's mandatory detention scheme. The notion that Rudd, and later Gillard, were 'soft' on asylum seekers is plainly incorrect.[20] Former Prime Minister Julia Gillard herself has stated that conditions for asylum seekers in Australia are deliberately harsh. Ms Gillard said:

That's why people aren't able to work, and people are given the most basic of benefits – absolutely the most basic of benefits – the lowest benefit available in our social security system. And that, too, is done deliberately because we don't want the degree of support to in any way be used by a people smuggler to spruik the benefits of getting on a boat.[21]

More importantly, the emphasis on 'pull' factors understates the importance of 'push' factors. The 'push' factor of ongoing violence and repression is one of the most important reasons driving people to seek asylum overseas. If we take Sri Lanka, Afghanistan and Iraq as examples, it is evident that the ongoing conflicts within these countries have forced – and will continue to force – people to flee for their own safety and security. Rising levels of violence in these countries coincide directly with the uptake of asylum applications in Australia.

Strangely, throughout this period, the fact that the Afghan asylum seekers were fleeing the very regime that Australia and the United States were then fighting in Afghanistan – and other war-torn and violence-riddled regimes – seemed to have been ignored in the conversation.

The political narrative: 'We will decide'

The rise of Pauline Hanson in the late 1990s cut into the voting base of the Liberal Party. Her One Nation party campaigned heavily against boat people 'coming in their thousands', branding them as 'queue jumpers' and calling for the boats to 'be sent packing'.[22] At the time, the Liberal Party could not rely on One Nation preferences flowing to them and John Howard realised he needed to win back the primary votes he had lost to One Nation supporters.

John Howard had personally experienced (in Washington DC) the effects of 9/11, as he was in the United States at the time. It is understandable that the imagery of that day was burned into the consciousness of many Australians. A direct political link to Australia came in the form of comments by Peter Reith (the then Defence Minister) just 48 hours after the incident. He warned that unauthorised boat arrivals to Australia could be a 'pipeline for terrorists'.[23] This political turning point for the Howard government pivoted around the now infamous *Tampa* incident, in which Australia refused permission to enter Australian waters to a Norwegian commercial ship carrying refugees it had rescued at sea.

The MV *Tampa* incident

Much has been written about the August 2001 incident involving 433 asylum seekers rescued from their sinking wooden vessel by the Norwegian container ship MV *Tampa*.[24] It might have been expected that the captain of the *Tampa* would be lauded for an act consistent with maritime law 'rescue at sea' responsibilities and reflecting humanitarian concern. But, in an unexpected turn of events, the Norwegian vessel, the parent company and the Norwegian government found themselves locked in a battle with the Australian prime minister, who was in the midst of the run-up to a federal election that was being fought on platforms of border security and refugees (themes which had assumed prominence given post-9/11 concerns around terrorism).

Responding to calls on 26 August for assistance from Australian search and rescue authorities, the captain of the *Tampa* diverted his ship to pick up the refugees from their disabled and overcrowded vessel. He then sought medical and urgent assistance from Australia, as many of the passengers were unwell, including two pregnant women, 43 children, a number of barely conscious adults, and a man with a broken leg. Over the course of the next few days many of the refugees became very ill. A humanitarian crisis quickly enveloped the captain and crew of the *Tampa*, which, as a container ship, was unable to cope with the huge number of passengers.

The *Tampa* sought permission from the Australian government to unload the refugees at Christmas Island. The Australian government argued that the rescued asylum seekers were the responsibility of Norway or Indonesia and denied permission to enter Australian waters. An instruction was issued to the captain to take the refugees to a port in Indonesia. The captain insisted it wasn't safe to travel back to Indonesia and, indeed, when he turned the vessel around to attempt to do so, many of the passengers became angry and unsettled and he feared for the safety of his ship and crew. The *Tampa* repeatedly sent messages to the Australian government regarding the deteriorating health of the passengers (the Royal Flying Doctor Service was prevented by the Australian government from providing direct medical assistance). The crisis escalated to a conclusion at the three-day point in the standoff when the ship sent a 'mayday' message and headed for the Christmas Island port, despite the closure of the port and the Australian warning to stay outside the 12-nautical-mile exclusion zone. The captain took this action on the basis that he had passengers requiring urgent medical assistance.

The response from Australia was swift and militaristic. After entering Australia's territorial waters the *Tampa* was boarded by 45 members of the SAS. They demanded that the *Tampa* return to international waters before any medical assistance would be provided. Commentators later noted that this was in direct contravention of maritime law, since the number of persons on board meant the vessel was not seaworthy and could not lawfully sail. The captain did not concede and the incident was finalised through the transferral of the refugees to an Australian navy vessel which transferred them to detention facilities in Nauru.

The Australian government's actions in relation to the *Tampa* incident drew international condemnation, while garnering strong domestic support for a 'tough on refugees' approach. In the subsequent reaction of shock and horror over the 9/11 terrorist attacks in the United States, the alleged security threat from unauthorised boat arrivals, and the threat of terrorism, specifically, featured heavily in the political discourse in Australia. This discourse was central to the revival of the Howard government's electoral fortunes.

Win at all costs

The *Tampa* incident was an interesting display of state power. The ship was sealed off from the outside world. A no-fly zone was imposed and the media denied access (largely via jamming the ship's satellite phone). Media imagery of the incident was carefully controlled. In their thorough-going examination of the case, *Dark Victory*, David Marr and Marian Wilkinson report that the Australian Defence Signals Directorate (DSD) monitored conversations between the *Tampa*, its owners and their lawyers and any communication between the ship and outside parties, while ASIO was granted a warrant to collect foreign intelligence ancillary to the DSD.[25]

The *Tampa* incident marked the start of a full-blown strategy to repel what the Howard government deemed unauthorised boat arrivals at all costs. It demonstrated the lengths that the government was prepared to go to in order to prevent asylum seeker boats from landing on Australian shores; to do so would activate onshore refugee processing and determination under Australian law as it then stood. The incident illustrated the government's depiction of refugee movements – a form of forced migration – as a security, sovereignty and border protection issue, rather than a humanitarian crisis.

The problem for aspirant refugees is that this incident and the subsequent 'Children Overboard' (and *SIEV X*) incidents, cemented a dominant political narrative which established a binary class of refugees, while at the same time narrowing the meaning of the term 'refugee'.[26] As Michael Clyne has argued, a specific discourse and selective use of terminology has labelled the contemporary boat arrivals not as legitimate refugees but as 'illegal refugees' (a term that is in itself both contentious and highly prejudicial to public attitudes towards the people concerned).[27] The use of such exclusionary language was no accident – it served a core political purpose. This was demonstrated in the Parliamentary debates around migration legislation, where both major sides of politics used inaccurate and misleading (but prejudicial) terms such as 'queue jumpers', 'illegals', 'illegal arrivals', 'illegal refugees'.[28] This was most starkly illustrated in the comment by the then Minister for Citizenship and Multicultural affairs:

> The people on board MV *Tampa* are not refugees, they are
> occasional *tourists*, who have contracted criminal elements
> or crime gangs who are often involved in the transportation

of drugs to our shores ... It is offensive to those who are genuine refugees who have come to this country and experienced the generosity that this nation has without a doubt offered them.[29]

So what was the cost of a 'win the election at all costs' mentality? The financial costs were significant, as was the assault on our international obligations. The personal burden carried by refugees whose lives had been endangered at sea or who were detained without charge or trial is also well documented. However, perhaps even more remarkable was the successful co-opting of Australia's military leaders into a domestic political campaign, as Marr and Wilkinson note in reference to the *Tampa* incident:

Australian soldiers and sailors had been ordered to do some of the worst work of their lives out on the Indian Ocean. Their leaders had been drawn into the Coalition's election strategy, compromising the political neutrality of the armed forces. Some of the most senior military men in the land were outwitted, outgunned and outmaneuvered in a military campaign designed to re-elect the Prime Minister.[30]

Political u-turn

The initial – and perhaps instinctive – Howard response to media calls to get even tougher on refugees (following a series of harsh measures) had, perhaps surprisingly, been quite different. In a mid-August interview with a Melbourne radio broadcaster – only a few days before the political opportunity afforded him by the *Tampa* incident – Mr Howard had clearly and unambiguously stated:

We are a humanitarian country. We don't turn people
back into the sea, we don't turn unseaworthy boats which
are likely to capsize and the people on them be drowned.
We can't behave in that manner. People say, well send
them back from where they came, the country from
which they came won't have them back. Many of them are
frightened to go back to those countries ... You see the
only alternative strategy I hear is really the strategy of in
the sense using our armed forces to stop the people coming
and turning them back. Now for a humanitarian nation
that really is not an option.[31]

But things subsequently changed. Perhaps there was a whiff
of an electoral opportunity in what was a tight electoral situation. The following month, just 48 hours after the 9/11 attacks
in Washington and New York, the Defence Minister Peter Reith
said in a radio interview that 'you've got to be able to manage
people coming into your country, you've got to be able to control that, otherwise it can be a pipeline for terrorists to come in
and use your country as a staging post for terrorist activities.'[32]
Polling around this time suggested that there may be electoral
advantage in exploiting a perception that so-called (and mistak-
enly called) 'illegal immigrants ... could be terrorists'.[33]

From here, it seems, an ugly form of politics took over. As
the election date approached, radio 'shock jocks' were quick to
get on the bandwagon, with top-rating Sydney breakfast host
Alan Jones specifically asking 'How many of these Afghan boat
people are "sleepers"?'[34] By the time of his official election campaign speech, delivered at the end of October 2001, John Howard's rhetoric had changed markedly. The forcefully delivered
line that 'we will decide who comes to this country and the

circumstances in which they come' cemented in the public's mind the links between refugees and terrorism that had been drawn.[35] It was just a few days before polling day that John Howard told Brisbane's *Courier Mail* newspaper 'You don't know who's coming and you don't know whether they do have terrorist links or not.' Mr Howard said it was a 'perfectly natural concern' and there was 'nothing alarmist or racist about that'.[36] The rest is history. John Howard went on to win the 2001 election (and the next election).[37]

Case(s) in Point: Sri Lankan refugees

Sri Lanka is a particularly useful example with regard to the myths surrounding the security threat that asylum seekers are said to pose to Australia. As a case study, Sri Lanka illustrates the existence of the 'push' factors driving refugee claims, as well as the complexity of the issues surrounding ASIO's assessments of individual refugees. There are currently only around 50 people in total who have been recognised as refugees but are still detained because they have been characterised by ASIO as a security threat. Many of these are Sri Lankan Tamils. By and large they are detained because they either fought for or had dealings with the Tamil Tigers during the Sri Lankan Civil War.[38] In part, this represents a blind spot in Australia's refugee laws in that we do not have a clear framework for dealing with former combatants, even though we know that many of them will be genuine refugees.

In Sri Lanka, Tamils are a minority population who have traditionally lived in the north and north-east of the island. The majority of Sri Lankans are Sinhalese Buddhists, and there is also a small Muslim minority. However, post-independence in 1947 a series of increasingly racist laws disenfranchised the Tamils.[39] There were also a number of communal riots in which the security forces did little to protect Tamil civilians from violence at the hands of Sinhalese rioters.[40] After attempts at a political resolution failed, segments of the Tamil population eventually took up arms against the majority Sinhalese government in the late 1970s.[41] Small skirmishes ensued, leading to the Black July riots of 1983 in which an estimated 3000 Tamils were killed by Sinhalese mobs, aided and abetted by the police and army.[42] Thereafter, a fully fledged civil war broke out between the Liberation Tigers of Tamil Eelam ('Tamil Tigers') and the Sri Lankan government. The resulting war left well over 100 000 people dead.

Over the course of the war the Sri Lankan Army committed a number of atrocities against Tamil civilians, including rape, murder, torture, disappearances and the destruction of property.[43] These crimes drew many Tamils to the insurgency.[44] Notably, the Tamil Tigers had a substantial number of female fighters, and strict rules of conduct and respect between the genders. This was in part a response to the Sri Lankan Army's use of rape as a weapon of war.

The Tamil Tigers styled themselves as the standing army of the Tamil people. In truth, while they enjoyed the support of large parts of the Tamil community, both in Sri Lanka and overseas, they also exercised power in the areas that they controlled with a degree of repression.[45] Nevertheless, between 1990 and 2008 the Tamil Tigers crafted an effective de facto state in the north of Sri Lanka.[46] This included a police service, a judiciary, and health and education systems. This meant no Tamil in LTTE-controlled areas could avoid having dealings with the Tamil Tigers. In the last stages of the war the Tamil Tigers kept some 300 000 Tamil civilians under their control.[47] These people were not free to leave the war zone and were denied the chance to flee to safety.

It is thought that the leader of the Tamil Tigers, Velupillai Prabhakaran, believed that though his troops were outnumbered and outgunned, if they kept a large civilian population with them the international community would be forced to intervene in order to save lives.[48] Such an intervention, like those which occurred in Libya and Kosovo, would have allowed the Tigers to regroup and fight again. Prabhakaran gambled on the international community, and lost badly. Tamil civilians and fighters paid the price. The United Nations has reported that an estimated 40 000 or more Tamil civilians died in the last stages of war, due to targeted bombings by the Sri Lankan military.[49] After the surrender of the Tamil Tigers, some 250 000 people were taken into camps.[50]

Having defeated the Tamil Tigers, the Sri Lankan government, led by President Mahinda Rajapaksa, enjoyed immense popularity among the majority Sinhalese. Yet Rajapaksa's regime has proved to be both corrupt and repressive. As the legitimacy of the regime depends upon its defeat of the LTTE, the Rajapaksa government has maintained a military occupation of Sri Lanka's north. In effect, Tamil civilians in the former conflict areas are still vulnerable to the repression that they suffered during the war years, but with the absence of any organised fighting force.

Consequently, a substantial number of Tamils have fled. Since late 2008, over 140 000 Tamils from the conflict areas have fled from Sri Lanka to India, Canada, the United Kingdom, Australia, Malaysia and a host of other countries. Notably, the Tamils who fled from Sri Lanka to India – where there is a very substantial Tamil population – have been unable to gain citizenship and permanent protection in that country. Similarly, a number of the transit countries offer only temporary respite and no path to long-term survival.

Choices available to refugees

We can glean a number of observations from the Sri Lanka case study that are relevant to our analysis of the security fears surrounding asylum seekers. First, many of the individuals in the conflict areas of Sri Lanka had little choice but to deal with the Tamil Tigers. The Tamil Tigers were effectively the governing authority in parts of northern Sri Lanka. Second, given the war crimes committed by the Sri Lankan Army, many Tamil civilians may have had valid reasons for joining or assisting the Tamil Tigers. It is not against public international law for a community to rebel against systematic oppression and violence. Third, there is no reason to suggest that the Tamil Tigers ever did or would carry on a military struggle in Australia. Notably, the one prosecution in Australia of three men suspected of financing the Tamil Tigers was less than successful. Fourth, the Rajapaksa government is a repressive regime. In order to maintain its legitimacy with the majority of Sri Lankans, it tends to inflate the threat of the Tamil Tigers, but in the five years since the end of the war it has been quite clear that the Tamil Tigers were well defeated.

The position that asylum seekers face is that serious ongoing conflicts within their home countries makes survival there increasingly difficult. These threats to safety and security can linger even after the formal end of a conflict, and where international intervention is ongoing. Having made the decision to flee, asylum seekers are then faced with the reality that many transit countries are not signatories to the Refugee Convention and will not offer them any prospect of long-term residence or citizenship. Likewise, the UNHCR-run refugee camps are poorly maintained and offer little real security. The quest to reach a final destination where there is the prospect of genuine refuge as afforded to asylum seekers under international law is understandable under these circumstances.

The legal narrative: humanitarian obligations

The protection of refugees under Australian law is governed by the *Migration Act* and the Refugee Convention. The Refugee Convention does not have direct effect in Australia's domestic laws. However, as Australia is a party to the Convention, the relevant provisions of the *Migration Act*, dealing with the detention, processing, acceptance or exclusion of offshore arrivals, are designed to implement Australia's obligations under the Convention. Consequently, there exists within the *Migration Act*, insofar as it relates to refugees, a legal framework of protection.

Given the wording of particular provisions of the Act, its relationship with the Convention is quite important. It provides that a refugee to whom a protection visa may be granted is a non-citizen to whom Australia owes protection obligations under the Refugee Convention. In turn, the Refugee Convention defines a refugee as being a person who:

> owing to well-founded fear of being persecuted for reasons
> of race, religion, nationality, membership of a particular
> social group or political opinion, is outside the country
> of his nationality and is unable or, owing to such fear, is
> unwilling to avail himself of the protection of that country;

or who, not having a nationality and being outside the country of his former habitual residence, is unable or, owing to such fear, is unwilling to return to it.[51]

Clearly, according to the *Migration Act* and the Refugee Convention, it is not a crime to seek asylum.[52] Any person with a genuine fear of persecution in their home country can legally seek protection in a Convention country. However, even where a person has been assessed to be a refugee there is no obligation on any nation to provide them with a protection visa.[53] All states retain the sovereign right to determine how non-citizens may enter their country.

In two important recent cases, a majority of the High Court of Australia accepted that the *Migration Act* operates on the basis that Australia has protection obligations to individuals. In *Plaintiff M61/2010 v Commonwealth of Australia*, the High Court stated:

> [R]ead as a whole, the Migration Act contains an
> elaborated and interconnected set of statutory provisions
> directed to the purpose of responding to the international
> obligations which Australia has undertaken in the Refugees
> Convention and the Refugees Protocol ... [The Act] ...
> proceeds, in important respects, from the assumption
> that Australia has protection obligations to individuals.
> Consistent with that assumption, the text and structure
> of the Act proceed on the footing that the Act provides
> power to respond to Australia's international obligations by
> granting a protection visa in an appropriate case and by not
> returning that person, directly or indirectly, to a country
> where he or she has a well-founded fear of persecution for a
> Convention reason.[54]

This statement was again endorsed by the High Court in the M70 case, which knocked down the so-called Malaysia Solution.[55] Under the Malaysia Solution the Gillard government had sought to transfer a group of asylum seekers to Malaysia, in exchange for a larger group of asylum seekers who were held by Malaysia. The High Court struck down that plan on the basis that the Gillard government could not guarantee the safety of the asylum seekers in Malaysia. In M61, two Tamil applicants successfully challenged the Commonwealth's failure to consider their rights under the *Migration Act* owing to their having arrived in an area excised from Australia's migration scheme.

Limitations on protection

The implementation of Australia's obligations under the Convention is limited by specific provisions that have been designed in the post-*Tampa* environment. For example, an amendment to the *Migration Act* narrowed the scope of the Act so as to exclude persons who have not taken all steps possible to avail themselves of the right to enter and live in third countries where they do not have a well-founded fear of persecution.[56]

There are also provisions of the *Migration Act* that establish character test provisions robust enough to exclude from Australia anybody who poses a threat to the nation or to individuals and communities within it.[57] For example, the Minister has the power to cancel or reject a temporary safe haven visa for reasons such as the likelihood that the applicant might:

(i) engage in criminal conduct in Australia; or
(ii) harass, molest, intimidate or stalk another person in
     Australia; or

(iii) vilify a segment of the Australian community; or

(iv) incite discord in the Australian community or in a segment of that community; or

(v) represent a danger to the Australian community or to a segment of that community.[58]

The character test requirements are qualified by the obligation of a 'non-refoulment' obligation to not remove a person to whom refugee protections are owed to a country where that person has a well-founded fear of persecution.[59] The High Court has accepted in the M61 and M70 cases that Australia's non-refoulment obligation informs the interpretation of the *Migration Act*.[60] Accordingly, a person who successfully claims asylum as a refugee, but who fails the character test, cannot be returned to their home country if there is a real possibility that they will come to substantial harm. In such circumstances, another safe country must be found if Australia will not accept the refugee. This was the central issue that arose in another case: *M47 v Commonwealth*.

The ASIO case

The case of *M47 v Commonwealth* has come to be known as the 'ASIO case'.[61] In this case, a Tamil asylum seeker was found to be a genuine refugee but was also assessed by ASIO to be a potential security threat. The man in question had been an intelligence officer for the Tamil Tigers. However, he had left the Tamil Tigers and had subsequently refused to rejoin the organisation. In the aftermath of the civil war he genuinely feared reprisals from both the Sri Lankan government and former Tiger combatants.

ASIO assessed the man, known as M47, as a security risk in 2009 and again in 2011. At the second interview he was allowed to have a lawyer with him and he was informed of the general nature of the allegations against him. However, he was not informed of the specific incidents or information that was alleged to substantiate his negative assessment. In making their assessment, ASIO relied on a regulation made under the *Migration Act* that effectively provided that an adverse ASIO assessment means a visa applicant cannot be granted a visa.[62]

M47 and his lawyers challenged the validity of the regulation under which he was found to be a security threat. It is a general rule of law that regulations must be consistent with the legislation under which they are made and cannot go beyond the scope of the legislation. The relevant provisions of the *Migration Act* provided that the Minister was to review any decisions relating to adverse security assessments. However, under the regulations the decision was effectively made by an ASIO officer. Moreover, given the secrecy surrounding the assessments, the Administrative Appeals Tribunal – which has the power to review such decisions – could not effectively review them because the relevant information was suppressed. A majority of the High Court found that the regulation that ASIO relied upon was invalid because it exceeded the parameters of the *Migration Act*.

Questioning the threat narrative

A number of the findings in the M47 case directly challenge the threat narrative advanced by some politicians and media commentators. For instance, it was explicitly conceded by the Australian government that there was no evidence that M47 had engaged in war crimes.[63] There was no evidence that he intended to continue the Tamil insurgency in Australia, or that he would harm others in the country.[64] In short, there was little evidence on the public record that he presented any threat at all.[65]

Some pertinent points need to be made about the ASIO assessments scheme. First, there are legitimate concerns regarding the veracity of information supplied to ASIO by foreign governments. Asylum seekers have been the subject of adverse security findings based on information supplied by their home countries, when their home countries may have a vested interest in designating them as security threats. The earlier discussion of the situation in Sri Lanka is a case in point. Second, there has been a lack of procedural fairness in the way in which the scheme has been run. Given the secrecy that naturally applies to security screening, asylum seekers who have been adversely assessed may not have been afforded the opportunity to challenge their assessment.[66] Third, there have been instances where asylum seekers who have been assessed as a security risk by Australia have been safely admitted to other countries and have posed no problems in those countries.[67] Fourth, there is no reason to suggest, without more evidence to the contrary, that a former insurgent or combatant in a civil war or other conflict would wish to carry on that struggle in Australia just because they participated in that struggle in their home country.

More generally, despite the populist concern and rhetoric, there is nothing to suggest that anyone who comes from a country racked by conflict represents any greater terrorist, security or criminal threat that those already living in Australia. In fact, the evidence suggests that most refugees who flee violence and war – whatever the context – just want to get on with their lives in peace.

Stopping the next wave

It seems ironic that a relatively 'new' country founded on migrants (both legal and illegal) has a long history of latent fear of the next wave of immigrants. Historians have noted that Australia has never really faced the challenges of people flee-ing persecution and poverty in the way the more geographically accessible nations of the Americas, Continental Europe and the United Kingdom have done.[68] In fact, Australia has always tightly controlled who were regarded as 'genuine' refugees, and during the post–World War II period of the White Australia Policy, this tended to be defined by Australian officials sent to Europe to carefully choose 'suitable, white refugees'. Refugees were circumspectly selected and, ever since, Australians have seen 'genuine' refugees as those who wait patiently for us to come and collect them from far-away camps.[69]

Following the Vietnam War, Australia took many tens of thousands of Vietnamese refugees who arrived through formal processing channels, although public opinion polls at the time recorded negative attitudes on the part of Australians towards those who arrived by boat. By 1992, despite total boat arrivals for the entire decade of the 1980s numbering only a few thou-sand, Australia had introduced mandatory detention, which saw refugees detained for the entire time it took officials to deter-mine their claim for refugee status. This was at odds with the practice in other Western nations, which detained refugees only for the length of time required for health, identity and security checks.[70]

Despite mandatory detention breaching a number of inter-nationally recognised Conventions, polling figures and analy-sis show that the introduction of mandatory detention and the general policy of 'getting tough' on border protection issues was immensely popular with the electorate.[71] Polls showed an increasing trend in opposition to boat arrivals of asylum seekers over time.[72] By the late 1990s, polling showed the average Australian overestimated by 70 times the number of boat people arriving each year in the country. Politicians across the country also engaged in persistent low-level abuse of boat people as 'queue jumpers' for not waiting in foreign camps and 'illegals' for arriving without formal papers.[73] Thus it is clear that the seeds of any politically motivated reversion to a 'tough on refugees' approach are cast into fertile soil.

Fear of the other

What drives this fear of the 'other' in nations that in many other respects would be regarded as humane and compassionate? As noted sociologist Zygmunt Bauman has observed, the refugee, asylum seeker or impoverished exile is the personification of the 'resented stranger' in a globalised world.[74] Tribal wars and massacres, the proliferation of guerrilla armies, the hundreds of thousands who are chased from their homes and forced to escape their own borders through civil wars or external campaigns waged within sovereign nations – all of these result in the mass production of refugees.

For Bauman, refugees are stateless but in addition they are 'hors du nomos' – they are outside law, not the law of a particular country but outside law as such. They are 'outcasts and outlaws', the outsider incarnate of an entirely novel kind, the products of globalisation, a type of 'human waste of the global frontier'.[75]

They are resented and greeted everywhere with rancour
and spite. They are out of place everywhere except in places
that are themselves out of place – the 'nowhere places'
that appear on no maps that ordinary tourists use on their
travels. And once outside, indefinitely outside: a secure
fence with watchtowers is all that is needed to make the
'indefiniteness' of the out of place hold forever.[76]

This fear of the other is just one part of the contestable space
in which refugees and boat people find themselves. The other is
as fodder for the ruthlessness of political expediency. Australia
has seen governments of both persuasions use the concept of
security and national threat to justify various versions of territorial protection, particularly in recent times.[77] Bauman notes that
governments and various public figures have actively cooperated
in the 'aiding and abetting of popular prejudices' about asylum
seekers as a substitute for grappling with more genuine sources
of existential uncertainty that 'haunts their electors'.[78]

Asylum seekers have 'replaced evil-eyed witches and other
unrepentant evildoers, the malignant spooks and hobgoblins
of former urban legends'.[79] Through application of policy and
direct legislative intervention, Australian borders have been
policed against the threat of the other. Asylum seekers have been
politicised and relegated to the 'nowhere space' that Bauman so
eloquently describes. From here, we find it easy to forget – or
ignore – that they are human beings in need of care, protection
and safe haven.

Some have noted a seeming inverse proximity relationship.
That is, while displaced persons remain at a distance, compassion and sympathy can be harnessed and those peoples are often
appropriately judged to be victims of circumstance. However,

once they have the temerity to set out for our shores – or, worse, to arrive – the fact that they display resilience and independent agency is seen as a threat.

National insecurity

The political language that surrounds refugees and asylum seekers in Australia oscillates between two core ideas, both based on mistaken assumptions. The first is a traditional idea that Australians on the whole seem to be comfortable with. It depicts refugees as helpless victims without hope or entitlement, leading them to be passive recipients of the generosity that we may choose to bestow, and for which they are expected to be grateful. African victims of starvation or Asian victims of natural disasters, crowded into refugee camps, fit this bill nicely. The second core idea, which has become prominent in recent years, is that asylum seekers who arrive by boat as 'queue jumpers' pose a threat to Australia's security. They are not passive; they display 'a disagreeable degree of self-will ... willing to take action to address their situation, arrive uninvited'.[80] They are consequently represented as a threat and are often perceived in harshly negative terms. At best, these are people who need to be protected from their own desperation by being prevented from boarding rickety boats and thereby drowning at sea. No further generosity is to be afforded them. These are the people who, in the populist political narrative based on fear and insecurity, 'might be terrorists'.

The threat narrative insinuated by Pauline Hanson, taken up with gusto by the Howard government and extended through the Rudd and Gillard prime ministerships, is overstated and misleading. In fact, in 2008 a Parliamentary Committee found that of the 72 000 visa security assessments done by ASIO over the 2007–08 period, only two people were found to be security risks.[81] Similar figures have been found in other reporting years. Since the number of asylum seekers found to be potential security risks is exceedingly small, there is little reason for the exaggerated security fears that exist in relation to asylum seekers.

Moreover, while it is necessary for Australia to have laws in place to safeguard its national security, valid concerns have been raised about the way in which these laws are designed and administered. The effective narrowing of the way Australia treats its signatory obligations represents a backward step. The generation of policies motivated by political expediency rather than humanitarian obligations has seen the altruistic yet practical aims of the Refugee Convention take a back seat for the last two decades. Yet, as Zygmunt Bauman notes, while we may seek to secure our borders to keep refugees out, the real thing we seek is to fortify our own 'shaky, erratic and unpredictable existence'.[82] But this is unlikely to work. The hopes our politicians link to 'tough' new measures against refugees may provide some immediate political relief but it is likely to be short-lived, as our hopes for secure lives are dashed, our international reputation trashed and our own humanity diminished.[83]

1   John Howard, cited in D. Atkins, 'PM links terror to asylum seekers', *Courier Mail* (Brisbane), 7 November 2001.

2   The terms 'asylum seeker' and 'refugee' are sometimes used interchangeably, as may be the case in this chapter where the discussion relates to attitudes towards or treatment of 'asylum seekers and/or refugees', for example. In terms of status, an asylum seeker is an individual who seeks international protection as a refugee, but for whom this claim has not yet been determined. A refugee is an individual recognised as such under the 1951 Convention relating to the status of refugees: see J. Phillips (2013)

Asylum Seekers and Refugees: What Are the Facts? Background Note, Parliamentary Library, Department of Parliamentary Services, Canberra, p. 2.

3   T. Abbott, 'Tony Abbott's election 2010 statement', *The Australian*, 17 July 2010.

4   In preparation for the 2013 election, the language used by the Coalition opposition continued to imply a security threat from refugees: 'We will deliver stronger borders – where the boats are stopped – with tough and proven measures': Liberal Party of Australia (2013) *Our Plan: Real Solutions for all Australians. The direction, values and policy priorities of the next Coalition Government*, p. 5. At the same time, the governing Labor Party's policy of being tough on refugees arriving by boat 'has matched, if not exceeded, the Coalition's lack of humanitarianism when it comes to refugees, not to mention the disregard for international laws Australia has signed up to': Peter Van Onselen, 'Horrific policy ditches Labor's principle of equal opportunity for asylum-seekers', *The Australian*, 24 November 2012.

5   United Nations High Commission for Refugees (UNHCR) 1951 Convention relating to the Status of Refugees (the Refugee Convention) <www.unhcr.org/pages/49da0e466.html>; see also Australian Human Rights Commission, 'Migration Act amendments undermine Australia's international law obligations', media release, 1 November 2012.

6   This includes the International Covenant on Civil and Political Rights and Convention on the Rights of the Child: see Australian Human Rights Commission (2012) *Sri Lankan Refugees v Commonwealth of Australia: Report of an Inquiry into Complaints by Sri Lankan Refugees in Immigration Detention with Adverse Security Assessments; Report into Arbitrary Detention and the Best Interests of the Child*, AusHRC 56, Australian Human Rights Commission, Sydney; Australian Human Rights Commission (2012) 'Sri Lankan Refugees v Commonwealth of Australia (Department of Immigration & Citizenship)', media release, 6 December.

7   The process of ASIO undertaking security assessments is designed to provide a mechanism to include security considerations in regular government decision making in relation to areas such as the granting of visas. An adverse assessment means that ASIO has recommended that a certain 'prescribed administrative action'(such as the granting of a protection visa) be taken or not taken: see ASIO (undated) 'FAQs: Answers to your frequently asked questions' <www.asio.

gov.au/about-asio/faqs.html>; B. Saul (2012) 'Dark Justice: Australia's Indefinite Detention of Refugees on Security Grounds under International Human Rights Law', *Melbourne Journal of International Law* vol. 13, no. 2.

8   See Australian Human Rights Commission (2012), Sri Lankan refugees report.

9   D. Silove and Z. Steel (1998) *The Mental Health and Well-Being of On-Shore Asylum Seekers in Australia*, Psychiatry Research and Teaching Unit, UNSW, Sydney; see also D. Silove, P. Austin and Z. Steel (2007) 'No Refuge from Terror: The Impact of Detention on the Mental Health of Trauma-Affected Refugees Seeking Asylum in Australia' *Transcultural Psychiatry*, vol. 44, no. 3, p. 359.

10 L. Taylor and J. Ireland, 'Libs push for asylum crackdown,' *The Age*, 28 February 2013.

11 B. Hall, 'Liberals under hammer over asylum seeker claims,' *Canberra Times*, 28 February 2013.

12 B. Hall, 'Few asylum seekers charged with crime,' *Sydney Morning Herald*, 1 March 2013.

13 Angus Houston, Paris Aristotle and Michael L'Estrange (August 2012) *Report of the Expert Panel on Asylum Seekers*, Australian Government, Canberra, p. 19.

14 For example, an early action of the incoming Rudd government in 2007 was to abolish the Howard government's policy of issuing refugees with temporary rather than permanent visas: see Department of Immigration and Citizenship (2011) 'Fact Sheet 68 – Abolition of the Temporary Protection visa (TPV) and Temporary Humanitarian visas (THVs)' <www.immi.gov.au/media/fact-sheets/68tpv_further.htm>.

15 This is DIAC's preferred term: see Phillips (2013) *Asylum Seekers and Refugees*, p. 4.

16 Department of Immigration & Citizenship (DIAC) (2012) *Asylum Trends: Australia, 2011–2012*, Annual Publication, p. 25.

17 DIAC (2012) *Asylum Trends*, p. 31.

18 Phillips (2013) *Asylum Seekers and Refugees*, p. 6; DIAC (2012) *Asylum Trends*, p. 2; J. Phillips and H. Spinks (2013) *Boat Arrivals in Australia since 1976*, Background Note, Parliamentary Library, Department of Parliamentary Services, Canberra.

19 Phillips (2013) *Asylum Seekers and Refugees*; K. Koser (2010) *Responding to Boat Arrivals in Australia: Time for a Reality Check*, Lowy Institute for International Policy, Sydney.

20 This claim has continued to be used with great political effect by

the Coalition Opposition. For example, the Shadow Leader of the House, Mr Christopher Pyne, referred to the government's measures as acting as a 'sugar' that attracts asylum seekers: see Christopher Pyne, 'Government has only itself to blame for the boats', *The Australian*, 27 December 2011.

21   M. Kenny and B. Hall, B, 'Push to free refugee families as the boats keep coming', *Sydney Morning Herald*, 27 March 2013.

22   Marr and Wilkinson (2004) *Dark Victory*; I. McAllister (2003) 'Border Protection, the 2001 Australian Election and the Coalition Victory', *Australian Journal of Political Science*, vol. 38, no. 3; S. Jackman, 1998, 'Pauline Hanson, the Mainstream, and Political Elites: The Place of Race in Australian Political Ideology', *Australian Journal of Political Science*, vol. 33, no. 2, pp. 167–86; J. Minns (2005) '"We Decide Who Comes to This Country" – How the Tampa Election was Won' in J. Coghlan, J. Minns and A. Wells (eds) *Seeking Refuge: Asylum Seekers and Politics in a Globalising World*, University of Wollongong Press, Wollongong, NSW.

23   'Transcript of The Hon Peter Reith MP Radio Interview with Derryn Hinch – 3AK', 13 September 2001 <www.defence.gov.au/minister/8tpl.cfm?CurrentId=999>.

24   See, for instance, Marr and Wilkinson (2004) *Dark Victory*; M. Grewcock (2009) *Border Crimes: Australia's War on Illegal Migrants*, Institute of Criminology, Sydney; P. Mares (2002) *Borderline: Australia's Response to Refugees and Asylum Seekers in the Wake of Tampa*, 2nd edition, UNSW Press, Sydney; F. Brennan (2007) *Tampering with Asylum: A Universal Humanitarian Problem*, University of Queensland Press, Brisbane.

25   Marr and Wilkinson (2004) *Dark Victory*, p. 115.

26   Marr and Wilkinson (2004) *Dark Victory*; Grewcock (2009) *Border Crimes*; Mares (2002) *Borderline*; Brennan (2007) *Tampering with Asylum*.

27   M. Clyne (2005) 'The Use of Exclusionary Language to Manipulate Opinion: John Howard, Asylum Seekers and the Re-emergence of Political Incorrectness in Australia', *Journal of Language and Politics*, vol. 4, no. 2, pp. 73–96.

28   Clyne (2005) 'The Use of Exclusionary Language to Manipulate Opinion', p. 188; Phillips (2013) *Asylum Seekers and Refugees*.

29   The then Minister for Citizenship and Multicultural Affairs, Gary Hardgrave (Hansard, 30 August 2001) quoted in Clyne (2005) 'The Use of Exclusionary Language to Manipulate Opinion', p. 182, emphasis added.

30 Marr and Wilkinson (2004) *Dark Victory*, p. 384.

31 'Transcript of the Prime Minister The Hon John Howard MP Interview with Neil Mitchell – Radio 3AW', 17 August 2001 <www.sievx.com/articles/psdp/20010817HowardInterview.html>.

32 Transcript, radio interview with Derryn Hinch.

33 Gary Morgan, pollster, in F. Kelly, 'Howard's electoral fortunes turn around', *7.30 Report*, ABC TV, 20 September 2001.

34 Fran Kelly, 'Howard's electoral fortunes turn around'; P. Mares (2003,) 'What Next for Australia's Refugee Policy?' in M. Leach and F. Mansouri (eds), *Critical Perspectives on Refugee Policy in Australia*, Deakin University, Geelong.

35 'John Howard's 2001 Election Policy Speech', reproduced at AustralianPolitics.com <australianpolitics.com/2001/10/28/john-howard-election-policy-speech.html>.

36 D. Atkins, 'PM links terror to asylum seekers', *Courier Mail*, 7 November 2001.

37 Border protection and terrorism were significant issues in shaping the election outcome: see McAllister (2003) 'Border Protection, the 2001 Australian Election and the Coalition Victory'; Minns (2005) '"We Decide Who Comes to This Country" – How the Tampa Election was Won'.

38 Under the rules of public international law, a civil war is recognised as a non-international armed conflict. Provided that the hostilities reach a certain threshold of intensity and the rebels are sufficiently organised, they are recognised under international law as insurgents and not as mere terrorists. The Tamil Tigers were a genuine insurgency, though they also committed numerous acts of terror within Sri Lanka. International law also sets rules on the conduct of hostilities. For a discussion of the rules of war under international law, see C. Gray (2000) *International Law and the Use of Force*, Oxford University Press, London. Both the Tamil Tigers and the Sri Lankan Army breached these rules by directly targeting civilians.

39 W. McGowan (1993) *Only Man Is Vile*, Picador, New York.

40 A. Pratap (2001) *Island of Blood*, Viking Press, New Delhi; see also L. Sabaratnam (2001) *Ethnic Attachments in Sri Lanka*, Palgrave, New York.

41 M.R. Narayan Swamy (2010) *The Tiger Vanquished: LTTE's Story*, Sage, London.

42 For an account of the 'Black July' riots of 1983, albeit a somewhat partisan one, see E.M. Thornton and R. Niththyananthan (1984) *Sri Lanka, Island of Terror: An Indictment*, Eelam Research

Organisation, London; see also George Alagiah (2007) *A Passage to Africa*, Abacus, London.

43 Thornton and Niththyananthan (1984) *Sri Lanka, Island of Terror*; see also Human Rights Watch, 'We Will Teach You a Lesson: Sexual Violence Against Tamils by Sri Lankan Security Forces', 26 February 2013 <www.hrw.org/reports/2013/02/26/we-will-teach-you-lesson>.

44 An account of the considerations that inspired resistance can be found in Niromi De Silva (2011) *Tamil Tigress*, Allen & Unwin, Sydney.

45 A detailed and impartial account of the crimes committed by the Tamil Tigers is available from the Sri Lankan NGO group 'University Teachers for Human Rights'; see also Narayan Swamy (2010) *The Tiger Vanquished*.

46 See Narayan Swamy (2010) *The Tiger Vanquished*; see also N. Malathy (2012) *A Fleeting Moment in My Country: The Last Years of the LTTE De-Facto State*, Clarity Press, Toronto.

47 G. Weiss (2011) *The Cage*, Picador, Sydney; see also F. Harrison (2012) *Still Counting the Dead*, Portobello Books, London.

48 Weiss (2011) *The Cage*.

49 United Nations, Report of the Secretary-General's Panel of Experts on Accountability in Sri Lanka, 31 March, 2011 <www.un.org/News/dh/infocus/Sri_Lanka/POE_Report_Full.pdf>.

50 This included male and female fighters of the Tigers. Some of these fighters had been forcibly recruited in the last stages of the war. Subsequently, credible allegations of rape and murder were levelled against the Sri Lankan Army. It has been reported that a number of female fighters were gang raped and murdered after the surrender: see United Nations, Report of the Secretary-General's Panel of Experts; see also US Department of State (2009) 'Report to Congress on Incidents during the Recent Conflict in Sri Lanka'; Channel Four, 'Sri Lanka's Killing Fields' <srilanka.channel4.com>; European Centre for Constitutional and Human Rights (2010) 'Alternative Report on the Implementation of the UN Convention on the Elimination of Discrimination against Women (CEDAW) – Sri Lanka'; University Teachers for Human Rights (2009) 'Let Them Speak: Truth about Sri Lanka's Victims of War', p. 142.

51 Article 1A(2).

52 The right to seek asylum is recognised under Article 14 of the Universal Declaration of Human Rights.

53 *Minister for Immigration and Multicultural Affairs v Khawar* (2002) 210 CLR 1, [42].

54 243 CLR 319.

55 *Plaintiff M70/2011 v Minister for Immigration and Citizenship* (2011) 280 ALR 18, [44] and [90].

56 Subsections 36(3), 36(4) and 36(5) of the *Migration Act*.

57 For example, sections 500A and 501 set out grounds upon which asylum seekers can fail to satisfy the character test. The character test provisions are also reflected in the Refugee Convention itself. Article 32 of the Convention permits a member state to expel a refugee on the basis of public order and national security,

58 Subsection 500A(1)(c). Notably, all of these considerations fall within the broad rubric of Article 32 of the Refugee Convention.

59 Article 33 of the Refugee Convention contains the non-refoulment obligation.

60 Refugee Convention, Article 33.

61 (2012) 86 ALJR 1372.

62 See the explanation of adverse security assessments in note 7.

63 M47, [16].

64 If M47 had in fact represented such a threat, the Commonwealth could have expressly relied on section 500A(1)(c) of the *Migration Act*. No evidence was presented in the M47 case that the plaintiff presented any such threat. In cases such as that of M47, it is likely that the adverse security assessment relates to past conduct: see Saul (2012) 'Dark Justice', p. 706.

65 The outcome of the M47 case caused a rethink of the way in which security assessments are undertaken and administered. In the aftermath of M47 a review system, headed by a retired Federal Court judge, was put in place, in order to make the security assessment scheme fairer and more effective: see ABC News online, 'Government to allow reviews of ASIO assessments,' 15 October 2012 <www.abc.net.au/news/2012-10-15/government-to-allow-reviews-of-asio-assessments/4314652>.

66 Australian Human Rights Commission (2012), Sri Lankan refugees report.

67 This concerns Mohammad Sagar. He was found to be a security risk by ASIO but was later resettled by the UNHCR to Sweden: see Joint Standing Committee on Migration Report, *Immigration Detention in Australia: A New Beginning*, 'Criteria for release', p. 40.

68 Grewcock (2009) *Border Crimes*.

69 Marr and Wilkinson (2004) *Dark Victory*, pp. 44–45.

70 Phillips and Spinks (2013) *Boat Arrivals in Australia since 1976*; Phillips (2013) *Asylum Seekers and Refugees*.

71   McAllister (2003) 'Border Protection, the 2001 Australian Election and the Coalition Victory'; Phillips and Spinks (2013) *Boat Arrivals in Australia since 1976*; Minns (2005) '"We Decide Who Comes to This Country" – How the Tampa Election was Won'.

72   K. Betts (2001) 'Boatpeople and Public Opinion in Australia', *People and Place*, vol. 9, no. 4, pp. 34–48.

73   Marr and Wilkinson (2004) *Dark Victory*, p. 48.

74   Z. Bauman (2009) *Does Ethics Have a Chance in a World of Consumers?* Cambridge University Press, Cambridge, Mass.

75   Bauman (2009) *Does Ethics Have a Chance in a World of Consumers?*, p. 39.

76   Bauman (2009) *Does Ethics Have a Chance in a World of Consumers?*, p. 39.

77   See Carmen Lawrence (2005) 'Fear of the "Other" and Public Policy' in Coghlan, Minns and Wells (eds) *Seeking Refuge*.

78   Z. Bauman (2007) *Liquid Times: Living in an Age of Uncertainty*, Polity, Cambridge, p. 43.

79   Bauman (2007) *Liquid Times*, p. 43.

80   P. Mares (2002) 'Reporting Australia's Asylum Seeker Crisis', *Media Asia*, vol. 29, no. 2, p. 74.

81   Joint Standing Committee on Migration, *Immigration Detention in Australia*, p. 39.

82   Bauman (2007) *Liquid Times*, p. 85

83   M. Grattan and B. Hall, 'New crackdown on refugees', *The Age*, 22 November 2012.

4

CYBER-TERRORISM: THE PHANTOM MENACE

Daniel Baldino

'Cyber-attacks will end the world as we know it.'

DOES NOT COMPUTE. The notion that governments must move to a war footing, and radically reorganise security ideas, to limit wholesale destruction stemming from active threats in cyberspace is a fashionable talking point. In the 21st century, the computer mouse has been depicted as creating as much havoc as old-fashioned bullets and car bombs. Many have speculated that technology-based threats like advanced, offensive cyber-weapons are insidious, ever-increasing and will soon rival traditional wars. Some, such as former US defence secretary Leon Panetta, have warned about a future 'cyber-Pearl Harbour' that will cripple society, compromise national defence and destroy critical national assets.[1]

The new reality is that we are being told to prepare for a decades-long war against mounting digital dark forces, including online terrorists, state-sponsored cyberhackers and perhaps the rise of an irreversible cyber–Cold War – with the United States and China at centre stage. Cyberspace is the ultimate battlefield. These automated waves of intentional (and unforeseeable) cyber-assault will be nimble, networked and can be launched from anywhere in the world, including by thrill-seeking hackers sitting alone in dark basements or cyberwarriors working diligently in small groups in locations like an isolated government building. Others, like whistle-blower Edward Snowden, who revealed the National Security Agency's massive secret spying machinery in the United States in June 2013, have also been accused of undermining national interests in this new world of interconnectivity.

In this way, the inherent vulnerabilities of global computer networks are projected to lead to an imminent world of 'cyber-9/11s' that will 'shut down power grids, freeze money supplies, cripple transportation systems and imperil nuclear plants'.[2] At the very least, cybersecurity has become a hot topic – a trendy buzzword. For instance, tech research firm IDC predicted that 2003 would be the 'year of cyber-terrorism', and that extended attacks would bring the Internet 'to its knees'.[3] In 2010 the US Director of National Intelligence cautioned that the United States would be threatened by cyber-operations of 'extraordinary sophistication'.[4] In 2013, a sampling of computer security professionals forecast a 'major' cyber-attack on modern infrastructure in the United States by the end of the year.[5] So how real and dangerous are these cyber-threats in a technology-dependent world? Could an intentional cyber-attack be launched by the 'push of a button'? Will newfangled forms of sustained online warfare involve a type of 'electronic jihad' against Australia and like-minded nations?

Slippery definitions

A core drawback regarding an item like cyber-terrorism is its elastic definition. It is evident that a variety of cybersecurity-related topics – such as cyberweapons, cyber-protest, cyber-power, cyber-crime, cyber-espionage and cyber-enabled sabotage – all tend to be lumped into one booming threat. As a result, cyber-metaphors become blurred, imprecise and distorted. Taipale has argued that 'cyber-terrorism' itself has become a 'useless' expression.[6] An automatic by-product of misleading analogies is that we don't really know what it is that we are essentially fighting against. Another problem relates to resource allocation: are we prioritising budget commitments, contingency plans and intellectual resources to the 'right' type of repeated strategies, and on what targets?

As a starting point, the concept of cyber-terrorism might be applied to actions involving the intersection of terrorism and cyberspace. It can involve a criminal act to create fear and bully or coerce people in order to influence decision making. It might be motivated by political objectives or religious impulses, or stem from personal and trivial goals. Generally, to be associated as a class of cyber-terrorism, computer or information systems should either be used to conduct the attacks or will be the target of the attack. The Department of Foreign Affairs and Trade (DFAT) has also correctly mooted that future terror groups could use cyber-attacks as an ancillary option; a cyber-tactic to provide a decoy or to work in conjunction with a larger kinetic (physical) attack.[7] This might lead to a larger conclusion – that cyberwarfare is best seen as a supplementary tool that will operate in conjunction with traditional forms of warfare.

Nonetheless, it is clear that various groups are using

computers to disrupt network systems. Elsewhere, reports have claimed that some countries – Israel, for example – are currently being attacked 1000 times a minute by people targeting its critical infrastructure – including attempts to cut its electricity supply.[8] Interestingly, security experts have highlighted that these attempted hacks are regularly unable to mount any sort of meaningful assault on major systems. Instead, in addressing national requirements, they tend to view these limited attacks as 'a strategic threat, not a threat to our survival. Our task in the cyber-war is to ensure the continued operation of computers and systems.'[9] In other words, cyber-attacks are not envisaged as an existential threat; such cyber-intrusions will not cause cyber-Armageddon and paralyse Israel. There is also an implicit recognition that Israel can have only a limited degree of control over the operations of cyberspace.

It is worth noting that the instigators of such cyber-attacks against Israel may not purely involve transnational terrorist groups or the obvious nation-state culprits (like Iran), but might consist of organised crime, or state-sponsored espionage driven by conventionally friendly and allied nations (or even derive from citizens within Israel itself). 'The countries where the attacks originate from are not necessarily the ones we are at war with, including the US, China and Korea.'[10] Further, as technology evolves, it is not unreasonable to suggest that online intrusions like the stealing of commercial or military secrets will remain an ongoing and genuine security challenge. Yet this should not be equated with war. It is espionage. Cat-and-mouse foreign spy games have never been regarded as an act of war.[11]

Equally, cyber-terror does not directly result in injury, death and violence. About the only thing specialists can seem to agree on about terrorism is that it involves violence, or the threat of violence. By comparison, should items like email disruption or website defacement or hacking that intends to disrupt service for a period of time be equated to an act of terror? A denial-of-service attack refers to the flooding of an online server with false requests until it is completely down and non-operational. Yet low-level denial-of-service operations do lead to another fiddly dimension of debate: should 'primitive' activism or internet vandalism, which might cause delays to non-essential services and is not characterised by violence, be called cyber-terrorism?

To date, the consequences of denial-of-service attacks against Internet-connected systems have, at best, a marginal impact on national security. A target is not irreparably destroyed. Any fallout, while unquestionably bothersome, has been contained. For example, in August and September 2012, the hacker group Anonymous launched a series of attacks on Australian government websites to protest against the government's plans to store customer data and record how citizens used the internet. Most of this 'internet warfare' involved the shutting down of affected websites, including ASIO's official public homepage. While the defacement of websites would be irritating to the target, the ultimate end result was relatively minor. The web pages were all back up within 24 hours. The hack itself had zero impact on security operations. While ironically encouraging authorities to work harder to better shield their systems, ASIO acknowledged that the public website did not host sensitive information, nor did the digital disturbance represent any risk to its core business – gathering information and producing intelligence.[12]

E-terror

It is incredibly difficult to locate a real-life cyber-terror event that has had an overwhelming impact on critical infrastructure, let alone caused a loss of human life.

Perhaps one of world's first examples of an arguably success-ful cyberweapon has been used against, rather than perpetrated by, the 'rogue state' in Iran. In 2010, Iran had experienced a cyber-attack – the work of the complex Stuxnet computer worm, designed by the United States and Israel, who aimed to hurt Iran's nuclear facilities at Natanz.[13] The advanced malware code was launched to sabotage uranium enrichment operations (by destabilising critical centrifuges that appeared to be func-tioning normally) and stealthily incapacitate Iran's budding nuclear research program.

Yet it is worth noting that the attack still required physical involvement. The virus had to be manually injected into Iranian networks to infect networks (for example, via a portable USB device) because nuclear control systems are 'air-gapped' – not physically connected to the Internet. Additionally, despite the code's cleverness in exploiting security loopholes, Stuxnet had clear-cut limitations. It took a very long preparation time (and a great deal of trial and error), required high-level technologi-cal expertise and intelligence know-how and entailed significant financial outlay.[14] Interestingly, despite the security lapse, most of the centrifuges in fact survived the attack. In effect, the Stux-net worm initiated only a temporary hindrance for the Iranian nuclear program – a limited one-shot attack from which it com-pletely recovered.

The *Bulletin of the Atomic Scientists* added: 'how ironic that the first acknowledged military use of cyberwarfare is ostensibly to prevent the spread of nuclear weapons.'[15] Nonetheless, beyond debate whether such a recorded computer virus was the first step towards the age of covert cyberwar, the fact that Israel and the United States were jointly behind the state-produced sabotage raises another age-old dilemma – that 'one person's terrorist is another person's freedom fighter'.

Many extra questions remain. Was Stuxnet an act of war? What is the profile of a cyber-terrorist? How can we best protect and preserve our latest threat landscape, the cyber-world – alongside traditional land, sea, air and space domains? What is the likelihood and impact of an enormous cyber-terrorist attack in Australia and other Western countries? And to what extent are military ideas and revamped concepts like cyber-deterrence a logical first-step plan to counter computer vulnerabilities?

According to Dorothy Denning, cyber-terrorism consists of targeted and 'politically motivated hacking operations intended to cause grave harm such as the loss of life or severe economic damage'.[16] Terrorists will adapt tactics to suit their objectives or situation at any given time. The apparent push towards cyber-attacks is seen as a highly attractive prospect for modern-day or could-be terrorists. Terrorists can exploit the anonymity of an Internet-based world, spreading propaganda, raising funds, recruiting followers online and sharing terror plots with a lower risk of capture. Concurrently, in 2012, the US Department of Homeland Security reported that it had received more than 50 000 reports of cyber-intrusions or attempted intrusions in less than a 12-month period – an increase of over 10 000 reports when compared to the previous year.[17] At the same time, similar reports claimed that disruptive hacking attempts are being made on Australian defence networks at least 20 times each day.[18]

The repeated assumption about future battlelines is that as

ultraviolent terrorist organisations become more computer literate and learn state-of-the-art programs, their potential cyber-strike options will multiply and they will become more digitally active. The establishment of new and previously undiscovered IT advancements will permit enemies to conceal their identities, with early warnings against these types of launched attacks remaining near impossible. Terrorists will be able to both modify and implement Internet-based attack plans on critical data and communications networks. In the near future, this blurring of digital and physical words will take advantage of frail but high value national infrastructure projects in industrialised nations. These cyber-weapons will be deployed on the financial sector, gas pipelines, health services, air traffic control centres, military installations and water supply systems.

In 2002, Richard Clarke, a former US National Coordinator for Security, Infrastructure Protection, and Counter-terrorism, warned a predominantly business-orientated crowd of future perils: 'if you spend more on coffee than you do on security you will be hacked; what's more, you deserve to be hacked.'[19] Malware is malevolent software designed to damage or disrupt a system. Malevolent computer codes that are able to copy themselves and infect an ordinary computer are called viruses. Most generic viruses are triggered by unintentional actions taken by the recipient (for example, opening a rogue email). Another intrusion is spyware, a kind of malware that can instantly collect small pieces of information about users without their knowledge. Alternatively, a Trojan horse is the name given to a program that masquerades as a harmless tool or innocent game but can, for instance, record what is being typed in order to capture sensitive data (for example, a user's passwords).

Similarly, policymakers in Australia have warned about

alleged cyber-disasters based on the permanently shrinking gap between a terrorist's wish list and their growing 'fire-power' capability. In fact, the 1951 ANZUS alliance has recently been modernised to address cyberwarfare within a changing threat landscape.[20] The Australian government has also been steadily exploring proposals to increase surveillance on citizens and extend the powers of police and security agencies to retain emails, text messages and other data used in possible cybercrimes. Further, in 2013, former Prime Minister Julia Gillard announced the construction of an Australian Cyber Security Centre to better coordinate a concerted campaign to defend cyberspace as a strategic asset, although critics claim that the much-hyped centre is a budding bureaucratic Frankenstein's monster with 'no central leadership, no legislation and no clarity around different roles'.[21]

Regardless, the image that today's digitally vulnerable world is facing an unprecedented cyber-meltdown has been bolstered in popular culture. The imminent dangers of technology have been neatly captured in a number of popular big-screen Hollywood films – *Tron*, *Wargames*, *Swordfish*, *Live Free or Die Hard*, *Untraceable*, *Eagle Eye*, *Independence Day* and *Sneakers*, just to name a few. Prominent screenwriters and directors have skilfully captured, and arguably reinforced, an atmosphere of fear and uncertainty about poor defence shields against cyber-dangers and the possible consequences of infected information networks: the obliteration of the share market; the triggering of chemical plant explosions; the infiltration of the Pentagon's classified defence systems and launch of multiple missile strikes.

Without doubt, in the real world, cybersecurity, including safeguarding government agencies against hacking attempts and unauthorised access to network systems, is an important issue.

Year by year, various stakeholders are rethinking steps to better protect, and restore the functions of, critical computer networks and infrastructure. And discussion about the consequences of cyber-tricks that might steal commercial or military secrets should lead to open discussion about systems failures, appropriate responses and best practice guidelines.

But many hyped threats like cyber-terrorism remain hypothetical, unsubstantiated or overblown. For instance, cyber-attacks by non-state terror actors still face significant technical hurdles like in-built system redundancies. A wide variety of cyber-attack options remain unable to directly cause mass death and lasting physical destruction. Conflated cyber-intrusions, such as website defacement, are relatively inconsequential and should not be presented as high-end threats to national security. Extended statistics on items like trends in cyber-crime remain highly dubious and imprecise. And despite new hacker tools and plenty of attractive targets, the capabilities of mooted challengers like Al-Qaeda to harm national security interests should not be overstated. As George Lucas put it: 'To be blunt, neither the 14-year-old hacker in your next-door neighbor's upstairs bedroom, nor the two or three-person Al-Qaeda cell holed up in some apartment in Hamburg are going to bring down the Glen Canyon and Hoover dams.'[22]

At the very least, with governments pushing for Internet data retention and stronger control and regulation of cyberspace, it is worth reflecting on the scope and implications of sweeping cybersecurity prescriptions, the potential loss of individual privacy, censorship issues and the prospects for misuse of new covert government powers in the name of crushing forecasted cyber-chaos.[23] Emergency-level panic about anticipated cyber-attacks will need to take into account the fact that not only are many worst-case projected scenarios highly questionable, but that fevered imaginations could propel resource misallocation, policy mismanagement and the excessive militarisation of cyberspace.

The E-fear industry

In light of this, there are a number of key reasons why the threat of cyber-terrorism does tend to lend itself to a bias which is prone to inaccuracy and overinflation.

Firstly, no politician wants to be seen as on the wrong side of history by compromising national security. In this case, policymakers are conscious of being judged by their opponents and peers as 'soft' on terror. This leads to tough-sounding talk about ambiguous-although-looming dire threats and an over-emphasis on 'what could happen', rather than a push for sensible risk-based assessments and measured policy adjustments.

And ironclad declarations to 'smash' terrorism have generally been warmly received in a post-9/11 world. An emotionally stressed public has repeatedly indicated a knee-jerk preference for the presumed delivery of better security standards to catch terrorists over the preservation of long-standing democratic rights and legal protections. Nonetheless, irrational fear, or the exploitation of that fear, remains a highly counterproductive starting point for the formation of working policy.

Alternatively, a less cynical perspective might argue that today's distracted society is unprepared or indifferent to emerging problems like IT fraud. Policymakers and other interested groups are therefore simply attempting to raise public awareness about vulnerabilities in operating systems, so ongoing risks are sometimes dramaticised or overplayed, with the aim of hopefully igniting public readiness and stimulating forward-thinking about – in this case – personal online security. Perhaps more people might be encouraged to take computing courses, install anti-virus software or be less naive when confronted with internet scams. Regardless, the overdramatisation of such threats also has significant costs and blowback.

Glib news reporting too often channels a poorly targeted and overstated emphasis. Elements of the media feed the 'mystique' of terrorism and magnify its alleged capacities. Media stories are deliberately overplayed to create the latest exclusive headline. This can feed into public uncertainty that 'it's only a matter of time' before something terrible will happen. For example, news stories happily ran the story that manuals full of supervisory control and data acquisition (SCADA) information (computer-based control systems) relating to dams had been discovered at Al-Qaeda training camps. Yet a more detailed analysis revealed that the terrorist group had no actual concrete plan to disrupt water distribution systems. Nor did it have the nous or ability to be a serious near-term cyber-threat.[24]

In addressing the escalating push for cyber-threat inflation, some point to self-serving economic incentives that persist in playing up modern cyber-dangers as a vast leviathan unleashing random violence. In short, cyber-safety is a lucrative business.[25] Elevated warnings about the climbing scale of cyber-threats will generate extra demand for additional resources and protective countermeasures by groups who perceive themselves as probably vulnerable. The worldwide sale of security products like anti-virus software and the demand for expert consultative advice to help fend off the latest strand of cyber-attack can be expected to skyrocket. It is a highly competitive and highly profitable market to compete in – and exploit.

Government agencies are also accused of regularly feeding into or manipulating a climate of cyber-angst. Intense cyberwar scenarios can act as an extra justification for a bigger slice of the budget pie, new powers and related legislative and budget-ary rearrangements. In turn, doomsday scenarios feed the 'mil-itary-industrial complex' and the expansion of military ideas and operations to justify boosted defence expenditures. As Jerry Brito and Tate Watkins say, 'The alarmist scenarios dominating policy discourse may be good for the cybersecurity-industrial complex, but they aren't doing real security any favors.'[26] But those advocating funding cuts might find themselves crudely accused of compromising national security.

Finally, it can be argued that there is a lack of concise, rea-sonable discourse on multidimensional cyber-issues. Instead, the default is political chest-beating and general public confusion over how to interpret warnings about cyber-conflict and, more broadly, the unwanted, intrusive side effects of an information age. It is no surprise that the new Q in James Bond is a tech-savvy, young and unashamed computer nerd. Old-fashioned Q was given the boot. This could be interpreted as reflecting valid generational gaps and the varying levels of suspicion or accept-ance in the minds of citizens regarding their relationship with a decentralised cyber-world.

At the extreme end, 'Luddite' is a phrase used to label people who distrust progress or resist technology. It was coined in the late 1700s and characterised any individual or group who opposed new, and rapidly changing, technology during the Industrial Revolution. The impact of machinery was seen as creating con-ditions that harmed social and cultural life. So while a person's feeling towards computer technology today will manifest itself in a variety of ways, and is certainly not static, longstanding doubts and worries about accelerating technological change (feeling 'out of touch') can be easily intertwined with more abstract scenarios of uncharted peril to life and work. Psychological reactions and cultural attitudes will continue to play a key part in threat assessments and the direction of security patterns.

Cyber-terror

It is acknowledged that security planners do need to be forward-thinking in calculating threat assessments. Given this situation, it is worth considering whether cyber-attacks remain on the agenda of terrorist groups like Al-Qaeda (and imminent offshoots) in order for them to achieve strategic goals. The short answer is 'Probably'. But concerns are not always level-headed or well-founded. Experts like Kathryn Kerr and Dorothy Denning highlight a range of reasons why any heightened interest by terrorists in using cyber-terror will be hard to sustain and tricky to implement. And as evident in the Stuxnet case, low entry costs should not be simply assumed. Taken as a whole, effective large-scale cyber-terror attacks remain problematic, and appear to be less likely than physical attacks – 'the actual magnitude and pace of the attacks do not match popular perception.'[27] Cyber-terror scenarios should therefore not be portrayed as a highly feasible, easily applied and manifestly convenient weapon in a terrorist's arsenal.

Kerr raises the subject of 'plausible deniability' – how disguising intrusions may be a plausible option for the owners and operators of any crippled network system.[28] Terrorists wish to send a noticeable message – to generate terror. They place a high value on the psychological impact and emotional grab of violent action. But cyber-attacks are not necessarily 'spectacular' – they do not readily leave a trail of injured people, and media coverage is not automatically certain. In other words, the ability to instill fear and create violent 'theatre' is significantly diluted. As Denning says, 'Unless people are injured, there is … less drama and emotional appeal.'[29] Pure cyber-terrorism lacks a stringent 'shock value' message that is key to a terrorist's cost-benefit analysis; it involves investing in a situation that will entail no loss of life and, at the same time, no mental harm, due to the possibility that effects could either denied or deflected.

Denning adds that cyber-terror attacks, in contrast to physical methods, are much more complicated to coordinate, control and calculate. 'Although cyber terrorism is certainly a real possibility, for a terrorist, digital attacks have several drawbacks. Systems are complex, so controlling an attack and achieving a desired level of damage may be harder than using physical weapons.'[30] Many forms of terrorism are attracted to 'soft', opportunistic openings where a lethal blow can be delivered with an amplified impact – 'low-hanging fruit' that might be difficult to secure and protect, like a shopping centre or outdoor sporting event. In contrast, a successful large-scale cyber-intrusion on a government installation might rely, in part, on access to high technology, target surveillance and specialised knowledge about the explicit design and operation of a particular (and possibly updated) network and its fail-safe systems. And crystal ball visions about the aftermath of cyber-intrusions (and collateral damage) will remain cloudy.

Ultimately, the physical (and psychological) damage caused by methods such as bullets and bombs remain easier to anticipate, and calculable. Compared to physical attacks, in launching a targeted cyber-assault, 'it is much more difficult for an attacker to be certain his actions will achieve the desired result.'[31] This uncertainty can translate into a strong disincentive to invest time, money and energies into potential cyber-plots – especially if 'older' activities like improvised explosives can be more readily tested and executed and are estimated as instrumental (to capture attention, to cause destruction and to kill people for strategic purposes).

An extra angle to consider is that cyber-intrusions do not appear to have the lasting, destructive impact of other more conventional threats like kidnapping, hijacking and homemade explosives. Recovery from deliberate interference on networked assets – aided by precautions such as planned back-up systems – should translate to a far easier restoration of assets as opposed to a physical (or chemical, biological or nuclear) attack on critical infrastructure and shared facilities. As summarised by Giampiero Giacomello, setting up cyber-terror tactics might be an unsatisfactory option for a simple reason: 'high costs and meagre returns'.[32] The bottom line is that 'if recovery is able to occur quickly, then from a terrorist perspective, the attack may be less effective as a means of instilling fear or causing serious damage.'[33]

Such types of assessments do not advocate ignoring online security challenges. Instead, such investigations contribute to a better understanding of capabilities and add some perspective to the consideration of actual and potential problems. At the same time, rather than thinking about computer security in absolute terms, there is obvious value in establishing flexible response plans to absorb system disruption and allow the timely restoration of operations to pre-breakdown conditions – a task which also remains highly relevant in addressing accidents and failures such as flight delays or power blackouts. Such damage to systems and networks can, and will, stem from ordinary occurrences like storms and floods. Finally, varying cybersecurity breaches should entail analysts strengthening control and detection elements as quickly as possible, thereby making a repeat performance even harder.[34]

Who's who?

From a different angle, it is not always easy to instantly identify the 'enemy'. It is not unusual to conclude that the best way to defend against cyber-attack is to be prepared to take swift counter-action. The principle of 'retaliation' refers to a concrete coercive capacity, sitting alongside an emphasis on one's own power to make any cyber-attack highly costly for the original architect.

Such deterrence practices should not be discounted. But this is also not the same world as the 1950s and 1960s. The accurate recognition of who attacked ('attribution') in the context of cyberspace might also be easier said than done. Attribution will frequently entail guesswork. There is no guaranteed smoking cyber-gun because of, for example, the use of proxy servers to cover or erase tracks. A correlated issue is threat measurement: is the digital attack aimed at cyber-shenanigans, stealing data or the disruption of computers to affect national security? Is the purpose of the cyber-attack online protest, spying, to coerce a government, or is it a precursor to a larger, physical attack? Tactical counterstrikes against a small-time amateur hacker who has caused minimal damage – an act of vandalism that is completely disconnected to military operations – appear grossly disproportionate (and time-consuming).

Computer network exploitation might stem from locally based criminals, transnational business groupings, patriotic small-fry hackers or state-sanctioned overseas intelligence services – suspected in places like China. And even if brazen hack attempts can be traced to a 12-story facility in Shanghai, are particular cyber-intrusions being directed by the Chinese government or is it the work of an independent, bored hacker? 'Are the attackers curious teenagers, criminal gangs, a foreign power – or … a criminal gang sponsored by a foreign power? Deterrence becomes meaningless when the identity of an attacker is unknown.'[35]

Cyber-deception may also be a likelihood. Perhaps a supposed culprit like China has itself been victim of a clever cyber-intrusion – maybe routed through a third nation by a third party – with the instigator wishing to frame China as the centre of blame, with the aim of escalating underlying international tensions. In backtracking cyber-events to obtain evidence about 'who did it' the possibility of deliberate mischief needs to be taken into account, as do tremendous grey areas that could led to misattribution. 'The forensic work necessary to identify an attacker may take months, if identification is possible at all.'[36]

Talk about the need for better offensive or second strike capabilities (that turns into cyber-deterrence) to deal with potential problems needs to be carefully weighed against the inconclusive evidence and inappropriate escalation.[37] An overlapping predicament is that the rules of what is offending behaviour – which will shape expectations about retaliation – remain unclear, inconsistent and arbitrary.[38] Thus the old school instinct to punish cyberwarriors lacks a well-designed strategic doctrine and diplomatic foothold with which to navigate the 'global cybercommons'. Response must contend with a high degree of anonymity, lag time, questionable evidence, possible violations of international law and potential unintended political consequences that might accompany retaliation designs.

Y2K

Recent history does point to some pertinent examples of society's disconsolate orientation towards an online future. In 1999, the alarms bells surrounded an ominous 'millennium bug' or the 'Y2K' problem (an alleged glitch in the way computers stored data). As a result, all computers were expected to crash and burn at midnight on 31 December 1999.[39]

The Y2K problem neatly captured a pervasive sense of unease within broad sections of society about unfamiliar IT threats and seemingly uncontrollable technological catastrophes on the horizon.[40] Some media guesswork included recommendations that people stockpile food. Y2K crisis call centres were set up. Bestselling books were written about bug-prevention measures and how to survive the coming cyber-catastrophe (and presumed looting). One of the more colourful conspiracy theories floating around was that the US government was planning to take advantage of the Y2K bug by launching a campaign that declared martial law and suspended all civil liberties![41]

Some accused software companies and security consultants of crying wolf in 'sales pitch' countdown towards Y2K.[42] Various countries and companies spent heavily on products and services to better protect computer programs and to sort out existing network holes. Media stories about upgrading old applications and patchworked systems were definitely not as eyecatching as pessimistic headlines about possible banking meltdowns. As the clocks hit midnight, no serious problems to computer systems were reported, civil anarchy did not erupt and several doomsayers were left red-faced (although some did make a few quick bucks).

It can be argued that much of the confusion surrounding the elevation of cyberspace as a combat zone is based on a similar pattern of paranoia, poor research and rumour-mongering. Frustratingly, a number of past examples of cyber-horror stories that have been debunked continue to surface as clear-eyed truth – despite evidence being thin or non-existent.

For instance, cyber-doomsayers claim that the fast-spreading Blaster worm virus in 2003 was responsible for massive power blackouts in the north-eastern United States and parts of Canada. Yet a 2004 investigation concluded that this was not the case. While the blackout may have highlighted vulnerabilities in computer control systems, a US–Canada task force found zero evidence that malicious actors had caused or contributed to problems with power delivery.[43] The detailed report stressed human error, and that there was no connection between Al-Qaeda (who reportedly claimed responsibility for the attack after the fact) and the cascading blackout. Others have concluded that, at best, the contributions of the Blaster worm virus were 'incidental'.[44] From a psychological perspective, if there were a less dazzling culprit – like trees that had fallen over power lines and caused mass blackouts – would we be drawn to an apocryphal narrative that overgrown plants were a significant risk to national security?

Ankle-biters

Hackers (and hacktivists) are also commonly compared to, or characterised as, the equivalent of cyber-terrorists.

But again, cyber-terrorism should relate to conventional 'terrorism' – and long-established terrorist scenarios are violent, or involve threats of violence, with a distinct political objective. The bottom line is that hacking by computer-literate groups should not be conflated with an act of terror without at least considering context and the intention of the provocateur. Many hackers are simply thrillseekers looking for a high-profile challenge, maybe fuelled by ego or glory-seeking. They can be motivated by openly demonstrating skill sets in order to gain some 'street cred' or notoriety. Much of their mischief is benign. Rather than a homogeneous group, hackers might be better likened to 'an amorphous collection of internet enthusiasts, pranksters and activists'[45] rather than correlated with terrorist groups that aim to spread fear, destroy infrastructure and kill people.

For instance, in December 2012 a lone hacker stole details of up to 20 000 Australian military staff. Stolen personal information included names, birthdays, identification numbers, passwords and email addresses. The mainstream media categorised the security failure as 'one of the worst known cyber-attacks' on a government organisation within Australia.[46] This was in spite of the fact that Defence acknowledged that most of the stolen information was out of date, and not confidential. The hacker, known as Darwinare, boasted online that the hack was for 'fun', and that they infiltrated networks primarily out of sheer boredom.

Or in November 2002, UK citizen Gary McKinnon was indicted by a US grand jury for hacking into a number of US military computers, including at NASA. He faced a prison sentence of up to 70 years under US law, but the British Home Secretary later withdrew an extradition order to the US on human rights grounds. It was discovered that McKinnon had Asperger's syndrome and was suffering from severe mental illness. While depicted as 'one of the biggest military computer hacks of all time', 46-year-old McKinnon had infiltrated the overseas computers from his home bedroom. He had caused the data breach through childlike curiosity based on the desire to discover the existence of UFOs.[47]

Another famous case was that of a disgruntled Australian man, Vitek Boden. From March 2000, Vitek had hacked into a computerised waste-pumping control system in Queensland. He had released hundreds of thousands of litres of raw sewage into surrounding rivers and parks. He used stolen software and remote radio transmissions to spill the pollution. In fact, Vitek was an ex-employee who had hands-on experience and intimate knowledge of the specific computer systems involved, as he had installed the plant's SCADA system. It was later discovered that Vitek's unauthorised cyber-intrusion was driven by revenge over a rejected job application.[48] (It is worth noting that his capture was also sluggish – he repeated intrusions over a period of three months before he got caught.)

Conceivably, hackers might be split into amateurs and professionals. Their operations might be classified as criminal or not-criminal in nature. They may or may not have highly specific inside knowledge of targeted systems. They might be driven by forces like a sense of bravado or curiosity, or by dollars. The background and the intentions of any sort of hack attack are crucial in determining a better operational classification of the threat (as well as then identifying appropriate steps for policy response). The consequences of nuisance hacks – like 'electronic graffiti' on a host's webpage – are not severe. They do not qualify as a major threat to national security.

The public needs to remain alert to the opportunistic political or media manipulation that aims to fuel cyber-angst about vicious hackers in the digital age:

> It is the hacker – a sort of modern folk devil who
> personifies our anxieties about technology – who gets all
> the attention. The result is a set of increasingly paranoid
> and restrictive laws and regulations affecting our abilities

to communicate freely and privately online, to use and control our own technology, and which puts users at risk for overzealous prosecutions and invasive electronic search and seizure practices.[49]

Aiding the enemy?

The WikiLeaks saga is another that has been labelled by some as cyber-terrorism or a precedent for future cyber-clashes. Wiki-Leaks co-founder and Australian ex-hacker Julian Assange was seen as a real-world cyber-terror poster child by his enemies, and as a First Amendment crusader by his fans (see also chapter 8). Sarah Palin, a former American vice-presidential candidate, bluntly stated that US authorities should 'hunt him down like a terrorist'.[50]

WikiLeaks is basically an organisation that aims to publish leaks. The WikiLeaks incident emphasises the extended drama of 'insider' knowledge – a type of digital-age dilemma that is linked to poorly trained or disgruntled insiders, contractors or ex-employees. The Edward Snowden saga is another clear example of a discontented government contractor (rather than the much-maligned foreign hacker) who exposed top-secret government programs with significant security and political consequences.

The political storm was started by Bradley (now Chelsea) Manning, a low-ranking US officer who had unrestricted access to classified data. This data included military and incident reports and diplomatic cables. Manning had downloaded thousands of secret documents on a small, portable music CD at his workstation. These copied documents were then easily carried outside and shared, uploaded and published online by

Assange (and soon every major newspaper outlet in the world). A focus on far-away foes distracts from the less spectacular issue of unhappy employees (or former employees) as threat agents. A 2003 study illustrated that 'disgruntled insiders, not foreign terrorists, posed the greatest cyber-security threat to companies ... Even the most comprehensive IT security technology cannot stop the careless, uninformed or disgruntled person with access to the network from wreaking havoc.'[51] Like Vitek and Snowden, Bradley had privileged access to specific systems. In regards to his impetus, Bradley claimed that he acted according to his conscience. He had hoped to make the world a better place through improving transparency about the 'underground realities' of US combat operations.[52]

Regardless, in December 2010, former Australian Prime Minister Kevin Rudd, rather than scapegoating Assange, correctly pinpointed the United States's responsibility for poor security procedures and the subsequent security lapse that triggered the larger political and diplomatic uproar. 'I think there are real questions to be asked about the adequacy of their security systems and the level of access that people have had to that material over a long period of time.'[53]

Cyber snake oil?

Many worst-case cyber-terrorism situations are not grounded in the underlying strengths of a variety of safety precautions.[54] While not a perfect antidote, security commitments can include installing up-to-date cyber-armour like network firewalls, data encryption, proxy screens and anti-virus software – although it is recognised that improvements are never-ending and will inevitably raise points about restrictions on access to information. Likewise, system hardening (the removal of redundant applications and unnecessary services) and whitelisting (using only authorised software), combined with a capacity to quickly bounce back from successful cyber-intrusions (resilience), will have a very powerful deterrent and defensive impact.

In regard to other 'big picture' concerns and estimates, some have highlighted the uniqueness of many computer installations and questioned the plausibility of cyber-attack scenarios on multipart, widely distributed critical infrastructure. In other words, even if computer networks are not completely invulnerable, this does not translate to a high risk of shut-down or structured manipulation of different network technologies – for instance, a single centralised pathway to cause sustained cyber-chaos against multiple systems is not a plausible development:

> Cyber-terrorism is likely not what movies make it out
> to be. Think of movies like 'Die Hard 4' where attackers
> launch a sophisticated, synchronised attack where they
> disrupt traffic lights, phone lines and TV broadcasts at
> the same time. The truth of the matter … is that many of
> these systems depend on different technology (hardware
> platforms, software, etc.) and different vulnerabilities need
> to be discovered to take control [of] such systems.[55]

Certainly, governments, as well as companies and private network owners, should work to upgrade basic infrastructure; they should strive to adopt flexible risk management approaches to protect computer products, as well as investing in sensible disaster recovery plans to recover crippled systems. Security planners were not born yesterday – unlike television actors, they do not store entire payloads of sensitive information in one location or on a single hard drive. Generally, OPSEC (or 'operations security') practices are well-rehearsed functional tasks that are used to safeguard critical information in defence and intelligence establishments.[56] At the same time, the reality of non-computerised fail-safe mechanisms ('air-gaps' that make unconnected computer systems impossible to be externally hacked) within suggested targets like air traffic control centres or nuclear power plants tend to be entirely underplayed.[57]

When hackers have been able to cause unexpected or unpredictable lower-level disruptions – such as the crashing of government or banking sites – network functions have recovered quickly, and such intrusions do not qualify as cyber-terrorism. Microsoft founder Bill Gates has spoken about the alarmist scenarios that promote inaccurate or outdated reports about failing national safety protocols.

> There are safeguards that can be put in place. This is
> something that the rich countries have the same goals in
> mind. You won't have to spend like you spend on an army
> – it's just a group of experts spreading best practice. So
> with the right approach, it shouldn't be something people
> will have to worry about.[58]

In contrast, the language of military aggression can give rise to countless myths. An avalanche of magnified fears about computer technology is in danger of entrenching a 'call-to-arms' outlook obsessed with the pursuit of clandestine cyber-terror bogeymen.

> A danger lies at the heart of cyber-war rhetoric. Declaring
> war, even cyber-war, has always serious consequences.
> Since war is acknowledged as the most severe threat to the

survival and well-being of the society, war rhetoric easily creates and feeds an atmosphere of fear, provokes a raise in the emergency level and launches associated counter-measures.[59]

Finally, some observers have raised doubts about the willingness in the private sector for voluntary participation to prioritise cyber-safety, and question the extent to which businesses will self-protect without better guidance and regulation. So while some cite a preference for the magic of the free market to lead 'cyber-resilience' platforms, several point out that the private sector has been sluggish in gearing towards vulnerability management and related business continuity plans.[60] Numerous hacking incidents remain classified by governments and under- (or non-) reported by companies who do not wish adverse publicity or to alarm stakeholders.[61] This lack of transparency about security breaches will feed into a loss of trust, and ingrain public confusion about the nature of digital vulnerabilities, the likelihood of compromised computer systems and the impact on privacy protections for customers.

Taken as a whole, security education and a differentiated detection, identification, preventive defence and recovery game – which will also need to balance society's privacy expectations – might be considered a better option than lumping together a loose federation of separate threats, fixating on doomsday scenarios and elevating offensive sabre-rattling to address real or presumed computer technology faultlines.

Conclusion

Threats to cyberspace do exist. But the sky is not falling. Australia is not a mouse-click away from a cyber-meltdown. Many assumptions about vulnerabilities are plain wrong. And there have been no instances of cyber-terror on critical infrastructure in Australia – and mooted international examples have been extremely rare and manageable, and have not had long-term effects. Other forms of cyber-panic appear linked to short-lived nuisance disruptions like hacks that do not cause bloodshed, or are in reaction to age-old spy games that now entail sophisticated forms of cyber-snooping. Scores of elaborate 'what if' scenarios remain more imaginary rather than real. The bottom line is to avoid overinflating the threat of cyber-attack: to keep a sense of proportion, stick to the facts, enhance e-security awareness, strengthen long-term mechanisms for public–private co-operation, and commit to research that enables a more accurate analysis of trends in order to find better ways to access, detect, mitigate and respond to emerging and evolving cyber-risks.

1   L. Panetta, cited in E. Bumiller and T. Shanker, 'Panetta warns of dire threat of cyberattack on US', *New York Times*, 11 October 2012.
2   Associated Press, 'Retiring rep. Norm Dicks warns of cyber 9/11', *Seattle Times*, 11 October 2012.
3   E. Frauenheim, 'IDC: cyberterror and other prophecies', *CNET News*, 12 December 2002.
4   Cited in M. Thompson, 'U.S. cyberwar strategy: the Pentagon plans to attack', *Time Magazine*, 2 February 2010.
5   S. Gallagher, 'Security pros predict "major" cyber terror attack this year', *Ars Technica*, 4 January 2013.
6   K. Taipale (2010) 'Cyber-Deterrence' in E. Gelbstein and P. Reich (eds), *Law, Policy and Technology: Cyberterrorism, Information Warfare, Digital and Internet Immobilization*, Information Science

Reference (IGI Global), Hershey, PA.

7   DFAT (2004) *Transnational Terrorism: The Threat to Australia*, Chapter 2 <www.dfat.gov.au/publications/terrorism/chapter2.html>.

8   D. Shamah, 'Israel fights off 1,000 cyber-attack hits a minute', *The Times of Israel*, 6 September 2012.

9   Ron-Tal cited in Shamah, 'Israel fights off 1,000 cyber-attack hits a minute'.

10   Shamah, 'Israel fights off 1,000 cyber-attack hits a minute'.

11   J. Carr, cited in M. Ruiz, 'Weapons of mass disruption', *El Ojo Digital*, 22 March 2001.

12   A. Colley, 'Hacker group Anonymous targets ASIO and Australian defence bodies', *The Australian*, 10 August 2012.

13   D. Sanger, 'Obama order sped up wave of cyberattacks against Iran', *New York Times*, 1 June 2012.

14   C. Williams, 'Stuxnet: cyber attack on Iran was carried out by Western powers and Israel', *Telegraph*, 21 January 2011.

15   K. Benedict, 'Stuxnet and the bomb', *Bulletin of the Atomic Scientists*, 15 June 2012.

16   D. Denning (2001) 'Activism, Hactivism, and Cyberterrorism: The Internet as a Tool for Influencing Foreign Policy' in J. Arquilla and D. Ronfeldt (eds), *Networks and Netwars*, Rand, Santa Monica, CA, p. 241.

17   J. Cloherty 'Virtual terrorism: Al Qaeda video calls for electronic jihad', *ABC News*, 22 May 2012.

18   H. Cooper, 'Hackers targeting Australia's electronic secrets', *ABC News*, 25 September 2012.

19   S. Lemos, 'Security czar: button up or get hacked', *CNET News*, 19 February 2002.

20   S. Mann, 'Cyber war added to ANZUS pact', *Sydney Morning Herald*, 16 September 2011.

21   B. Packham, 'Julia Gillard announces cyber security centre, warning a long fight lies ahead', *The Australian*, 23 January 2013 and B. Keane, 'The new ACSC: a "reasonable illustration" of a cybersecurity hub?', *Crikey*, 15 March 2013.

22   G. Lucas, cited in P. Singer (2012) 'The Cyber Terror Bogeyman', Brookings Institute, November <www.brookings.edu/research/articles/2012/11/cyber-terror-singer>.

23   See A. Baker, 'You've got mail. ASIO wants to read it. All of it', *Punch*, 19 July 2012.

24   A. Peritz, 'Fears aside, al-Qaeda ill-equipped for a major cyber attack', *Philadelphia Inquirer*, 20 March 2011.

25 'Obama budget makes cybersecurity a big priority', *Reuters*, 11 April 2013.

26 J. Brito and T. Watkins, 'Cyberwar is the new yellowcake', *Wired*, 14 February 2012.

27 B. Valeriano and R. Maness (2012) 'The Fog of War', *Foreign Affairs*, November.

28 K. Kerr, 'Putting cyberterrorism into context', 24 October 2003, available at <www.auscert.org.au/render.html?it=3552> (last accessed 22 July 2013).

29 D. Denning (2000) 'Cyberterrorism: The Logic Bomb versus the Truck Bomb', *Global Dialogue*, vol. 2, no. 2, Autumn.

30 Denning (2000) 'Cyberterrorism'.

31 Kerr, 'Putting cyberterrorism into context'.

32 G. Giampiero (2004) 'Bangs for the Buck: A Cost-Benefit Analysis of Cyberterrorism', *Studies in Conflict and Terrorism*, vol. 27, no. 5.

33 See J. Lewis, 'Assessing the risks of cyber terrorism, cyber war and other cyber threats', Center for Strategic and International Studies, December 2002.

34 Kerr, 'Putting cyberterrorism into context', 2003.

35 Thompson, 'U.S. cyberwar strategy: the Pentagon plans to attack'.

36 W. Lynn III (2010) 'Defending a New Domain', *Foreign Affairs*, vol. 89, no. 5; see also J. Michaels, 'Pentagon seeking "rules of engagement" for cyber-war', *USA Today*, 4 April 2013.

37 H. White, 'Arming the country for cyber attack', *The Age*, 13 September 2011.

38 T. Barnett, 'The new rules: don't fear U.S. cyber deterrence', *World Politics Review*, 20 June 2011, last accessed 22 July 2013 <www.worldpoliticsreview.com/articles/9217/the-new-rules-dont-fear-u-s-cyber-deterrence>.

39 T. Long, 'Dec. 31, 1999: horror or hype? Y2K arrives and world trembles', *Wired*, 30 December 2007.

40 K. Poulsen, 'The Y2K solution: run for your life!!', *Wired*, August 1998.

41 J. Monroe, 'Y2K paranoia runs rampant in Arkansas', CNN, 29 December 1999 and J. Karl, 'Y2K precautions: successful or excessive?', CNN, 2 January 2000.

42 'Everyone pays a price for Y2K hype', *CNET News*, 4 November 1999.

43 Brito and Watkins, 'Cyberwar is the new yellowcake' .

44 S. Lemos, 'MSBlast not to blame for blackout, report says', *CNET News*, 5 April 2004.

45 R. Satter, 'Watching the watchers: hackers breach FBI, Scotland Yard', *Sydney Morning Herald*, 4 February 2012.

46 M. Mannheim, 'Military personnel data hacked for fun', *The Age*, 11 December 2012.

47 L. Travis and O. Bowcott, 'Britain defies US over biggest military computer hack of all time', *Sydney Morning Herald*, 17 October 2012.

48 T. Smith, 'Hacker jailed for revenge sewage attacks', *Register*, 31 October 2001.

49 M. Sauter, 'If hackers didn't exist, governments would have to invent them', *Atlantic*, 5 July 2012.

50 M. Beckford, 'Sarah Palin: hunt WikiLeaks founder like al-Qaeda and Taliban leaders', *Telegraph*, 30 November 2010.

51 See G. Walters (2008) 'Protecting Information Infrastructures' in G. Walters et al., *Australia and Cyber-Warfare*, ANU E Press, Canberra.

52 P. Dorling, 'I take full responsibility', *Courier*, 1 March 2013.

53 B. Malkin, 'Wikileaks: Kevin Rudd blames US for release of diplomatic cables', *Telegraph*, 8 December 2010.

54 See T. Rid and P. McBurney (2012) 'Cyber-Weapons', *RUSI Journal*, vol. 157, no. 1.

55 D. Manky cited in S. Poremba, 'Cyber terrorist threat looms 10 years after 9/11', *NBC News*, 1 September 2011.

56 See also S. Pierce, 'How real is Skyfall's portrayal of cyber-terrorism', CNN, 14 November 2010.

57 For a detailed range of complexities, see T. Rid (2012) 'Cyber war will not take place', *Journal of Strategic Studies*, vol. 35, no. 1.

58 Gates cited in T. McDonald, 'Governments on alert for cyber terror threat', *The World Today*, 19 October 2010, last accessed 22 July 2013 <www.abc.net.au/news/2010-10-19/governments-on-alert-for-cyber-terror-threat/2303774>.

59 J. Limnell, 'The danger of mixing cyber espionage with cyber warfare', *Security Week*, 22 May 2013.

60 See W. Jackson, 'To regulate or not to regulate? That is the question', *Government Computer News*, 26 February 2005.

61 See J. Menn, 'Exclusive: hacked companies still not telling investors', *Reuters*, 2 February 2012.

5

THE MAINSTREAMING OF EXECUTIVE-DIRECTED KILLINGS, OR: HOW THE WORLD LEARNED TO STOP WORRYING AND LOVE THE DRONE

Michael Mori

'The strategy of drone strikes is smart self-defence in accordance with international law.'

FALSE. The use of unmanned drones in taking out the 'bad guys' has headlined the news for the past several years. In fact, the Obama White House has utilised lethal drone strikes more than the previous Bush Administration. Such a means and method of warfare has been broadly applauded from within the United States as an effective tool in the so-called 'war on terror'. At the same time, legitimate concerns about the use and risks of drones – including collateral damage and the rise of a possible 'PlayStation mentality' – have been consistently downplayed or dismissed.[1] The equation of drone technologies with successful counter-terrorism remains widely entrenched.

The overall message is that Western societies can no longer afford to fight with their hands behind their backs. This picture of accelerated assassinations, alongside a 'green light' to circumvent the rule of law in order to make the world a safer place, has also not met any real criticism from many of the United States's strongest allies, including Australia. Yet drone attacks and executive-directed killings as part and parcel of US policy should raise many serious, and uncomfortable, questions.[2] While the legality of the trial, detention and interrogation methods under the laws of war are just as important, this chapter will focus on the issue of killing. In drawing attention to this new, deadly frontier of remote control warfare, it will be argued that drone strikes are not only morally troubling, but have a highly questionable legality and sharp political costs, and might lead to serious consequences.

Australia itself has not been immune to the allure of unmanned aerial vehicles for a variety of jobs that include attacking enemy targets, performing maritime patrols and conducting covert surveillance. Access to such hardware appears set to play a predominant part in Australia's civilian and military outlook, with the government planning to spend between $2 billion and $3 billion to propel drone technology usage.[3] Nonetheless, use of drones has again raised concerns about the protection of civilian populations and issues of privacy and accountability. At the same time, in engagements abroad like Afghanistan, the Australian Defence Force continues to refuse to release detailed rules of engagement (with Australian forces piloting unmanned US aircrafts) and the methods applied to complete target kill lists.[4]

Technology and war

Despite the media's recent fascination with drones, the basic concept underlying their use is not new. Radio-controlled planes and helicopters have filled the world's skies for years. Even before World War I, when powered flight was a new concept, the idea of an unmanned, automatically controlled 'flying bomb' or 'aerial torpedo', based on gyroscope technology, was circulated by a number of countries.[5]

The creation of a weapons system that allows the operator to remain at a safe distance has been sought after since wars began. Spears, slings, catapults, crossbows, longbows, rifles, cannons, mines and shoulder-fired rockets all represent advancements in technology designed to improve and develop methods of warfare. What is new – and what forms the basis of the rising popularity of drones – is the ability to kill pre-selected, specific individuals suspected of terrorist-related activities, far from any battlefield.

The challenges involved in responding to terrorist threats on urban battlefields in Iraq or rural terrains in Afghanistan are not particularly new; history is full of wars where it has been difficult to tell friend from foe. There were the rice fields of Vietnam and the same Afghan mountains in which the Russians faced Charlie Wilson's US-backed Mujahideen. The tactic of facing foes who may not confront us on the traditional field of battle was the same one employed by the patriots who hid behind the stone walls sniping the Red Coats as they marched back from Concord to Boston in 1775.

In 1969, *Life* magazine ran a photo depicting a South Vietnamese police general making the decision that the man handcuffed next to him had committed some kind of act that justified imposition of the death penalty.[6] This is an 'executive-directed killing' in its most basic, raw form: a member of the executive branch making a factual decision about the past, present or future conduct of a person, and deciding to impose the punishment of death for that conduct; certainly, an efficient and expedient system.

For those of you who can remember 1972, let's recall: the photo mentioned above was taken; 'American Pie' played on the radio; someone broke into the Watergate Hotel in Washington, DC; fourteen unarmed Catholic protestors were gunned down by the British Army on Bloody Sunday; and in September, at the Munich Olympics, a terrorist attack by the Black September group left eleven Israeli athletes dead.

The Israeli government responded to the attack with multiple executive-directed killings that took the form of a 'covert' operation aimed at eliminating those who the Israeli government believed were responsible. Ultimately, dozens of people were killed in connection with an operation authorised by then Israeli Prime Minister Golda Meir. The Israeli Prime Minister did not announce any of the kills on live TV; the operation was carried out secretly over 20 years, until the last known suspect had been killed.[7]

Why did the Israelis have to carry out this operation covertly? Why didn't Israel publicly accept responsibility? After all, if this was an acceptable means of warfare, there was no reason to shy away from hailing it as a victory. But in 1972, the idea of a government killing people without a trial was not legally and publicly acceptable.

In a more recent example, in January 2010, several men and women dressed in baseball caps and button-down shirts strolled in and out of a luxury hotel in Dubai to execute Hamas official Mahmoud al-Mabhouh.[8] This executive-directed killing was recorded on the hotel's CCTV system.[9] Philip Alston, the UN's Special Rapporteur on Extrajudicial Killings, came out swinging against those responsible: 'If a foreign intelligence agency was responsible for the killing of Mabhouh, the matter should clearly be classified as an extrajudicial execution. There is no legal justification for the cold-blooded murder of a man who, if alleged to have committed crimes, could have been arrested and charged.'[10]

Once the plans were discovered by the police, it came to light that fraudulent British and Australian passports had been used by the perpetrators. It was the use of these passports, rather than the killing itself, that caused the greatest outcry from each country. 'If Australian passports are being used or forged by any state, let alone for the purpose of assassination, this is of the deepest concern and we are getting to the bottom of this now,' Kevin Rudd told the ABC.[11] So while the Prime Minister of Australia viewed the killing as an assassination, his outrage was aimed at the use of forged Australian passports, and not the actual fact of the assassination.

Has the world changed so much that such a killing is being found legally and publicly acceptable?

Some 40 years earlier, the Israeli government had to respond secretly, yet today Israel isn't worried about their agents being recorded on CCTV carrying out an executive-directed killing. The US openly admits that it is killing suspected terrorists, including it own citizens.[12] This new wave of US executive-directed killings culminated recently in the US President publicly claiming that the killing of bin Laden at his 'direction'[13] was an accomplishment 'in the pursuit of justice,'[14] as millions cheered around the globe.[15] The increased use of drones to kill suspected terrorists under the Obama administration has generated relatively little discussion; in 2012, the *Washington Post* described the drone campaign as an 'awkward open secret' in Washington; there appears to be acceptance or indifference from the general public towards executive-directed killings during the 'war on terror'.[16]

The post-9/11 mindset: judge, jury, executioner

Following September 11, 2001 the 'gloves [came] off' – the Bush administration acted to bring to trial, detain, interrogate and kill individuals under the law of war, while removing any legal protections that such a person might be entitled to.[17]

The Bush administration needed to make changes to achieve its goals in its new response to terrorism. First, there needed to be a war under which the United States could target people under the law of war. This was easily accomplished with President Bush's self-declared 'global war on terrorism', which is 'a war that spans the globe and includes many diverse campaigns'.[18] Second, the person they wanted to kill had to fit into a category of person that was participating in the new war but received none of the protections of the law of war, so 'unlawful enemy combatant' was born. A category, stated the Bush administration, well outside the protection of domestic laws as well.

Second, the person they wanted to kill could not be protected by the law of war, as domestic law interferes with executive-directed killings.

Before 9/11, acts of terrorism were covered by the domestic law of the country in which the terrorist activity took place; those suspected of carrying out such acts were treated like any other suspected murderer. A terrorist act would fall under the same legal category as internal disturbances and riots; there was no argument that it was a war – at least not until after 9/11. The Geneva Conventions defined only two types of armed conflict (war): non-international armed conflicts (such as civil wars) and international armed conflicts (one state against another), both of which provide protections to people. Since non-international armed conflicts take places within a state's borders, there is little need for the full body of the law of war to apply. However, people are still afforded basic protections by Common Article 3 of the Geneva Convention, which states that those who are not active participants in hostilities must be protected from violence and treated humanely.[19]

Since 2001, the United States has tried to establish that it is in a war with Al-Qaeda and its supporters, so that the domestic law restrictions on killing people are not applicable; in this new war, the enemy receive none of the legal protections they would ordinarily be afforded. For an example, take the war in Afghanistan. The United States invaded Afghanistan in October 2001, at which point there was an international armed conflict: the United States against Afghanistan. Since June 2002, when Hamid Karzai was selected as the Afghan President, the United States has technically no longer been at war with Afghanistan as a state.[20] But insurgents and rebels still pose a problem, so there is a non-international armed conflict.

Iraq was a similar situation. The United States invaded in 2003, and the international armed conflict stage ended quite quickly, with Bush declaring 'mission accomplished' in May and a provisional government established, but the continued violence from insurgents ensured that a non-international armed conflict carried on. Yet many of the current killings are occurring outside of Afghanistan, in countries such as Pakistan and Yemen.

The creation of a new war with Al-Qaeda was accomplished without much push-back, domestically or internationally. The invasions of Afghanistan and Iraq were clearly international armed conflicts, so the law of war applied until the re-establishment of central governments. The fabrication lay in creating a 'war on terrorism' which would permit the long-term window dressing for killing suspected terrorists outside of the domestic legal system of the United States. The media statements of President Bush and Secretary of State Donald Rumsfeld parroted comments from what would be made public and become known as the 'Torture Memos'.[21]

As detailed in a February 2002 memo, President Bush declared that 'the war against terrorism usher[ed] in a new paradigm' which 'require[d] new thinking in the law of war'.[22] This was not surprising, as his Attorney-General, Alberto Gonzales, had already described the Geneva Conventions as 'obsolete and quaint'.[23] President Bush asserted that the United States was in an armed conflict with Al-Qaeda, and removed any protections to those enemies.[24] He first determined 'that none of the provisions of Geneva *apply to our conflict with Al-Qaeda* in Afghanistan or elsewhere throughout the world because, among other reasons, Al-Qaeda is not a High Contracting Party to Geneva'.[25] Of course, no person or criminal organisation can be a high contracting party, as only a state can be a party; Al-Qaeda could not be a party, just as an organised crime family could not. This does not prohibit such a person from being protected by the Geneva Conventions if they fight in a war.

While President Bush determined that the Geneva Conventions applied to the 'conflict with the Taliban', he also decided that Common Article 3 of Geneva did not apply to Al-Qaeda since the conflict is 'international in scope' and Common Article

3 applies only to 'armed conflicts not of an international character'.[26] These presidential determinations were seen as necessary to protect those within the administration from potential criminal liability for its future actions. Attorney-General Gonzales warned President Bush in January 2002 that:

[i]t is difficult to predict the motives of prosecutors and independent counsels who may in the future decide to pursue unwarranted charges [against Bush Administration personnel] based on Section 2441 [US Criminal Code, the War Crimes Act]. Your determination [that the Geneva Conventions do not apply] would create a reasonable basis in law that Section 2441 does not apply, which would provide a solid defense to any future prosecution.[27]

No limits

This position remained unchallenged until June 2006. The US Supreme Court determined that if the Bush administration wanted to claim that there was a war with Al-Qaeda, then even if it was not an international armed conflict, it fell within the protections of Common Article 3 of the Geneva Conventions, which prohibit the killing of '[p]ersons taking no active part in the hostilities'.[28] In this Supreme Court case, there was no argument that the accused was not in Afghanistan when the international armed conflict was occurring; the question was about what part of the law of war applied to Salim Ahmed Hamdan, who was a bodyguard and driver for bin Laden. This contrasted with the situations of many of the current individuals subjected to executive-directed killings outside of Afghanistan – for these individuals, the unanswered question is whether there is even a war.

The central reason a war is required is because without one, there are all these pesky restrictions against killing people called laws. In 1976, President Gerald Ford issued Executive Order 11905 to clarify US foreign intelligence activities 'in response to the post-Watergate revelations that the CIA had staged multiple attempts on the life of Cuban President Fidel Castro'.[29] While these orders, last implemented by President Reagan, remained in effect, President Bush signed an intelligence order directing the CIA to undertake its most sweeping and lethal covert action since the founding of the agency in 1947, explicitly calling for the destruction of Osama bin Laden and his worldwide Al-Qaeda network, according to senior government officials.[30] 'White House and CIA lawyers believe that the intelligence "finding" is constitutional because the ban on political assassination does not apply to wartime.'[31]

In a White Paper recently made public, the US Justice Department continues to assert that '[t]he United States is in an armed conflict with al-Qa'ida and its associated forces.'[32] Following the US Supreme Court's decision in *Hamdan*, it asserts the type of conflict with Al-Qaeda is a non-international armed conflict. The memo lays out the Obama Administration's argument for its ability to kill a US citizen. Common Article 3's minimal protections only apply to those who are not 'actively participating' in the conflict; the decision-maker that determines what constitutes 'active participation', however, is the executive branch.

In an international armed conflict with one state's army facing the other state's army, the military can reliably identify who the opposing force is, and kill them. There is no need for the opposing army to pose a threat at the time of killing them; just being in the opposing army is enough. An enemy soldier in such a conflict can be sleeping, eating or engaging in no military-type activity, and still be legally killed. Opposing military forces on the ground can reliably determine where the enemy tanks, planes, bases and personnel are located in order to attack. This is not to say there are never mistakes. One need only look at the 'friendly fire' incidents from the 1991 war in Iraq to the present day.[33] Such mistakes should serve as a warning as to the difficulty in identifying an actual enemy that is only compounded in non-international armed conflicts, which may occur in urban areas among civilians who may have different cultures and languages.

Today, the majority of drone strikes are not being used to kill enemy forces shooting at our soldiers. With executive-directed killings being carried out far from the battlefield, a factual decision is being made about someone's past or potential future conduct, not on what the person is doing when they are killed. Intelligence services are trying to put together reliable information so that some authority in the executive branch can determine that the individual is actively participating in the armed conflict. This sounds very much like the role of the judicial branch.

The United States has carried out at least 350 executive-directed killings via drones in Yemen and Pakistan since 2003, with the resulting death toll claimed to be between 1900 and 3200 people. These individuals have been targeted under the presumption that because they are 'actively participating' in hostilities against the United States, they are afforded no protection under Common Article 3. What constitutes 'active participation', however, is a flexible and ever-expanding category of behaviour. It appears the full rationale of the United States's executive-directed killing program has yet to see the light of day.

It was recently alleged that there are at least eleven memos justifying such killings, with only one finding its way to the public eye and only three others actually being sighted by members of the US Congress.[34]

Drones don't kill people, people kill people

Drones are like super-snipers; among the most advanced weapons systems available, they maximise time over a target for surveillance, with the smallest chances of being discovered or subjected to successful attack. The operator is completely removed from any risk, while still carrying out knock-out impact. Current drone operators sit outside of Las Vegas operating drones in Afghanistan, allowing them to participate in combat operations without fear or the need for courage.[35]

What is not new, but is attracting more attention, is the US government's public declaration that it is using 'kill lists'.[36] The United States is following a precedent set by Israel despite its earlier renunciations of executive-directed killings. In July 2001, the American ambassador to Israel at the time, Martin S. Indyk, stated that the US government was very clearly on the record as 'against targeted assassinations […] they are extrajudicial killings, and we do not support that'.[37]

Of course, this denunciation took place before September 11, 2001. Twelve years into the 'war on terror', the kill lists are being approved by the President personally. President Obama 'signs off on every strike in Yemen and Somalia and also on the more complex and risky strikes in Pakistan – about a third of the total'.[38] Which leaves one wondering who is approving the other two-thirds, and where these two-thirds are occurring. The CIA is selecting and operating the drone program in Pakistan.

In the military, there are High-Value Target (HVT) lists used for capture-or-kill missions in Iraq and Afghanistan.[39] The criteria to get on one of these lists are vague and secretive, not unlike the Phoenix Program from Vietnam in which '[f]orces went to the villages and hamlets and attempted to identify the named individuals and "neutralise" them. Those in a list were arrested or captured for interrogation, or if they resisted, they were killed.'[40]

If you ask some servicemen and women about who has been placed on the HVT, they will respond by telling you that 'the target was a really bad guy'.[41] How do they know this? Well, because someone told them he was. How does the President know someone is a bad guy? Because someone told him so. It is the abdication of the factual decision-making to the unknown (and unaccountable) bureaucracy, instead of a judicial process, that should have people concerned.

I am not trying to imply that there are people intentionally trying to get innocent people put on HVT or kill lists. The targeting process within the military is regimented and reliable for determining traditional military targets.[42] Placing someone on an HVT or kill list implicitly involves the need to be able to determine what someone has done, or to predict a person's future conduct such that a person should be placed on such a list. This information is generated either by intelligence analysts from within the CIA or the US Department of Defense. So-called 'actionable' intelligence is fallible, since it is – rightly – based on information that would never make its way into a courtroom (also see chapter 6). Yet this information is being used to impose the ultimate punishment: death.

This is not the first time the United States has considered getting into the business of executive-directed killing. The United States contemplated using assassination as a means of fighting the threats of communism, at the very least developing hit lists: '[t]he [CIA] drew up lists of individuals for assassination, discussed training Guatemalan exiles for assassination teams, and conducted intimidation programs against prominent Guatemalan officials.'[43] During the 1980s, the covert war in Nicaragua led to more negative publicity, as the CIA mined harbours without providing Congress with adequate notification and published a guerrilla warfare manual – or 'the assassination manual', as it became known – on the 'selective use of violence' against targets such as judges, police and state security officials.[44] President Ronald Reagan's CIA director, William Casey, tried to organise a covert response to the 1983 truck bombing of the US Marine compound in Lebanon, which resulted in 241 dead American servicemen. The target was Muslim leader Sheikh Fadlallah, the head of Hezbollah, who was believed to have been connected to the attack. Retaliation took the form of a car bomb that exploded 45 metres from Fadlallah's Beirut residence, killing eight people and wounding 200. However, Fadlallah escaped without injury.[45]

Collateral damage: getting it wrong

Considering all the 'solid' evidence of Iraq's possession of WMDs, it might seem unfair – but it is probably necessary – to consider that governments and bureaucrats operating within intelligence communities or the military might get it wrong.

It shouldn't come as a shock, but authorities get it wrong much of the time, even when operating within their own country. One only need look at the February 2013 incident in California, when a former police officer, Christopher Dorner, was being hunted down for murders he had allegedly committed.

Eight Los Angeles police officers somehow mistook the aqua blue Toyota Tacoma of Margie Carranza and her 71-year-old mother, Emma Hernandez (who were 'delivering the *Los Angeles Times* before dawn near the home of a police officer named in Dorner's angry manifesto')[46] for the suspect's grey Nissan truck. Confusion and stress must have been high for the officers, who opened fire on the van. If this kind of simple misidentification or 'shoot first, identify the target later' incident is occurring on the streets of the United States, how many mistaken identifications of vehicles or 'shoot first, identify the target later' incidents have occurred, or are occurring, in Iraq or Afghanistan? That wasn't the end of the shooting for that night, either – half an hour later, a Redondo Beach man was also mistaken for Dorner and fired upon by officers.

Things get even more difficult when different languages and cultures are in play when interpreting someone's actions, potential actions, or whether they pose a threat. A snapshot of civilian deaths in Afghanistan during 2009–10 reveals that American and NATO troops 'firing from passing convoys and military checkpoints have killed 30 Afghans and wounded 80 others since last summer, but in no instance did the victims prove to be a danger to troops', according to military officials in Kabul. General Stanley A. McChrystal, who became the senior American and NATO commander in Afghanistan, said that '[w]e have shot an amazing number of people, but to my knowledge, none has ever proven to be a threat'.[47]

It would be reasonable to argue that the statistics for Iraq would not be much different – unfortunately, such numbers have not been reliably reported in the public media. It was not until 2008 that a change in tactics was prompted, due to concerns that US soldiers had killed and injured many hundreds of Iraqi civilians who unwittingly drove too close to convoys or checkpoints and triggered a reaction in gunners who considered them a threat. One statistic I came across in my time in Iraq was that for almost a four-year period (roughly 2004 through 2007), there were 4492 incidents when US convoys had to use force to stop what they believed to be an insurgent threat. In these incidents, which the military call 'escalation of force', 67 insurgents were killed, 285 civilians were killed, and 1038 were wounded. The accuracy of the US forces in determining what was a threat was 1.7 per cent. Statistically, the use of drones has not led to better results. Between 2005 and 2008, Pakistan claims, there were '50 civilians for every militant killed, a hit rate of 2 per cent'.[48]

Even Israel's response to the 1972 Olympic attack involved a mistake. The agents apparently believed that the man, Ahmed Bouchikhi, was Ali Hassan Salameh, suspected of masterminding the killing of 11 Israeli athletes during the 1972 Summer Olympics in Munich. Instead, by most accounts, he was an ordinary waiter living in Lillehammer, 170 kilometres north of Oslo. He was shot 13 times after he attended a movie with his wife, who was pregnant.[49] Had a judicial court been involved in punishing this man, there would have been a far greater likelihood that the mistaken identification would have been uncovered.

Regrettably, the use of drone strikes in Pakistan and Afghanistan has had its struggle with misidentification. In discussions with the delegation of tribal Maliks from North Waziristan the Special Rapporteur for the United Nations was informed that drone strikes routinely inflicted civilian casualties, and that groups of adult males carrying out ordinary daily tasks were frequently the victims of such strikes. They emphasised that to an outsider unfamiliar with Pashtun tribal customs there was a very real risk of misidentification of targets, since all Pashtun tribesmen tended to have a similar appearance to members of the Pakistan Taliban, including similar (and often indistinguishable) tribal clothing, and since it had long been a tradition among the Pashtun tribes that all adult males would carry a gun at all times. They considered that civilian casualties were a commonplace occurrence, and that the threat of such strikes instilled fear in the entire community.[50]

This misidentification is occurring in situations where no immediate risk is posed to service members. And one practice in particular demonstrates how the attitude of the leadership in the United States seeps down to the troops on the ground in regard to how to determine whether a person is 'good' or 'bad' when there is no immediate threat: 'baiting'.

The practice of 'baiting' involves targeting suspected insurgents by scattering 'pieces of "bait", such as detonation cords, plastic explosives and ammunition, and then killing Iraqis who picked[ed] up the items'.[51] This bright idea completely ignored the innocent reasons why an Iraqi civilian might pick up some detonation cord, plastic explosives or ammunition – such as the ability to sell the items for money, or to remove the dangerous item from their neighbourhoods. The military was only able to interpret such behaviour as posing a risk, even when the flaw in their logic was evident to everyone else.

'Baiting is putting an object out there that we know they will use, with the intention of destroying the enemy,' Captain Matthew P. Didier, the leader of an elite sniper scout platoon attached to the 1st Battalion of the 501st Infantry Regiment, said in a sworn statement. 'Basically, we would put an item out there and watch it. If someone found the item, picked it up and attempted to leave with the item, we would engage the individual as I saw this as a sign they would use the item against US Forces.'[52] This program was only made public through investigative documents uncovered in relation to murder charges filed against three snipers accused of planting evidence on Iraqis they killed.[53]

A dangerous precedent

The executive-directed killings being carried out by the United States in Pakistan, Afghanistan and Yemen may seem a world away from most western nations. Undoubtedly, the rest of the world is working on obtaining and employing drones for surveillance, which will easily have the ability to be armed. The aircraft are easily to obtain, and barriers to production are falling too quickly to place limits on the spread of the technology, which will transform warfare on a global scale. Currently, over 75 countries have remote piloted aircraft, and more than 50 countries are building nearly a thousand different types of aircraft. At a recent trade show display in Beijing, China showed off 25 different unmanned aerial vehicles.[54] The development of drones is within the reach of all countries, not just the US government and its close allies, as they are cheap to develop and readily available.[55]

The legal framework surrounding executive-directed killing that has been developed by Israel and adopted by the United States provides an unsettling precedent for the employment of drones. America has now adopted a war-making process that involves a secret program based on legal advice never properly vetted and never publicly discussed. In fact, former White House Press Secretary Robert Gibbs has stated that the Obama administration effectively banned him from speaking about drones; he was not allowed to discuss it in any way, or even acknowledge the program's existence.[56]

Implementing this covert program has involved lowering the threshold for use of lethal force by reducing the cost and risk involved in combat. Use of drones in counter-terrorism efforts to kill people 'outside of traditionally defined battlefields and established protocols for warfare, has given friends and foes a green light to employ these aircraft in extraterritorial operations that could not only affect relations between the nation-states involved but also destabilise entire regions and potentially upset geopolitical order.'[57] China is not far off from employing a drone for its own executive-directed killings. The *Global Times*, a Chinese state-run newspaper, reported that China had considered conducting its first drone strike against a man suspected of involvement in the 2011 murder of thirteen Chinese soldiers, but ultimately authorities decided that they wanted to keep the man alive so that he could be put on trial – a course of action the United States could not envision in the handling of Osama bin Laden.[58]

Full steam ahead, in March 2013 the United States opened a new drone base in Niger. While it claims that the base is for unarmed surveillance only, it doesn't take much to attach a Hellfire missile on the Predator.[59] Currently, the US government maintains two drone programs – one run by the CIA, and the other by the Department of Defense. A plan has been put forward to shift the CIA's program to the Pentagon, which would 'unify the command and control structure of targeted killings and create a uniform set of rules and procedures. The CIA would maintain a role, but the military would have operational control over targeting.'[60]

The key is: who will be selecting the targets? It is being

reported that the CIA would 'remain involved in lethal target-ing, at least on the intelligence side, but would not actually con-trol the unmanned aerial vehicles.' Yet the issue of how targets are selected and who selects them is more problematic than the mere use of drones.

In February 2013, a Department of Justice memo was leaked to news channel NBC. The memo outlines the circumstances in which a United States citizen who is allegedly a member of Al-Qaeda or an associated group can be legally targeted: when the target poses an 'imminent threat', capture is not feasible, and if the operation would be conducted consistently with law of war principles. The media has heavily criticised the memo's caveat to the 'imminent threat' requirement, which 'does not require the United States to have clear evidence that a specific attack on US persons and interests will take place in the imme-diate future'. Again, this is the standard set to target American citizens – one can imagine that the standards for non-citizens will be even less stringent.

After the release of the Department of Justice memo, the White House promised to disclose additional information on the memo to congressional intelligence committees, providing assurances that strikes against US citizens were 'legal, ethical and wise'.[61] Some senators have called for the establishment of 'drone courts' to oversee executive-directed killing decisions in relation to US citizens, or for the drone program to be moved from the CIA to the Department of Defense's purview, which would provide it with greater oversight. However, others have been less demanding; Dick Durbin, a senator from Illinois, stated that '[w]e have to find a new constitutional balance with the challenges we face today.'[62] Even before the memo was leaked, Congress was largely accepting of the Obama administration's 'trust us' stance, with few calls for oversight or transparency made.

Checkmate

The only political resistance the US's executive-directed killing program has met with was a thirteen-hour filibuster by Senator Rand Paul over President Obama's nominee for CIA director, John Brennan. A letter written by US Attorney-General Eric Holder to Senator Paul suggests that in 'extraordinary circumstances'[63] it would be lawful and within the President's authority to use a weaponised drone to carry out a lethal strike on an American citizen on US soil. Though dismissing the potential for such a strike as 'unlikely to occur', Holder suggested that in a situation similar to the attack on Pearl Harbour or 9/11, it could be conceivable that the President would be forced to use drones to attack Americans domestically in an effort to 'protect the homeland'. The letter to Rand was a response to the senator's threat to filibuster the Brennan nomination until the President '[answered] the question of whether or not the President can kill American citizens through the drone strike program on US soil'.[64]

Senator Paul had one more question: 'Does the President have the authority to use a weaponised drone to kill an American not engaged in combat on American soil?' Attorney-General Holder finally answered that question with a 'no',[65] but what the senator forgot to ask is how the White House will define 'combat'. Senator Graham 'said flatly that Obama would not use a drone against a noncombatant sitting in a café somewhere in the United States'.[66] Again, the real question is how 'noncombatant' will be defined, and how collateral damage will be applied within the United States – these definitions and concepts have proved very malleable when applied to Iraqis and Afghans.

The United Nations and Pakistan have not been shy about critiquing the US program. In response to drone attacks in Pakistan, the Pakistani government informed the UN's Special Rapporteur on Human Rights and Counter-terrorism that Pakistan does not consider the situation in the Federally Administered Tribal Areas, where many of the strikes have taken place,[67] to amount to an armed conflict, either international or non-international. Rather, 'Pakistan considers that its own military forces operating in the region are engaged in a law enforcement operation aimed at countering terrorism in support of the civilian administration.'[68] Within a week of these comments, the US defiantly responded by unleashing a further drone strike in Pakistan, 'fir[ing] two missiles at a vehicle in Pakistan's northwestern tribal belt ... killing four militants'.[69]

In fact, there has been more US congressional resistance and public outcry over the new medal former Secretary of Defense Leon Panetta proposed for drone operators. The new Distinguished Warfare Medal would honour drone pilots and 'cyberwarriors' who work far away from the traditional battlefield. In response, the Senate's leaders on military affairs, in a letter to Defense Secretary Chuck Hagel, said that the new medal 'should not be ranked higher than combat awards, including the Bronze Star and the Purple Heart'.[70] This criticism brought an immediate response from Hagel, who had been a Purple Heart recipient in Vietnam, who stopped production of the controversial medal intended to honour drone pilots pending a review of its official rank above some combat valour medals in the military's 'order of precedence'.[71] Secretary Hagel was quick to nix the proposed medal after the review.[72]

Conclusion

After 9/11, a more permissive way of thinking set about to justify a new type of warfare against Al-Qaeda and its associates. A policy of killing targeted suspected terrorists – relatively cheaply and without directly spilling US blood – has been elevated as an integral part of US national security strategy. At the same time, legal irritants like the Geneva Conventions would no longer apply to US conflicts in Afghanistan and beyond. The continuation of a politically expedient 'war on terror' continues to underpin executive-directed drone killings that are conducted in secret.

Sadly, most of these drone strikes are not being used to kill enemy forces shooting at American troops. 'Kill lists' are usually based on guesswork by the military about someone's past or potential future conduct, rather than what the person is doing when they are actually killed. Such actions sidestep basic principles of international humanitarian law. Further, justifications are compiled behind a bureaucratic wall that bypasses judicial process and legal systems. At the same time, intelligence about these drone targets should not be equated as evidence and should be recognised as imperfect. Mistakes and misidentification have killed and wounded many hundreds of civilians. And the ongoing practice of 'baiting' has obvious downfalls, including the rise of anti-US sentiment.

The implementation of a covert drone program has lowered the threshold for use of lethal force. Such a fragile basis for 'surgical' killings dismisses the applicability of traditional legal and political standards; a lower of rule of engagement can be (and is) easily copied by other countries. Critically, the issue of how targets are selected and who selects them remains both awkward and problematic – unless we simply choose to continue to turn a blind eye to secret wars while embracing a blind faith in the conduct of executive power with arbitrary ethical boundaries, with little oversight and with no clear governing laws and policies.

Thank you to Kamala Rangarajan, a Juris Doctor student at Melbourne Law School, for all her assistance. Also to Professor Tim McCormack, Melbourne Law School, Professor George E. Edwards, Indiana University, Robert H. McKinney, School of Law, Indiana University, and Dr Daniel Baldino, The University of Notre Dame Australia.

1   D. Walsh, 'Leading UN official criticises CIA's role in drone strikes', *Guardian*, 3 June 2010.

2   This article uses the term 'executive-directed killing' to describe such actions, though other terms used include 'targeted killing' or 'extrajudicial killing'.

3   I. McPhedran, I, 2013, 'Australia to stock up on US drones', *News Limited Network*, 16 May 2013, last accessed 22 July 2013 <www.news.com.au/technology/sci-tech/australia-to-stock-up-on-us-drones/story-fn5fsgyc-1226644838899>.

4   'Revealed: Australians at the console of Kill TV, when drone strikes take out Afghan targets', *Sydney Morning Herald*, 5 September 2011, last accessed 22 July 2013 <www.smh.com.au/technology/sci-tech/revealed-australians-at-the-console-of-kill-tv-when-drone-strikes-take-out-afghan-targets-20110904-1jslm.html>.

5   K. Werrell (1985) *The Evolution of the Cruise Missile*, Air University Press, Alabama.

6   Available at <www.thetimes.co.uk/tto/multimedia/archive/00293/14803019_eddie_adam_293641b.jpg> (last accessed 10 April 2013).

7   K. Beyer, 'The myths and reality of Munich', *Time*, December 2005.

8   'Dubai names suspects wanted for killing of Hamas man', *BBC News*, 16 February 2010.

9   See 'CCTV footage: the assassination of Mahmoud al Mahbouh in Dubai', YouTube video, posted by 'DUBAISESSION',

15 February 2010, last accessed 10 April 2013 <www.youtube.com/watch?v=kzzzTtpo8AY>.

10 'Targeted for death: military and human rights lawyers weigh in on the legality of the killing of Hamas' Mahmoud al Mabhouh', *Los Angeles Times*, 21 February 2010.

11 'Dubai Hamas assassination: Australia angry over use of fake passports', *Telegraph*, 25 February 2010.

12 M. Mazzetti, 'How a U.S. citizen came to be in America's cross hairs', *New York Times*, 9 March 2013.

13 M. Phillips, 'Osama Bin Laden dead', White House blog, 2 May 2011, last accessed 22 July 2013 <www.whitehouse.gov/blog/2011/05/02/osama-bin-laden-dead>.

14 Phillips, 'Osama Bin Laden dead'.

15 See 'Osama Bin Laden killed: worldwide reactions', *The Atlantic*, 2 May 2011, last accessed 22 July 2013 <www.theatlantic.com/infocus/2011/05/osama-bin-laden-killed-worldwide-reactions/100058/>.

16 G. Miller, 'Under Obama, an emerging global apparatus for drone killing,' *Washington Post*, 27 December 2011.

17 Statement of Cofer Black, Joint Investigation into September 11, Joint House/Senate Intelligence Committee Hearing, 26 September 2002.

18 US Department of Defense Office of the Assistant Secretary of Defense (Public Affairs), 'DoD announces criteria for Global War on Terrorism medals', news release, 26 February 2004.

19 In the case of armed conflict not of an international character occurring in the territory of one of the High Contracting Parties, each Party to the conflict shall be bound to apply, as a minimum, the following provisions:

'(1) Persons taking no active part in the hostilities, including members of armed forces who have laid down their arms and those placed "hors de combat" by sickness, wounds, detention, or any other cause, shall in all circumstances be treated humanely, without any adverse distinction founded on race, colour, religion or faith, sex, birth or wealth, or any other similar criteria.

To this end, the following acts are and shall remain prohibited at any time and in any place whatsoever with respect to the above-mentioned persons:

(a) violence to life and person, in particular murder of all kinds, mutilation, cruel treatment and torture; ...

(b) taking of hostages;

    (c) outrages upon personal dignity, in particular humiliating and degrading treatment;

    (d) the passing of sentences and the carrying out of executions without previous judgment pronounced by a regularly constituted court, affording all the judicial guarantees which are recognised as indispensable by civilised peoples.'

20 'Hamid Karzai – fast facts', *CNN Online*, 17 December 2012.

21 An index to many of the torture memos can be found at 'A Guide to the Memos on Torture', *New York Times*, last accessed 22 July 2013 <www.nytimes.com/ref/international/24MEMO-GUIDE. html?_r=0>.

22 <www.pegc.us/archive/White_House/bush_memo_20020207_ ed.pdf> (last accessed 10 May 2013).

23 A. Gonzales, 'Decision re application of the Geneva Convention on Prisoners of War to the conflict with Al-Qaeda and the Taliban', Memorandum for the President, 25 January 2002.

24 President Bush even went so far to create Global War on Terror medals for the US military: US Department of Defense Office of the Assistant Secretary of Defense (Public Affairs), 'DoD announces criteria for Global War on Terrorism medals', 26 February 2004.

25 'Humane treatment of Taliban and Al-Qaeda detainees', White House Memorandum, 7 February 2002.

26 'Humane treatment of Taliban and Al-Qaeda detainees'.

27 A. Gonzales, 'Decision re application of the Geneva Convention on Prisoners of War to the conflict with Al-Qaeda and the Taliban'.

28 *Hamdan v Rumsfeld*, 548 US 557, 2006.

29 'U.S. policy on assassinations', *CNN News (Online)*, 4 November 2002, last accessed 22 July 2013 <archives.cnn.com/2002/ LAW/11/04/us.assassination.policy/>.

30 B. Woodward, 'CIA told to do "whatever necessary" to kill Bin Laden', *Washington Post*, 21 October 2001.

31 'U.S. policy on assassinations', *CNN News (Online)*.

32 US Department of Justice, *White Paper: Lawfulness of a Lethal Weapon Operation Directed against a U.S. Citizen Who Is a Senior Operational Leader of Al-Qa'ida or an Associated Force*, 10 May 2013.

33 'Friendly Fire: A Recent History', *CBS News (Online)*, 16 February 2007.

34 R. Reilly, 'Seven other targeted-killing memos still undisclosed,' *Huffington Post*, updated 13 February 2013, last accessed 22 July 2013 <www.huffingtonpost.com/2013/02/13/targeted-killing-memos_n_2679397.html>.

35 R. Blackhurst, 'The air force men who fly drones in Afghanistan by remote control', *Telegraph*, 24 September 2012.

36 J. Newman, 'CIA "kill list" shrouded in secrecy', *CBS News Online*, 6 October 2013, last accessed 22 July 2013 <www.cbsnews.com/8301-503543_162-20116691-503543/cia-kill-list-panel-shrouded-in-secrecy/>.

37 J. Greenberg, 'Israel affirms policy of assassinating militants', *New York Times*, 5 July 2001.

38 J. Becker and S. Shane, 'Secret "kill list" proves a test of Obama's principles and will', *New York Times*, 29 May 2012, last accessed 23 July 2013 <www.nytimes.com/2012/05/29/world/obamas-leadership-in-war-on-al-qaeda.html?pagewanted=all&_r=0>.

39 Spc. Ben Hutto, 'Soldiers capture High-Value Target during night raid', American Forces Press Service, 18 March 2008.

40 A. Finlayson, 'A retrospective on counterinsurgency operations', Central Intelligence Agency: Centre for the Study of Intelligence <www.cia.gov/library/center-for-the-study-of-intelligence/csi-publications/csi-studies/studies/vol51no2/a-retrospective-on-counterinsurgency-operations.html>.

41 Hutto, 'Soldiers capture High-Value Target during night raid'.

42 United States Army Training and Doctrine Command, 'Field Manual FM 3-60 (FM 6-20-10): The Targeting Process', November 2010.

43 Gerald K. Haines, *CIA and Guatemala Assassination Proposals 1952–1954*, CIA History Staff Analysis, June 1994.

44 Woodward, 'CIA told to do "whatever necessary" to kill Bin Laden'.

45 Woodward, 'CIA told to do "whatever necessary" to kill Bin Laden'.

46 H. Chang and S. Tata, '8 LAPD officers involved in shooting after Dorner "case of mistaken identity"', *US News (Online)*, 22 February 2013, last accessed 22 July 2013 <usnews.nbcnews.com/_news/2013/02/22/17058326-8-lapd-officers-involved-in-shooting-after-dorner-case-of-mistaken-identity?lite>.

47 Richard A. Oppel Jr., 'Tighter rules fail to stem deaths of innocent Afghans at checkpoints', *New York Times*, 27 March 2010.

48 David Kilcullen and Andrew McDonald Exum, 'Death from above, outrage down below', *New York Times*, 16 May 2009.

49 'Israelis to compensate family of slain waiter', *New York Times*, 28 January 1996.

50 United Nations Office of the High Commissioner for Human Rights, 'Statement of the Special Rapporteur following meetings in Pakistan', press release, 14 March 2013.

51 J. White and J. Partlow, 'U.S. aims to lure insurgents with "bait"',
    Washington Post, 24 September 2007.

52 White and Partlow, 'U.S. aims to lure insurgents with "bait"'.

53 White and Partlow, 'U.S. aims to lure insurgents with "bait"'.

54 K. Roberts, 'When the whole world has drones,' *National Journal
    (Online)*, 21 March 2013.

55 See, e.g., the 'Build your own drone' website at <www.
    buildyourowndrone.co.uk> (last accessed 11 May 2013).

56 J. Miller, 'Former White House press secretary Robert Gibbs: I
    had gag order on drone program', *CBS News (Online)*, 24 February
    2013.

57 K. Roberts, 'When the whole world has drones'.

58 T. Zakaria, 'As drone monopoly frays, Obama seeks global rules',
    Reuters (Online), 17 March 2013, last accessed 22 July 2013
    <www.reuters.com/article/2013/03/17/us-usa-security-drones-
    idUSBRE92G02720130317>.

59 C. Whitlock, 'Drone base in Niger gives U.S. a strategic foothold in
    West Africa', *Washington Post*, 22 March 2013.

60 D. Klaidman, 'Exclusive: no more drones for CIA', *Daily Beast*,
    19 March 2013.

61 M. Bruce, 'Drone strikes on US terror suspects "Legal",
    "Ethical", "Wise", White House says', *ABC News (Online)*,
    5 February 2013, last accessed 22 July 2013 <abcnews.go.com/m/
    blogEntry?id=18412905&sid=77&cid=77>.

62 'Obama allies urge greater scrutiny of drones policy', *Guardian*,
    10 February 2013.

63 E. Holder, Office of the Attorney-General, letter dated 4 March
    2013.

64 K. Herting, 'Holder: drone strikes on US soil legal in "extraordinary
    circumstances"', *Jurist (Online)*, 6 March 2013, last accessed 22 July
    2013 <jurist.org/paperchase/2013/03/holder-drone-strikes-on-us-
    soil-legal-in-extraordinary-circumstances.php>.

65 United States Senator Rand Paul, 'Sen. Paul Reaches Victory
    Through Filibuster', press release, 7 March 2013.

66 T. Curry, 'McCain, Graham assail Rand Paul on targeted killings
    policy', *NBC Politics (Online)*, 7 March 2013, last accessed 22 July
    2013 <nbcpolitics.nbcnews.com/_news/2013/03/07/17225441-
    mccain-graham-assail-rand-paul-on-targeted-killings-policy?lite>.

67 L. Charbonneau, 'US drone strikes violate Pakistan's sovereignty:
    UN', *Reuters*, 15 March 2013.

68 'Statement of the Special Rapporteur following meetings in

Pakistan', UN press release, 14 March 2013.

69 'US drones kill four in Pakistan: officials', *Global Post*, 21 March 2013.

70 K. DeYoung, 'Top military affairs senators ask Chuck Hagel to downgrade new Distinguished Warfare Medal', *Washington Post*, 12 March 2013.

71 J. Koebler, 'Hagel to order review of drone medal', *US News (Online)*, 12 March 2013, last accessed 22 July 2013 <www.usnews.com/news/articles/2013/03/12/hagel-orders-review-of-drone-medal>.

72 K. Wong, 'Hagel nixes medal for drone pilots, cyberwarriors', *Washington Times (Online)*, 15 April 2013, last accessed 22 July 2013 <www.washingtontimes.com/news/2013/apr/15/hagel-nixes-medal-drone-pilots-cyber-warriors/>.

6

BIGGER BUDGETS = BETTER INTELLIGENCE?

Peter Leahy

*'The old national intelligence system in place
on September 11 was destined to fail.'*

MAYBE. But spy agencies do not necessarily get it all wrong, all of the time. Intelligence is not the same as hard evidence. And given inherent and fixed limitations, some intelligence failures and mistakes will be inescapable. Further, while it can be argued that many Western intelligence communities had been facing significant resourcing problems in a post–Cold War era, which included a chronic shortage of experienced analysts and high-calibre linguists, it is equally wrong to presume that increased budgets will automatically lead to better intelligence.

Certainly, in Australia after the events of 9/11, former Prime Minister John Howard introduced a comprehensive web of unprecedented criminal and national security laws with a focus on pre-emptive surveillance and offensive engagement. The Australian Intelligence Community (AIC) was elevated as the 'best weapon' to stamp out the likelihood of future attacks on Australian soil. As part of an urgent upgrading process, the budget of organisations like Australia's main domestic spy agency – the Australian Security Intelligence Organisation (ASIO) – skyrocketed. More broadly, in January 2013, the Gillard government announced that in the wake of 9/11 'our overall intelligence budgets tripled'.[1] The equation appeared simple – intelligence failures threaten national security; therefore, increase the budget, get better intelligence and remove threats to national security.

Jigsaw pieces

In simple terms, intelligence is knowledge. Intelligence fulfils a vital role in contributing to national security, defined by Prime Minister Gillard in 2013 as 'fundamentally about protecting Australia from harm'.[2] In a more detailed and useful definition, in 2008 the then Prime Minister Kevin Rudd defined national security as 'Freedom from the threat of attack; the maintenance of our territorial integrity; the maintenance of our political sovereignty; the preservation of our hard-won freedoms; and the maintenance of our fundamental capacity to advance economic prosperity for all Australians'.[3]

Without timely and accurate intelligence to help inform decision-making on a wide range of security, defence, economic, diplomatic, trade and criminal threats Australia would be a less secure and prosperous place. Without intelligence, a nation is blind to developing threats, unable to secure its own secrets and clueless about how to adapt to changing circumstances. As Richard Betts says, 'It is the role of intelligence to extract certainty from uncertainty and to facilitate coherent decision in an incoherent environment.'[4] Nonetheless, while there is a definite need for intelligence, questions on how much, what sort and how the intelligence system should be organised and assessed are difficult to answer. Of course, we must also decide if we can ever expect to know everything and will be able to perfectly predict the future.

In Australia, intelligence has been described as 'useful information' by the Director General of the Office of National Assessments, Allan Gyngell;[5] as 'secret information gleaned without the official sanction of the owners of that information' by the Director General of the Australian Secret Intelligence Service, Nick Warner;[6] and as 'Information that enables you to protect your interests or to maintain a valuable advantage in advancing your interests over those posing threats to them' in the 2011 Independent Review of the Intelligence Community by Robert Cornall and Rufus Black.[7]

In another basic form, intelligence is the ability to obtain and apply knowledge and skills to assist policymaking. It can be used to describe a particular attribute of individuals and to describe the process of acquiring, analysing and disseminating information for political, military, economic, commercial or private reasons. The timely provision and use of intelligence can inform the future and offer an advantage over an opponent (or friend). Intelligence is at its best when it is timely, accurate, relevant and distributed.

Intelligence is either covert or overt. Covert intelligence is obtained without the knowledge of the individual, organisation or government. Overt intelligence is obtained from open source information such as television, newspapers, radio, internet and diplomatic reporting. Overt intelligence is becoming a much more important element of gathering information, with the recent exponential increase in the amount of publicly available information on the internet. 'To open source advocates, up to 95% of intelligence sought by governments is freely available –

if you've got the time and expertise and know where to look. It's less cloak and dagger, more mouse-click and blogger.'[8]

There are three basic types of intelligence: human, which involves contacts between individuals; signals, which involve eavesdropping on signals and electronic communications; and imagery, which involves the collection of photographs or satellite information. Following the collapse of the Soviet Union, in an effort to harness the so-called 'peace dividend', many nations ran down their human intelligence networks in favour of the more technical and supposedly less expensive signals and electronic products. In recent years, especially in the wake of 9/11, this has been seen as a mistake. As a result, there has been a reversal of the trend and an increased focus on human intelligence. Human intelligence is often preferred, as it can provide a guide to both capability and intent.

Intelligence is not just about collecting information and gathering facts. The facts are important but what is more significant is the process of evaluating and analysing the facts into useable assessments and then ensuring that the assessments are distributed in a timely manner to the people who need them. In 1977, in a report from his seminal Royal Commission, Justice Hope stated that 'Intelligence is produced for the consumers. Otherwise it is a waste of time and money. It would be well for the intelligence agencies to remember this and to impress on their staffs its importance.'[9] Cornall and Black in their 2011 review of intelligence agreed and noted, 'any helpful definition of intelligence has to go well beyond the collection and dissemination of useful information. Intelligence has to be clearly linked to the needs of the individual customers and tailored for purposes to which they can apply it.'[10]

Assessment is the real work of intelligence. It requires loyal, mature and experienced people with good judgment and excellent research and analysis skills. People like this are difficult to find and retain, and don't come cheap. Intelligence assessments are used to provide warning of impending conflicts, uprisings and terror attacks and to enhance the understanding of the global, regional and domestic environment of the nation's decision-makers. Intelligence assessments also support decisions regarding security and defence strategies, force structure decisions and capability and acquisition planning.

Finally, it is valuable to note that intelligence is not an end product in itself. It is an intermediate product used to inform policy advisers and decision-makers. Decisions are taken on the basis of intelligence, not exclusively because of intelligence. In addition to intelligence, policy advisers and decision-makers are influenced by their own background, training, prejudices and cultural experiences, plus other sources of information. So again, the equation bigger budgets = better intelligence = better security can be a highly deceptive premise. While better intelligence might be required, it is equally valid to argue that so too are better decisions by government, the consumers of intelligence.

A lack of intelligence

It is not controversial to suggest that intelligence failure can threaten national security. But caution needs to be taken in assuming that bigger budgets will mechanically amount to better intelligence. Such an approach can wrongly presume an intelligence system is hopelessly broken. Critically, it can fail to appreciate that intelligence will never be perfect. Also, as former US Defense Secretary Donald Rumsfeld has said, 'If you think about it, what comes out of intelligence is not fixed, firm con-clusions. What comes out are a speculation, an analysis, proba-bilities, possibilities, estimates.'[11]

Intelligence analysis remains a complex mix of both art and science; it might be described as trying to find the needle in the haystack. At the very least, the threat landscape is constantly changing and enemies do actively work to hide their capabili-ties and deceive about their actual intentions. At the same time, there remains ongoing public discussion about whether the AIC is performing in a morally, professionally and politically accept-able fashion. As one journalist put it, 'There have been claims that turf wars and rivalries, and an alleged willingness to shape intelligence to political agendas, are undermining Australia's ability to navigate its way through a more troubled world.'[12]

Certainly, intelligence failures are not new. There have been plenty of past intelligence missteps at the centre of pivotal events: the failure to forecast the Japanese assault on Pearl Harbour on 7 December 1941; the surprise at the Argentinian invasion of the Falkland Islands in 1982; the failure to comprehend the absence of weapons of mass destruction (WMD) in Iraq in 2002; and the inability to foresee the 'green on blue' attacks on Australian soldiers in Afghanistan in 2012. (A 'green on blue' attack is a rogue attack made on one's own side by a force regarded as neu-tral – in this case, violence by members of the Afghan security forces against NATO coalition soldiers.)

Nearer to Australia, serious question have been raised about why policymakers did not know more about the growing prob-lems in our own backyard, such as political and social break-down in the Solomon Islands. As of this moment, it appears malicious cyber-activity and internet-based espionage is being promoted as a new national security priority. And this does not take into account more elastic viewpoints of security that point to a lack of comprehension of non-traditional problems like climate change, information security and global pandemics.

As such, bigger budgets to improve intelligence must be carefully targeted, require improved coordination and should be sensibly adjusted to keep pace with emerging threats and new challenges to national security. Spending more money to get more timely and reliable intelligence may be part of the answer, but it is not the entire answer – or an instant panacea. The complexity of the task of formulating operational priorities and optimising the core procedures of our intelligence agencies should not be understated, and care must be taken to ensure that extra money doesn't just build bigger and more unwieldy bureaucracies, or reinforce inward-looking or outdated workplace habits, or unnecessarily duplicate already available information.

Top secret

One ever-present hurdle does deserve a special mention: the role of secrecy. Intelligence works hand-in-hand with official secrecy. Sporadic government reports on the performance of the intelligence agencies and oversight by Parliamentary committees and the Inspector General of Intelligence are generally reassuring about the AIC, but understandably vague about what is really going on (see chapter 10). Interested outside observers will often have to try to 'read between the lines'. Unfortunately, this type of blueprint is somewhat unavoidable. The quandary is discerning the degree of necessary secrecy required to protect intelligence work. Further, from a security policy standpoint, 'the difficulty of assessing whether these agencies are performing is that agencies such as ASIO are unaccountable – you never know what they're doing and we're not entitled to know, and it makes it very difficult for the community to make an assessment ... What government is going to cut back money for the security agencies? Then it'll leak out: "Sources say government risks terror attack." So they've got them over a barrel.'[13]

For security reasons, those who produce and consume intelligence seldom declare their failures or celebrate their successes. For the same reasons, it is difficult to determine how much is actually spent on intelligence. Australia's current total intelligence budget is artfully hidden deep within annual reports and spread across multiple agencies. Commentators and analysts cannot be absolutely sure of the accuracy of publicly available figures and have to contend with layers of opaqueness and even undeclared or 'black' programs designed to confuse and deceive the enemy. This makes it difficult to judge the value for money provided by the nation's intelligence agencies. Nonetheless, what is certain is that there has been a remarkable increase in intelligence budgets in the last decade.

One final point regarding secrecy is worth contemplating. Robert Gates, Director of Central Intelligence from 1991 to 1993, commented that a bloated cocoon of secrecy can cripple accountability while producing a 'groupthink' mindset which can impair government planning and conduct:

> I sat in the Situation Room in secret meetings for nearly twenty years under five Presidents, and all I can say is that some awfully crazy schemes might well have been approved had everyone present not known and expected hard questions, debate and criticism from the Hill. And when, on a few occasions, Congress was kept in the dark, and such schemes did proceed, it was nearly always to the

lasting regret of the Presidents involved. Working with the Congress was never easy for Presidents, but then, under the Constitution, it wasn't supposed to be. I saw too many in the White House forget that.[14]

The Australian Intelligence Community

The AIC is generally accepted to consist of six security and intelligence agencies. The agencies vary in role, size, collection method, reporting responsibilities, legislation, administrative control and budget. One relatively minor Defence intelligence agency, not listed as a member of the AIC, is the Defence Security Agency. The accepted members of the AIC are:

The Office of National Assessments. ONA provides assessments to the Prime Minister and senior ministers in the National Security Committee of Cabinet, based on an analysis of global political, strategic and economic developments that affect Australia's national interests. It incorporates information from other intelligence agencies, diplomatic and other government sources and the news media. ONA is an independent body, with its own legislation, directly accountable to the Prime Minister. Because of its direct access to the Prime Minister and the members of the National Security Committee of Cabinet, it is regarded as the most influential of Australia's intelligence agencies. Acknowledging the recent proliferation of publicly available information, ONA has recently established an Open Source Centre to collect, validate and produce reports based on this freely available information.

Australian Security Intelligence Organisation. ASIO has the primary responsibility of collecting, analysing, and reporting on activities or situations that might threaten Australia's national security. Its primary role, as defined in the *ASIO Act*, is to protect Australia and its people from domestic threats such as espionage, sabotage, politically motivated violence, the promotion of communal violence, attacks on Australia's defence system, or acts of foreign interference.[15] ASIO is not a law enforcement body and works closely with the Australian Federal Police and the state police authorities. It provides security assessments for individuals requiring national security clearances, access to sensitive areas and those who wish to become Australian citizens. In a departure from its primary role, which is the collection of domestic intelligence, at the request of the Foreign Minister it is also responsible for the collection of foreign intelligence in Australia. Since the Sydney Olympics, the 9/11 attacks on New York and the attacks in Bali, ASIO has increased its focus on preventing a terrorist attack in Australia.

Australian Secret Intelligence Service. ASIS, the most secretive of Australia's intelligence agencies, collects and distributes foreign intelligence, primarily from human sources, about the capabilities, intentions and activities of individuals or organisations outside Australia which may impact on Australia's interests and the well-being of its citizens. In addition, ASIS contributes to efforts against terrorism, the proliferation of weapons of mass destruction and transnational issues such as people smuggling. It also undertakes counter-intelligence activities to protect Australia's national interests.

The organisation has acknowledged the need to adapt and expand to meet the growing number and diverse range of threats facing Australia and its citizens. Nick Warner, the Director General of ASIS, in an unprecedented speech in July 2012 acknowledged the need for ASIS to 'increase its operational capacity, and to become more innovative, creative and flexible'.[16] An example of this approach is the provision of support to the Australian Defence Force military combat efforts in Iraq and Afghanistan. As described by Warner, these efforts, ranging from force protection at the tactical level to strategic level reporting on Taliban leadership, are important tasks for ASIS, which has 'a major commitment in Afghanistan, and this will remain as long as the ADF is deployed there'.[17]

The last three agencies making up the AIC are administered by the Department of Defence.

Defence Signals Directorate. DSD supports military and strategic decision making by collecting and analysing foreign signals intelligence (Sigint) for the Australian Defence Force and Australian government. In a significant and growing role, it also supports national cyber- and information security (InfoSec) by providing the following: advice and assistance to federal and state authorities on matters relating to the security and integrity of information; a greater understanding of sophisticated cyber-threats; and the coordination of and assistance with operational responses to cyber-incidents of national importance across government and systems of national importance.

Defence Intelligence Organisation. DIO provides all-source independent intelligence assessments to the Defence Minister, government policymakers, defence planners and battlefield commanders. Advice is provided to support the planning and conduct of ADF operations, defence capability and policy development and wider government planning and decision-making on defence and national security issues. This includes general intelligence on the ability of other countries to wage war or to threaten regional and international stability; scientific analysis on the identification of weapons and defence systems; and technical intelligence on nuclear, radiological, chemical and biological weapons proliferation and proliferators. Over the last decade DIO has been exceptionally busy supporting multiple global ADF deployments. Another related development requiring additional effort has been the provision of intelligence directly from the strategic level to operational and tactical commanders in the field.

Defence Imagery and Geospatial Organisation. DIGO provides geospatial and imagery intelligence to provide information on the intentions or activities of people or organisations outside Australia; to meet the operational, targeting, training and exercise requirements of the ADF; and to support Commonwealth and state authorities in carrying out national security activities.

Other agencies

While the AIC is traditionally acknowledged to consist of six primary agencies, there are other agencies with active intelligence functions and responsibilities. These additional agencies are becoming increasingly important as new threats and challenges to Australia's national security appear in a more broadly defined national security environment. Although they were mentioned briefly in Cornall and Black's most recent review of Australia's intelligence agencies, they were not evaluated. They are:

Australian Federal Police. Intelligence is acknowledged as one of the key national functions of the AFP, which maintains an in-house intelligence capability headed by an Assistant Commissioner. Within the AFP, intelligence is 'an enabling function that directly contributes to AFP operational outcomes and, more broadly, Australian national security'.[18] The AFP intelligence element supports national and international investigations, analyses global organised crime and produces an Annual Intelligence Assessment; it engages with international partners to prevent crime and arrest criminals and with Australia's whole-of-government intelligence community in producing national security and criminal intelligence.

Australian Crime Commission. One of the goals of the ACC is to maintain a leading-edge capability in national criminal intelligence and information services. To achieve this goal, the ACC manages the Australian Criminal Intelligence Database (ACID) and the Australian Law Enforcement Intelligence Network, to provide federal, state and territory law enforcement and other regulatory authorities with a framework to securely store, retrieve, analyse and share criminal information and intelligence on a national basis.

Australian Customs and Border Protection Service. ACBPS is developing and embedding a strategic planning process that realises the intelligence-led, risk-based approach of the agency. One of the Service's senior managers is the National Director of Intelligence and Targeting, who is responsible for the assessment of new and emerging threats to the border and the provision of intelligence and targeting that underpin risk mitigation.

Department of Immigration and Citizenship. DIAC maintains an intelligence network to combat people smuggling, fraud and unauthorised arrivals in Australia. The network consists of national intelligence officers and overseas compliance officers, who collect and disseminate information and intelligence relating to immigration activities.

Cyber Security Operations Centre. The CSOC is the newest and arguably the most important of Australia's intelligence initiatives. Although it is established within the Defence Signals Directorate, it is considered here as a separate entity. This is because of the immediate and significant nature of the cyber-threat and the likelihood that the CSOC will, in the future, attract significant resources, potentially distorting other intelligence budgets. Cybersecurity is mentioned in the 2008 National Security Statement as one of Australia's national security priorities and has witnessed a further rise in profile and focus by again being emphasised in the 2013 National Security Strategy.

Diplomatic reporting. While not a formal intelligence agency, diplomatic reporting from Embassies and High Commissions through the Department of Foreign Affairs and Trade is a vital raw material for other agencies in gathering information and informing their assessments and decisions. It is widely recognised that the Department of Foreign Affairs is under considerable budget pressure, and is having difficulty achieving the myriad tasks required to represent Australian interests and provide consular support to the enormous number of Australians travelling overseas. DFAT budgets have been in decline over a period of time, and two studies from the Lowy Institute have reported on disarray, overstretch and deficit within DFAT.[19]

Boosted budgets

Over the last decade Australia's expenditure on intelligence has tripled. This is a remarkable increase by any measure. The end result is that the Prime Minister reported that in 2011–12 the total expenditure on intelligence was $1519 million.[20] The government claimed that this dramatically enhanced budget was a response to, in part, transnational criminals, multiple and lengthy deployments of the ADF and what now appeared to be an entrenched 'war on terror'. As Graeme Dobell colourfully captured it:

Cast your eyes over ASIO's new central office, big enough for 1800 people, the largest monument to what the 9/11 decade did to Canberra. The new office can still be defined as part of the parliamentary triangle – a geographic zone that is home to the institutions with true power in the national capital – and depending on the way the symbolism is worked, ASIO's staff will stare across the lake at the High Court or lift their eyes to the giant flag that flies above Parliament House.[21]

The bigger budgets have been evident across the entire intelligence community but, as noted earlier, the figures can be difficult to track and explain. Three relatively recent official reports provide a guide to the scope, consistency and breadth of the overall increase in money spent on the AIC. In 2004, Philip Flood noted that intelligence was the key element in Australia's response to the changing security environment and that there had been a doubling of the intelligence budgets since the year 2000, with over $650 million invested in the intelligence community in 2004–05. Staff numbers in the AIC rose by 44 per cent over the same period. Overall, the government committed more than $3 billion in additional funding for national security from 2001–02 to 2007–08.[22] Confirming the scale of the increase, Cornall and Black noted that 'Overall, the combined annual budgets of the intelligence agencies grew by $753 million from 2000 [to] 2010 at a compound annual growth rate of 14.6% a year to a total of $1.07 billion.'[23]

The Parliamentary Joint Committee on Intelligence and Security, in their 2012 Review of Administration and Expenditure of the Australian Intelligence Agencies, reported that this trend continued later in the decade when they noted that 'Of the agencies other than ASIO, two received a significant increase in their budget for 2009–10, with the other three receiving modest increases.'[24] Additional comments noted that ASIO program expenses in 2009–10 were $368 million, an increase of 5 per cent from 2008–09, while the estimated cost for 2010–11 was $413 million – an increase of 12 per cent from 2009–10. Separately ASIO also received capital injections for telecommunications interception systems, capability enhancements and asset replacement, as well as boosting counter-espionage capabilities (counter-intelligence can be defined as intelligence gathered about an adversary's intelligence activities).

Public commentary confirms the broad budget growth and speculates that in the decade after the September 11 terrorist attacks Australia's bill for fighting terrorism was estimated to be edging towards $30 billion, consisting of the money spent on the wars in Iraq and Afghanistan, and the rivers of cash poured into the police and intelligence agencies. Semi-official reporting from the Australian Strategic Policy Institute's *Australian Defence Almanac* of 2011–12 calculates the nominal nine-year budget increase for elements of the AIC to be:

Agency	% increase in dollars
Department of Defence	101
Overseas Development Assistance	135
Australian Federal Police	167
Department of Foreign Affairs and Trade	57
Australian Security Intelligence Organisation	471
Australian Secret Intelligence Service	355
Office of National Assessments	400

Under any accounting method, significantly bigger budgets have been allocated to the AIC since the year 2000.[25]

Effectiveness

So what did the bigger budgets actually buy? Australia's intelligence community is unique, extensive, and over the last decade has grown at a rapid rate. It has evolved over time to meet Australia's particular constitutional and structural requirements and over the years has been subject to a number of rigorous and extensive reviews. These reviews provide a rare insight into the effectiveness of this secretive area of government.

Hope Royal Commissions. Justice Hope conducted two Royal Commissions into the AIC, one in the 1970s and another one in the 1980s. In 1977, for instance, Hope found deep-seated problems with ASIO. ASIO had departed from 'principles of propriety, including legality, to which ASIO should have regard when fulfilling its functions'.[26] While some argue that his work has little relevance in the present day context, Hope's overall assessment of the effectiveness and conduct of the AIC remains highly important, as it lays the foundations for, and has helped to shape, the standards expected by the AIC today. These principles include the requirement for robust and independent intelligence; the separation of collection from assessment; the separation of assessment from policy formulation; the collection of human and signals intelligence by different agencies; and the principle that intelligence activity should be conducted in accordance with the laws of Australia.

The Flood Review of 2004. The Flood Review was conducted at a time when there was concern about the quality of intelligence advice provided to government. The judgments and comments made by Flood give an insight into the effectiveness of the AIC at the time. With reference to perceived intelligence failures, Flood found that Australia 'shared in the allied intelligence failure on the key question of Iraq WMD stockpiles'; that intelligence on Jemaah Islamiyah was 'inadequate' prior to December 2001; that there was 'no evidence' to support a claim that a pro-Jakarta lobby existed in DIO; and that intelligence advice on the Solomon Islands was 'generally of a very high quality'.[27]

In his conclusion Flood wrote that 'Australian intelligence agencies are performing well overall, and represent a potent capability for government.'[28] He found that all the agencies had adapted to the major challenges posed by global terrorism and increased requirements for support to deployed Australian forces, and that overall the quality of assessment provided to government has been generally 'very good'. Nevertheless, he also highlighted the continuing need for intelligence analysts to be challenged, confronted by different perspectives and alerted to flaws in their arguments. But some argued that key questions remained unanswered.

> Flood confirms that any mistakes in assessing intelligence on Iraq's WMD were not the result of pressure exerted by ministers to ensure that intelligence assessments were in line with their policy agenda ... But it leaves open big questions about the nature of the policy process which led to decisions about Australia's commitment to Iraq and about the complex relationship between intelligence and policy.[29]

Cornall and Black 2012. Unlike the Flood Review, which had intelligence failures to concentrate on, the Cornall–Black Review was a programmed and broader investigation. The public version of the report is a slight document and overall is effusive in its praise of the performance of the AIC. 'As a nation we now possess a new range of well tested intelligence capabilities. Those capabilities have made Australia and Australians far safer than they would otherwise have been and have also made significant contributions to global security.'[30] Cornall and Black also make note of other benefits, such as creating a capability multiplier effect by being able to access combat 'partners' in dealing with a range of contingencies.[31]

In slightly less hagiographic tones, the authors note that the challenge for the AIC is to meet both our existing and expanding security challenges in an era of constrained resources. Cornall and Black see opportunities to increase the efficiency and effectiveness of the AIC most evident in 'improved policy setting, mission integration and intelligence distribution'; 'more efficient and rigorous performance evaluation'; 'outside input to support innovation'; 'new strategies for managing intelligence collection in an age of abundant information'; and 'continuing to deepen the quality of working relationships with the wider national security community'.[32]

In their conclusion they note that 'the investment made in the intelligence agencies has resulted in improved capability and performance' and that the challenge for the next five years or so 'will be to better align the AIC's priorities with the new geo-political and technological realities facing Australia as a middle power with global interests'.[33] It is noteworthy that these observations relate to ways of improving the performance of the AIC that can be achieved largely through administrative and bureaucratic action to improve coordination, rather than through dramatically bigger budgets. Further, it is worth acknowledging that the report did hint at unresolved ethical questions and human rights roadblocks.

> The use of Intelligence Surveillance and Reconnaissance platforms has been subject to criticism from human rights organisations. Close analysis of their concerns suggest that this is an area that requires considerably more deliberation. If the use of important new capabilities like these is to retain public support, there needs to be a clear articulation of any ethical issues involved in managing them effectively and the way they are used.[34]

A number of critics did express strong reservations about the overall ambit and substance of the public review, as well as the absence of lucid recommendations.

> A big lack in Cornall–Black is any discussion of the contestability of assessments coming out of the intelligence agencies … How well is the Australian system doing today on achieving contestability? If you are charged with doing a follow-on study to Flood, then contestability is a primary gauge of what Flood sought. All the key issues Cornall and Black were charged with examining (supporting national interests, reforms, working arrangements, practices, collaboration) would have a contestability dimension. Yet the word 'contestability' does not appear.[35]

Paddy Gourley, a former deputy secretary of the Defence Department, was blunter, saying: 'The highly censored public Black–Cornall report is a woeful document.'[36]

No room for complacency

While some of the achievements of the intelligence community over the last decade are laudable, there is no room for complacency or self-congratulation. The world of intelligence is a two-way firing range, and the enemy gets a vote. The intelligence agencies must be vigilant, and there is always room for improvement. It is often said that the enemy only has to be lucky once, but we have to be lucky every time. Even Allied access to German military codes during World War II did not guarantee success in some of the biggest battles of that war. Intelligence will hardly ever be flawless, and even with the best intelligence in the world, government officials and politicians can still make bad decisions.

Rather than the budget largesse of the last decade, the future budget outlook is likely to be one of fiscal stringency as forecast by Prime Minister Julia Gillard when launching the 2013 National Security Strategy. Any future budget increases for intelligence will be on the basis of changing national interests, specific threat events, increasing risk, the introduction of new technologies such as drones, and developing requirements such as the many more Australians travelling overseas and increased commercial and mining interests such as in Africa, an area not routinely covered by the AIC. Even while demanding fiscal stringency, governments are unlikely to accept any decrease in the standard of intelligence. The challenge for the AIC will be to maintain the present high standard of intelligence product. To cope with steady state or reduced budgets, the intelligence supremos will be faced with hard decisions related to strict adherence to intelligence priorities, increased international cooperation and the acceptance of evolving, non-traditional security challenges.

Brave new world

The most spectacular recent failure of intelligence was the inability of the US intelligence community to forecast the terror attack on the United States in what Osama bin Laden called the 'Manhattan Raid'. In the voluminous report of the events surrounding the 2001 raid it was concluded that 'the 9/11 attacks revealed four kinds of failures: imagination, policy, capabilities, and management.'[37] The major problem identified by the Commission Report was that US intelligence gathering was fragmented and poorly coordinated, and that the intelligence agencies often operated independently of each other. As a result, connections were missed and dots were not joined that might have warned of the attack. US authorities have made many changes on the basis of the Commission Report. Priority changes included improving coordination between intelligence agencies, establishing a Department of Homeland Security, and reinstating human intelligence capabilities.

These US remedial actions provide a guide for Australian actions. While sensibly not establishing a department of homeland security, Australia has already acted to ensure better coordination between the existing national security departments, agencies and capabilities. As a result of the National Security Statement of December 2008, a National Security Adviser was appointed to 'build on the existing community of relatively small, separate agencies, ensuring they remain nimble, accountable and, above all, properly joined up'.[38] A priority action for the National Security Adviser was to improve coordination and share intelligence between the intelligence agencies. As part of this process, a National Intelligence Coordination Committee was established to ensure that the national intelligence effort is fully and effectively integrated.

Other suggested actions as outlined by Cornall and Black include improved policy settings, mission integration and intelligence distribution; performance evaluation; and deepening the quality of working relationships with the wider national security community. These are all sensible steps which build on the larger staff and enhanced capabilities of the agencies.

The first decade of the 21st century saw an unprecedented growth in expenditure on Australia's intelligence agencies. Bigger budgets were used to expand and meet new threats and demands for intelligence on a global scale. One success appears to be increased level of cooperation and coordination between the various intelligence agencies. But there should be no respite in efforts to institutionalise this improved coordination and cooperation. There remains a persistent need for the AIC to avoid internal competition, alert other public agencies and commit to improving national cooperation, with the withholding or concealment of information as the exception rather than the rule. Even the rankest optimist would have to admit that the biggest budgets will never deliver perfect intelligence. There can be no guarantee of being able to predict a strategic shock such as the Arab Spring or a lone wolf terrorist intent on causing damage to Australia. Nevertheless, government should demand a high degree of reliability, accuracy and consistent success from its intelligence agencies. This high standard of intelligence will require consistent budgets, careful and attentive management and frequent critical evaluation.

After 9/11 the world became a more complicated and dangerous place and Australia, in pursuit of its national interests, has expanded its role as a global actor through military and police deployments across the globe. Global deployments require global intelligence. Interestingly, in January 2013, even as Prime Minister Gillard declared the end of the 9/11 decade, she spoke of 'a new era of national security imperatives'.[39] According to this vision, this will be an era when Australia will need to focus on its own region while recognising that the behaviour of states, rather than non-state actors, will be the most important driver, and in which diplomacy will be critical in a multipolar world. Sounds like no rest for the intelligence agencies. If any future government is looking for easy savings from intelligence in an era of 'fiscal stringency', it is likely to be disappointed.

1   Prime Minister J. Gillard, 2013, 'Australia's national security beyond the 9/11 decade', speech, last accessed 22 July 2013 <crawford.anu. edu.au/news/132/prime-minister-julia-gillards-speech-national-security-college>.

2   Department of the Prime Minister and Cabinet (2013) *Strong and Secure; A Strategy for Australia's National Security*, Commonwealth of Australia, Canberra, p. 3.

3   K. Rudd (2008) 'National security statement to the Parliament', *Hansard*, House of Representatives, 4 December, p. 12549.

4   R. Betts (1978) 'Analysis, War and Decision: Why Intelligence Failures are Inevitable', *World Politics* vol. 31, no. 1, pp. 61–89.

5   A. Gyngell, 'The challenges of intelligence', lecture, Lowy Institute for International Policy, Canberra, 2011.

6   N. Warner, 'ASIS at 60', speech, Lowy Institute's Distinguished Speakers Series, 19 July 2012.

7   R. Cornall and R. Black (2011) *Independent Review of the Intelligence Community*, Australian Government, Canberra, p. 6.

8   T. Hyland, 'Money for nothing and your clicks for free', *The Age*, 8 March 2008.

9   R. Hope (April 1977) *Third Report of the Royal Commission on Intelligence and Security: Abridged Findings and Recommendations of Mr Justice Hope, Royal Commissioner*, Australian Government Printing Service, Canberra, p. 9.

10 Cornall and Black (2011) *Independent Review of the Intelligence Community*, p. 27.

11 D. Rumsfeld, Department of Defense press briefing, 27 October 2001.

12   B. Nicholson, 'Can our spies come in from the cold?', *The Age*, 24 April 2004.

13   Greg Barnes, cited in S. Neighbour, 'Hidden Agendas', *The Monthly*, November 2010.

14   R. Gates (1996) *From the Shadows*, Simon and Schuster, New York.

15   Australian Security Intelligence Act 1979, last accessed January 2013 <www.austlii.edu.au/au/legis/cth/consol_act/asioa1979472/s4.html - security>.

16   Warner, 'ASIS at 60'.

17   Warner, 'ASIS at 60'.

18   Australian Federal Police Annual Report 2011–12, p. 60.

19   Lowy Institute, 'Diplomatic disrepair: rebuilding Australia's international policy infrastructure', 2011, last accessed 15 July 2013 <www.lowyinstitute.org/publications/diplomatic-disrepair-rebuilding-australias-international-policy-infrastructure> and Lowy Institute, 'Australia's diplomatic deficit', 2009, last accessed 15 July 2013 <m.lowyinstitute.org/publications/australias-diplomatic-deficit>.

20   Department of the Prime Minister and Cabinet (2013) *Strong and Secure*, p. 15.

21   G. Dobell, 'Hope's ghost lingers in a secret security world', *Inside Story*, 11 April 2012, last accessed 15 July 2013 <inside.org.au/hopes-ghost-lingers-in-a-secret-security-world/>.

22   Philip Flood (2004) *Report of the Inquiry into Australian Intelligence Agencies*, Ch 8, last accessed 15 July 2013 <www.dpmc.gov.au/publications/intelligence_inquiry/chapter8/1_findings.htm>.

23   Cornall and Black (2011) *Independent Review of the Intelligence Community*, p. 16.

24   Parliamentary Joint Committee, *Review of Administration and Expenditure: No 9 – Australian Intelligence Agencies*, 13 June 2012, para. 3.11.

25   Australian Strategic Policy Institute, *Defence Almanac 2011–2012*, p. 126.

26   R. Hope (April 1977) *Third Report of the Royal Commission on Intelligence and Security*, p. 70.

27   Claim made by Lieutenant Colonel Lance Collins, supported by the conclusion of Captain Martin Toohey RAN in the *Report of Investigation – Redress of Grievance* submitted by Lieutenant Colonel Lance Collins. Also see Flood (2004) *Report of the Inquiry into Australian Intelligence Agencies*.

28   Flood, (2004) *Report of the Inquiry into Australian Intelligence Agencies*.

29 W. Hugh, 'More a failure in policy-making than intelligence', *Sydney Morning Herald*, 26 July 2004.

30 Cornall and Black (2011) *Independent Review of the Intelligence Community*.

31 Cornall and Black (2011) *Independent Review of the Intelligence Community*, p. 16.

32 Cornall and Black (2011) *Independent Review of the Intelligence Community*, p. 20.

33 Cornall and Black (2011) *Independent Review of the Intelligence Community*, p. 22.

34 Cornall and Black (2011) *Independent Review of the Intelligence Community*, p. 37.

35 G. Dobell, 'Intelligence review not a pinch on Flood', *Interpreter*, 3 February 2012, last accessed 22 July 2013 <www.lowyinterpreter. org/post/2012/02/03/Intelligence-review-not-a-pinch-on-Flood. aspx>.

36 P. Gourley, 'I spy another intelligence whitewash', *Sydney Morning Herald*, 3 April 2012.

37 *9/11 Commission Report*, p. 339, last accessed 15 July 2013 <www.9-11commission.gov/report/911Report.pdf>.

38 K. Rudd (2008) 'National security statement to the Parliament', *Hansard*, House of Representatives, 4 December, p. 12549.

39 Prime Minister J. Gillard, 2013, 'Australia's national security beyond the 9/11 decade'.

7

TELLING THE TRUTH ABOUT TORTURE

Jude McCulloch and David Vakalis

'Torture is an effective intelligence-gathering tool.'

VERY WRONG. Imagine you work for the country's top domestic spy agency, tasked with gathering and analysing intelligence to prevent threats to national security. You are aware that there have been discussions between certain people about a bomb that is set to detonate, but you do not know when or where.

You are, however, holding someone in incommunicado detention who has valuable information that may assist in discovering the bomb, and thus potentially saving many, perhaps even thousands of lives. You have tried some standard questioning techniques without success. You become increasingly anxious about the looming possibility of a bomb explosion. The detainee refuses to talk or denies all knowledge and you are unconvinced they are telling the truth. The clock – and you fear the bomb – is ticking. You start to think the only way to get the information you need is to use 'enhanced interrogation techniques' – the CIA's preferred euphemism for torture. Torture, you conclude, in line with a theme in the contemporary 'torture debate', is the 'lesser of two evils'; regrettable and morally tainted, but not as bad as taking no action and risking many innocent lives.[1]

The 'ticking bomb' scenario is often used to argue in favour of torture as an indispensible and morally defensible tool for gathering timely and reliable intelligence in order to prevent catastrophe in support of national defence.[2] Despite its frequent recital, however, the scenario bears so little resemblance to reality that it should be considered entirely hypothetical. Intelligence and police agencies rarely, if ever, have in custody someone they 'know' has planted a bomb or has information about such a bomb which they 'know' is ticking. Extensive examination of the history and contemporary context of intelligence gathering do not reveal any such examples.[3]

Even apart from representing an entirely unlikely set of facts as a pressing problem for intelligence agencies, the scenario fails to take into account the nature of torture and the purposes for which it is used. Torture is a systematic state practice, not a desperate response to an extreme or exceptional emergency situation. Torture is not typically used to gather intelligence, but instead targets reviled individuals and groups, most frequently minorities and political dissidents.[4] Further – and significantly – the hypothetical assumes that torture is an effective means to gain intelligence, and, beyond this, more effective than other, less brutal means. These assumptions are not supported empirically, and there is much evidence to the contrary.

What is torture?

Although torture is extensively practised, and often glorified in movies and television shows like *24*, it has long been condemned by international law. The United Nations's 1984

Convention against Torture defines torture as:

> any act by which severe pain or suffering, whether physical
> or mental, is intentionally inflicted on a person for such
> purposes as obtaining from him [sic] or a third person
> information or a confession, punishing him [sic] for an act
> he [sic] or a third person has committed or is suspected of
> having committed, or intimidating or coercing him [sic] or
> a third person, or for any reason based on discrimination
> of any kind, when pain or suffering is inflicted by or at
> the instigation of or with the consent or acquiescence of a
> public official or other person acting in an official capacity.
> It does not include pain or suffering arising only from,
> inherent in or incidental to lawful sanctions.[5]

This international law definition is limited in a number of significant ways. It does not apply to non-state actors such as corporations.[6] Likewise, it does not apply to private individuals, so that major forms of gendered violence such as family violence and most sexual assaults don't fall within the definition, though rape (in some circumstances) can come within the international law definition. Nonetheless, the right not to be tortured is one of the few that is universally applied and cannot be derogated from, whatever the nature of any purported threat to national security.[7] Statements made as a result of torture are banned in any legal proceedings.

In short, despite its prohibition under international law, torture and the ill-treatment of people do remain widespread. For example, Amnesty International reports that between 1997 and 2000, it received reports of torture from 150 countries, with people dying as a result in over 80 countries.[8] Various case studies included Israeli security services torturing Palestinian detainees, extrajudicial executions of alleged criminals by government officials in Peru, and the torture of political prisoners by police in India. The reality is that although torture is strictly prohibited under international law, 'torturers are very rarely punished, and when they are, the punishment rarely corresponds to the severity of the crime.'[9]

Torture and tyranny

Torture is considered one of the most heinous of state crimes and is often conceived of as a form of state terror or terrorism. Torture is strictly prohibited under international law largely because of its close association with cruelty and tyranny. It has 'always been bound up with military conquest, royal revenge, dictatorial terror, forced confessions, and the repression of dissident belief'.[10]

It is a mistake, however, to conclude that democratic states rarely engage in torture. Liberal democracies have long participated in regimes of torture by proxy funding, training or equipping paramilitaries and regimes of state terror in outside, often poor, countries, in pursuit of national interests.[11] There is also a history of imperial countries maintaining repressive regimes, including programs of torture, in colonies, while maintaining the trappings of the rule of law domestically.[12] Democracy's link to torture is not confined, however, to foreign battlefields. Darius Rejali, in his comprehensively researched book *Torture and Democracy*, convincingly demonstrates the way modern democracies have developed a range of what he calls 'stealth' or 'clean' torture techniques which have subsequently spread to more overtly repressive regimes. Such practices include 'water-boarding', dry choking (using plastic gags over the head so as not to leave visible marks), temperature manipulation, stress positions, drugs, sleep 'adjustment' or deprivation, noise, electroshocks, sensory deprivation, isolation, chemical irritants and 'nutrition control'. The techniques leave few traces on the body and, compared to standard torture techniques, are more readily cloaked in euphemisms that work to obfuscate the inherent brutality of all forms of torture.[13]

At the same time, as torture has come into the open as a topic considered suitable for rational debate as a policy choice in democratic countries there has been an attempt to narrow what constitutes torture. In a memo written by lawyers in the United States Justice Department in 2002, physical torture was defined to include only pain rising 'to the level of death, organ failure, or the permanent impairment of a significant bodily function'. In the case of mental torture it was defined as resulting 'in significant psychological harm of significant duration, e.g., lasting for months or even years'. These definitions are at odds with the canon of human rights law and longstanding humanitarian opposition to torture.[14]

Alongside these attempts at narrowing of the definition of torture, there has also been an attempt to exclude categories of people from the protections of international laws against torture. Former US President Bush's executive level lawyers argued that 'unlawful combatants' held at Guantanamo Bay are not protected by the Geneva Conventions against torture because they have no status in international law.[15] While Guantanamo Bay has been declared a 'legal black hole', various black sites beyond even the limited visibility of the Cuban island negate even further the protections of international law against torture.

New thinking on torture – from anathema to intelligence

In the years since the 9/11 attacks on the US, the idea of torture as a vehicle for cruelty and oppression has been incrementally eclipsed by the notion of torture as a vital aspect of intelligence in the fight against terror and imminent catastrophe. After 9/11 New York's *Newsweek* magazine declared it 'Time to think about torture'.[16] In short, torture has moved out of the shadows, to be increasingly debated, depicted and justified as part of an entirely rational and necessary national security strategy of liberal democratic states.

This new thinking is reflected in a rash of academic articles and books arguing in favor of torture in the face of serious threats to national security.[17] Popular culture is also awash with scenes of torture in the service of thwarting terrorists and saving innocent lives. The high-rating US television series *24* commenced only weeks after 9/11. Screening nearly 200 episodes over nine years, the drama courted controversy with its frequent scenes of torture as part of a successful counter-terrorism strategy. The series's main character is a popular hero, despite his association with torture.[18] The much-awarded 2011 US movie *Zero Dark Thirty* depicts torture in the hunt for information about bin Laden's hideout. The movie's CIA heroine bears witness to multiple torture episodes, while the film's torturer is depicted as a pleasant man doing his professional duty in the service of the greater good.[19]

Torture is now increasingly understood as a potential tool of Western intelligence agencies and counter-terrorism experts charged with the solemn burden of national security. No longer strictly anathema or officially denied, torture is considered by many a matter open for debate as a reasonable and credible policy choice.[20] In a reversal of the association of torture with tyranny, some now claim that liberal democracies must use torture in self-defense against terror and tyranny.

Debate about torture and intelligence has been most intense in the United States, where such practices have been embraced as part of former President George W. Bush's so-called 'war on terror'. Since 2001 the United States, in Afghanistan, at Guantanamo Bay, and Abu Ghraib in Iraq, has been torturing prisoners, to 'exploit [them] for actionable intelligence'.[21] As a close ally of the United States, Australia has been implicated in controversies surrounding torture in the 'war on terror'. The UN Committee against Torture has raised concerns over the Australian government's failure to investigate torture allegations made by Australian citizens, Mamdouh Habib and David Hicks, who allege ill-treatment at the hands of US officials overseas. In both cases, it is claimed that Australian officials were complicit in the kidnapping, illegal detention, torture and/or ill-treatment (see also chapter 9). The nature of the global media and information technology ensures that the popular culture depictions, along with academic and political commentary, particularly emanating from the United States, have international resonance.

A lexicon of denial

While the new thinking about torture has led to unprecedented public discussion, the victims continue to be 'disappeared' and the practice disguised through a lexicon of denial. (Enforced disappearance entails murder – it was a practice linked to the Nazi movement, used to instil terror, and later re-emerged in places like Colombia, Argentina and Chile.) Torture is frequently and deliberately mislabeled. Torture regimes frequently masquerade as counter-terrorism and crime fighting, while the techniques are referred to as lesser cruelties such as 'degradation', 'tough/rough interrogation', 'coercive questioning' and 'enhanced interrogations'. As pointed out above, Rejali maintains that contemporary tortures tend towards the 'stealthy' or 'clean'. The descriptions sound relatively benign – 'sleep adjustment', for example, which involves distorting a person's sleep cycles to produce extreme disorientation, or 'nutrition control', which means either providing food that contains just enough nutrition for survival or force-feeding prisoners a liquid nutritional supplement. But the methods are intended to cause intense psychological and/or physical pain. In addition, in leaving little or no trace on the body they undermine systems of accountability and the perceived veracity of victim/survivor accounts.

The proliferation of these types of torture methods, sometimes described as a type of 'torture lite', gives rise to the myth of a 'science of torture' – the idea that pain can be contained and controlled within some civilised level. However, as Rejali states, 'torture cannot be administered professionally, scientifically, or precisely.'[22] Tortures of all types inflicts severe suffering, frequently compounded by the victim's inability – especially in the case of 'stealth' and 'clean' methods – to prove the reality of their experience.

The way that torture is at once acknowledged and defended, while simultaneously being veiled in a misleading lexicon, is typical of the way narratives of denial are constructed around suffering caused by (and atrocities committed by) states. This 'seen but not seen' quality is a contradiction that is well explicated in the literature on torture. The officially denied yet selectively communicated nature of torture allows states to instill fear in the populations most likely to be the targets of disappearance, detention and torture, while still maintaining the moral high ground in terms of domestic authority and international reputation.[23] The combination of fear and denial works to silence and punish political dissidents and unpopular minorities, while maintaining state legitimacy. While in the past democracies hid their complicity or participation in torture by outsourcing to foreign nationals or external territories, today the link between torture and democracy continues to be rendered opaque through complicated and interlinking layers of official denial and rationalisation, compounded by multiple misunderstandings about the nature and purpose of torture.

Victims and perpetrators

In the face of misleading language, there remains a terrible array of violence that constitutes the world of torture. Apart from the 'stealth' or 'clean' categories outlined above, there are many overtly violent techniques, including beatings, stretchings, whippings, burnings, mutilation (especially of the genitals), rape, cuttings, hangings, breaking of bones, amputations, suspension, crucifixion, finger and teeth extractions, and attacks by animals, to list just some that make up the torturer's repertoire.[24]

Candidates and victims of torture are inevitably depicted as hardened criminals or unrepentant terrorists, bent on inflicting grievous injury on innocent victims. In the 1970s movie *Dirty Harry* a psychopathic murderer has buried a teenage girl alive and she is slowly suffocating. The culprit is captured but refuses to say where the girl is buried, instead taunting police with his knowledge. Torture, dished out by the police officer hero – played by Clint Eastwood – extracts the information. Harry's hands are dirty, but it is difficult not to applaud his noble cause.[25] The real-life profile of the torture victim rarely matches the stereotype propagated in popular culture and the academic and political or policy arguments in defense of torture. The victims of torture are most frequently the poor, minorities, and political dissidents, women and children included. Police are most often the perpetrators, and criminalised communities the target.[26] The rapid proliferation of less-than-lethal chemical weapons and electroshock devices – for example, capsicum spray and tasers – among police has expanded the capacity of police to engage in 'clean' and 'stealth' torture. It comes as no surprise that Indigenous Australians are massively overrepresented in the statistics of those on the receiving end of these weapons.[27]

Those detained and tortured post 9/11 were said to be the 'worst of the worst' – an appellation that was widely believed in the emotionally charged atmosphere after those attacks. Over time, however, it has become clear that most of those held at US detention sites such as Guantanamo Bay and Abu Ghraib had no information of any relevance; most seemed to have simply been in the wrong place at the wrong time.[28] States, when unable to outright deny torture, are able to paint the victims of torture as outside the moral community and non-deserving of human rights. Edward Herman points out that states, because of their resources, power, and authority, have 'great defamation edge' that leads to the ready acceptance of victims of torture as perpetrators of terror and serious crime, no matter how absurd the designation.[29]

When torture is unambiguously revealed, states tend to blame 'a few bad apples'. Sometimes such abuses are put down to sadistic individuals.[30] It is clear, however, that torture is a systematic practice that engages many levels of government and bureaucracy. To take just one historical example: a 1980 Amnesty International report on Argentina found that torture took place in sixty government and military facilities in that country in what became known as the 'Dirty War'. Others claim that the Argentine military kidnapped and tortured thousands of people, and that there were hundreds of torture centres and concentration camps at the height of that war.[31]

An effective intelligence tool?

At the heart of arguments in favor of torture is the myth that it is capable of providing timely relevant intelligence that saves lives. For those who reject the absolute moral position that torture is never justified, the assumption about the intelligence value of torture underpins the utilitarian argument for its use in pursuit of national security.[32] The idea that torture is effective in preventing catastrophe is a trope in much of the post 9/11 popular culture which focuses on counter-terrorism. As mentioned, in the movie *Zero Dark Thirty*, torture is depicted as vital in gathering clues in the hunt for Osama bin Laden. Yet the film, 'based on real events', has been roundly criticised for overstating the value of torture in that hunt. There is no empirical evidence to suggest that torture is effective in gaining reliable intelligence, and much to the contrary to suggest that the words of a tortured person are worthless.[33]

Torture gives rise to many false positives, as people say what is expected or demanded to avoid unbearable pain. False confessions under regimes of coercive questioning and torture abound through history. 'Witches' in their thousands confessed to devil worship and supernatural powers when subjected to tortures such as starvation, sleep deprivation and beatings.[34] In more contemporary times, conforming to modern-day myths, 'terrorists' likewise confess under unendurable regimes of pain and confinement. Three young British nationals held for months in isolation and subject to repeated coercive interrogations at Guantanamo Bay eventually 'confessed' to involvement in terrorist activities in Afghanistan. Subsequently, the British intelligence agency MI5 produced evidence that proved conclusively that they could not have been in Afghanistan at the relevant time, and they were released.[35]

There are a number of notorious Irish cases from the 1970s that demonstrate the phenomena of false confessions under regimes of coercion. The case of the 'Guilford Four' is the most infamous. In that case, four innocent Irish nationals were detained in England and subjected to various degrees of violence and psychological pressure, and as a result 'confessed' to a bombing carried out by the Irish Republican Army. The four served a combined total of more than sixty years in prison before the miscarriage of justice was finally acknowledged.[36]

Apart from the issue of unreliable information and false confessions, regimes of torture distract from investigative skills and processes capable of providing accurate and reliable information and evidence. Unreliable information obtained under torture can overwhelm investigators with false leads. False confessions likewise lead investigators astray and reduce the chance of identifying guilty parties. More generally, the resources directed at detention and torture can reduce the focus on investigations based on techniques capable of producing reliable evidence, rather than vague intelligence.

Torture is also likely to fuel the hostility that contributes to the type of threats to national security that it is said to be aimed at preventing. To succeed, torture has been linked to counter-terrorism needs to prevent incidents and identify perpetrators without increasing support for such actions or producing people willing to carry them out.[37] But the detention, torture and abuse of Muslims at Guantanamo Bay became a rallying cry for disaffected Islamists around the globe.[38] Similarly, the torture and abuse of Irish nationalists interned without trial in the early 1970s led to greatly expanded support for the Irish Republican Army in their conflict with the British.[39] While torture is justified on the hypothetical but ubiquitous ticking bomb, once sanctioned it is inevitably used more broadly. It is impossible to calculate any gains in intelligence under torture against the cost of fuelling conflict.

Torture: the lesser of two evils?

A final point in confronting the myths related to torture is the idea that in weighing terrorism and torture, the latter is the lesser of two evils. To endorse this position, it is necessary to put aside the weight of history, which demonstrates that harms committed by states are far more serious than those committed by non-state actors. In a 1985 trial of some of those responsible for atrocities in the Dirty War in Argentina, one of the implicated generals asked in his own defense: 'Wouldn't it [torture] be justified if a terrorist had planted a bomb in an apartment building that would kill 200 people?' The prosecutor responded, 'But if you can't identify the bomber you end up torturing the residents.'[40] The prosecutor's answer captures the reality of torture as a state practice far more precisely than the ticking bomb scenario; on the one side the risk of a mass casualty atrocity, and on the other the certainty of state terror, with the latter not guaranteed to diminish the risk of the former. A subsequent commission of inquiry set up after the ousting of the Argentine military regime in 1983 found that the terror of that regime was 'infinitely' greater than the terror of the guerilla movement it was allegedly combating.[41]

The capacity of state officials and institutions to kill, maim, exploit, repress and cause widespread human suffering is unsurpassed.[42] According to Jackson, Murphy and Poynting, 'the terrorism perpetrated by non-state insurgent groups ... pales into relative insignificance besides the hundreds of thousands of people killed, kidnapped, "disappeared", injured, tortured, raped, abused, intimidated and threatened by state agents and their proxies in dozens of countries across the globe.'[43] Counter-terrorism and crime fighting is frequently a Trojan horse for state terror; regimes of torture masquerading as intelligence gathering provide an emblematic example of such terror.

The truth about torture

The ticking bomb has become the lens through which the pros and cons of torture are weighed in much contemporary debate. 'America wants the war on terror fought by Jack Bauer. He's a patriot.'[44] But, despite its popularity, the assumptions underpinning the ticking bomb hypothetical, as well as notions of torture as an expedient response to terrorism more broadly, bear little resemblance to reality. Torture is not an intelligence tool. As Eric Stover and Elena Nightingale state in *The Breaking of Bodies and Minds: Torture, Psychiatric Abuse, and the Health Professions*: 'the purpose of torture is to break the will of the victim and ultimately to destroy his or her humanity.' Torture, and the state terror it embodies, causes far more human suffering than violence committed by non-state actors. Torture is not about finding the truth, but is instead a part of a larger system of control through terror.

1   See M. Ignatieff (2004) *The Lesser Evil: Political Ethics in the Age of Terror*, Edinburgh University Press, Edinburgh.

2   See H. Shue (2006) 'Torture in Dreamland: Disposing of the Ticking Bomb', *Case Western Reserve Journal of International Law*, vol. 37, pp. 231–39.

3   D. Luban (2007) 'Liberalism, Torture, and the Ticking Bomb' in S.P. Lee (ed.), *Intervention, Terrorism, and Torture: Contemporary Challenges to Just War Theory*, Springer, Dordrecht, The Netherlands; D. Rose (2004) *Guantanamo: The War on Human Rights*, The New Press, New York, pp. 249–62.

4   E. Herman (1993) 'Terrorism: Misrepresentations of Power' in D. Brown and R. Merrill (eds), *The Politics and Imagery of Terrorism*, Bay Press, Seattle, WA, pp. 47–65; E. Stanley (2004) 'Torture, Silence and Recognition', *Current Issues in Criminal Justice*, vol. 1, pp. 5–25.

5   M. Shaw (2006) *International Law*, 5th ed., Cambridge University Press, Cambridge, p. 304.

6   D. Rejali (2008) *Torture and Democracy*, Princeton University Press, Princeton, pp. 38–39.

7   R.K.M. Smith (2007) *Textbook on International Human Rights*, 3rd ed., Oxford University Press, Oxford, p. 208.

8   Amnesty International (2003) 'Combatting torture: a manual for action', Amnesty International Publications, London, p. 15, last accessed 3 April 2013 <www.amnesty.org/en/library/asset/ACT40/001/2003/en/1b2dee39-d760-11dd-b024-21932cd2170d/act400012003en.pdf>.

9   J. Conroy (2001) *Unspeakable Act, Ordinary People*, Vision, London, p. 228.

10 D. Luban (2007) 'Liberalism, Torture, and the Ticking Bomb', p. 251.

11 R. Jamieson and K. McEvoy (2005) 'State Crime by Proxy and Juridical Othering', *British Journal of Criminology*, vol. 45, no. 4, pp 504–27.

12 E. Saada (2003) 'The History Lessons: Power and Rule in Imperial Formations', *Items and Issues, Social Science Research Council*, vol. 4, no. 4, Fall/Winter.

13 D. Rejali (2008) *Torture and Democracy*, Princeton University Press, Princeton.

14 M. Danner, 'Torture and truth', *New York Review of Books*, 10 June 2004, last accessed 22 July 2013 <www.nybooks.com/articles/

archives/2004/jun/10/torture-and-truth/?pagination=false>; M. Danner, 'The logic of torture', *New York Review of Books*, 24 June 2004, last accessed 22 July 2013 <www.nybooks.com/articles/archives/2004/jun/24/the-logic-of-torture/?pagination=false>.

15   A. Gordon (2009) 'The United States Military Prison: The Normalcy of Exceptional Brutality' in P. Scraton and J. McCulloch (eds), *The Violence of Incarceration*, Routledge, New York, pp. 164–86.

16   J. Alter, 'Time to think about torture', *Newsweek*, 5 November 2001.

17   See A. Dershowitz (2003) *Why Terrorism Works: Understanding the Threat, Responding to the Challenge*, Scribe, Melbourne; M. Ignatieff (2004) *The Lesser Evil: Political Ethics in the Age of Terror*, Edinburgh University Press, Edinburgh; M. Bagaric and J. Clarke (2005) 'Not Enough Official Torture in the World? The Circumstances in Which Torture Is Morally Justifiable', *University of San Francisco Law Review*, vol. 39, pp. 581–616.

18   K. Dodds, 2010, 'Jason Bourne: Gender, Geopolitics and Contemporary Representations of National Security', *Journal of Popular Film and Television*, vol. 38, pp. 21–33; P. Brereton and E. Culloty, 2012, 'Post-9/11 Counterterrorism in Popular Culture: The Spectacle and Reception of *The Bourne Ultimatum* and *24*', *Critical Studies on Terrorism*, vol. 5, no. 3, pp. 483–98.

19   S. Coll, '*Zero Dark Thirty*: A film directed by Kathryn Bigelow', *New York Review of Books*, 7 February 2013, pp. 4–6.

20   Coll, '*Zero Dark Thirty*'.

21   General Antonio M. Taguba, quoted in Danner, 'The logic of torture'.

22   Rejali (2008) *Torture and Democracy*, p. 576.

23   P. Green and T. Ward (2004) *State Crime: Governments, Violence and Corruption*, Pluto Press, London.

24   E. Stanley (2009) *Torture, Truth and Justice: The Case of Timor-Leste*, Routledge, London, p. 156.

25   M. Punch (2000) 'Police Corruption and Its Prevention', *European Journal of Criminal Policy and Research*, vol. 8, no. 3, pp. 301–24; J. Kleinig (1996) *The Ethics of Policing*, Cambridge University Press, Cambridge, pp. 52–54.

26   See Green and Ward (2004) *State Crime*.

27   J. McCulloch, 'Tasers in the spotlight: Comforting Myths and Shocking Realities', The Conversation, 5 December 2012, last accessed 16 July 2013 <theconversation.edu.au/tasers-in-the-

spotlight-comforting-myths-and-shocking-realities-10735>;
J. McCulloch, 'Why the taser-related death toll is rising', The
Conversation, 22 March 2012, last accessed 16 July 2013
<theconversation.com/why-the-taser-related-death-toll-is-
rising-5965>.

28 See, for example, S. Poynting (2010) '"We Are All in Guantanamo":
State Terror and the Case of Mamdouh Habib' in R. Jackson, E.
Murphy and S. Poynting (eds), *Contemporary State Terrorism: Theory
and Practice*, Routledge, Abingdon, Oxon.

29 E. Herman (1993) 'Terrorism: Misrepresentations of Power' in
D. Brown and R. Merrill (eds.), *The Politics and Imagery of Terrorism*,
Bay Press, Seattle, WA, pp. 47–65.

30 See Danner, 'Torture and truth'.

31 M. Feitlowitz (1998) *A Lexicon of Terror: Argentina and the Legacies
of Terror*, Oxford University Press, Oxford, p. 8.

32 See Dershowitz (2003) *Why Terrorism Works*; Ignatieff (2004) *The
Lesser Evil*; Bagaric and Clarke (2005) 'Not Enough Official Torture
in the World?

33 See Rejali, (2008) *Torture and Democracy*, chapters 21 and 22.

34 K. Thomas (1973) *Religion and the Decline of Magic*, London,
Penguin.

35 D. Rose (2004) *Guantanamo: The War on Human Rights*, New Press,
New York, pp. 120–22.

36 C. Walker and K. Starmer (1999) *Miscarriages of Justice: A Review of
Justice in Error*, Oxford University Press, Oxford.

37 S.J. Pickering, J. McCulloch and D.P. Wright-Neville (2008)
Counter-Terrorism Policing: Community, Cohesion and Security,
Springer, New York.

38 Rose (2004) *Guantanamo: The War on Human Rights*, pp. 11–12.

39 R.W. White (1989) 'From Peaceful Protest to Guerrilla War:
Micromobilization of the Provisional Irish Republican Army',
American Journal of Sociology, vol. 94, no. 6, pp. 1277–1302.

40 Quoted in F. Graziano (1992) *Divine Violence. Spectacle,
Psychosexuality and Radical Christianity in the Argentine 'Dirty War'*,
Westview, Boulder, CO, p. 28.

41 Herman (1993) 'Terrorism: Misrepresentations of Power', p. 49.

42 E. Stanley and J. McCulloch (2013) 'Resistance and State Crime'
in E. Stanley and J. McCulloch (eds), *State Crime and Resistance*,
Routledge, New York, pp. 1–13.

43 R. Jackson, E. Murphy and S. Poynting (2010) 'Introduction:
Terrorism, the State and the Study of Political Terror' in Jackson,

Murphy and Poynting (eds), *Contemporary State Terrorism*, pp. 1–11.

44 Joel Surnow, cited in P. Sands, 'Torture is illegal – and it never works', *Guardian*, 25 November 2008.

8

WIKILEAKS: INFORMATION MESSIAH OR GLOBAL TERRORIST?

Ben Saul

'"Julian Assange is a heroic crusader for global freedom of information" versus "WikiLeaks is an attack on the international community that endangers global security".'

BOTH VIEWPOINTS ARE TOO ONE-DIMENSIONAL. Few topics cause political people to hyperventilate so much as WikiLeaks. Its supporters see WikiLeaks as a heroic, visionary crusader for global freedom of information, transparency and justice. WikiLeaks has exposed war crimes, corporate conspiracies, government transgressions, and America's 'war on whistle blowers'.[1] It has heightened the public's demands for more open government and stimulated calls for greater government openness, accountability and transparency.[2] Such appeals are particularly relevant in an era where surveillance powers are expanding and privacy is diminishing.[3]

Its detractors claim that WikiLeaks has committed grave crimes, threatened global security, and endangered the lives of informants and human rights defenders. Some have even called for WikiLeaks to be listed as a terrorist organisation, or for its Australian founder, Julian Assange, to be assassinated.[4] Government reactions to WikiLeaks may also have brought more secrecy and less openness; officials no longer write anything down and are less inclined to provide candid assessments.[5] And more information hasn't necessarily changed much.

The cultish personality of Assange is a particularly polarising factor. For some, Assange is 'the century's greatest journalist',[6] a modern-day 'Ned Kelly',[7] and a Casanova to boot. He is seen as the victim of a 'witch hunt' by a malevolent, vengeful United States, has been abandoned by Australia, and deserves asylum in Ecuador and protection from a conspiracy of courts and governments in (at least) Britain, Sweden, America and Australia.[8] For those outside his fan club, Assange slavishly reposts online what brave whistle-blowers (such as Bradley – now Chelsea – Manning) have passed to him, and is a 'predatory, narcissistic fantasist' or misogynist evading justice for sex crimes in Sweden.[9] Public sentiment in Australia is deeply divided about Assange, who hoped to be elected to the Senate in 2013 – despite accepting Ecuador's offer of asylum and implying that Australia is not safe for him.[10]

But there is a spectrum of more nuanced views in between these poles. The truth about WikiLeaks and Assange is both messier and more mundane.

What is WikiLeaks?

WikiLeaks describes itself as a 'not-for-profit media organisation' which aims 'to bring important news and information to the public', in part by providing 'an innovative, secure and anonymous way for sources to leak information to our journalists (our electronic drop box)'.[11] While WikiLeaks has been caricatured as a rogue, anarchist organisation bent on destroying government secrecy, it presents itself as a regular media organisation, albeit distinguished by its innovative methods and greater independence.[12] Ideologically, it claims inspiration from international human rights principles, particularly freedom of opinion, expression and information under Article 19 of the Universal Declaration of Human Rights 1948.[13]

Before and since its launch in 2007, WikiLeaks has published 'leaked' secrets on a monumental scale, including military, diplomatic and corporate information. At its best it has exposed war crimes – such as the infamous 'Collateral Murder' video of civilian killings in Iraq in 2007 by a US helicopter – and serious misconduct by governments or corporations.[14] At its worst, it has failed to properly vet documents, resulting in the publication of names of vulnerable informants, and putting lives at risk. It has also 'data dumped' troves of trivia of little public interest, including diplomatic gossip – who knew that Berlusconi is 'vain', Kim Jong-Il 'flabby', Gaddafi 'strange', Mugabe 'crazy', or Rudd a 'control freak'?[15]

Security threat?

It is clear that the US, Australian and various other governments believed that some WikiLeaks disclosures endangered their security interests, and there are radically different opinions about whether particular disclosures were justifiable. It is far more doubtful whether WikiLeaks or Assange committed national security crimes in the US or Australia.

The US and Australian governments have publicly accused WikiLeaks of crimes against security. US Vice-President Joe Biden called Assange a 'high-tech terrorist'.[16] Other US politicians called for WikiLeaks to be listed as a terrorist organisation and for Assange to be prosecuted for espionage.[17] A federal criminal investigation into WikiLeaks was launched, with reports of an ongoing secret grand jury investigation into espionage.[18] At the time, it was also speculated that the Department of Justice might be considering an indictment under the *Espionage Act*.[19] Nonetheless, while no charges have yet been laid against WikiLeaks, the United States is prosecuting the confessed source of its Iraq and Afghanistan 'war logs' and US diplomatic cables, US soldier Bradley Manning. Manning was charged in July 2010 with two overarching offences: transferring classified data to his computer and adding unauthorised software to a classified computer; and unlawful disclosures of classified information (including where it could injure the United States).[20]

Twenty-two charges were added in March 2011, including wrongfully obtaining classified material to post on the Internet, knowing that it would be accessed by the enemy; illegally transmitting defence information; and aiding the enemy. Manning pleaded guilty to ten lesser charges in February–March 2013, but contested more serious charges, including that he aided the enemy.[21] A judge ruled that the latter charge requires evidence that Manning knowingly helped Al-Qaeda, which is at odds with his professed motivation to expose US abuses. In July 2013, Manning was convicted of seventeen of twenty-two charges, including espionage and theft, but acquitted of aiding the enemy.[22] Manning's conditions in military custody have been strongly criticised for being inhumane.[23]

Manning's prosecution also aims to flush out any evidence of WikiLeaks's role in his decision to disclose US secrets. As in many democracies, security information is primarily protected by the law at its source, through obligations on those who owe duties of confidentiality not to breach those obligations. By disclosing US secrets, Manning took his chances, knowing that he was violating his legal obligations to keep government secrets safe: that is the very high price of acting on conscience where the law does not align with one's own ethics.

By contrast, WikiLeaks owed no such obligations to the US government. It seems that there are no successful US prosecutions of those who have published information leaked by others, although a bill before Congress seeks to criminalise the specific act of publishing the identity of any US intelligence asset. The US crime of espionage requires intent to injure the US or to advantage a foreign government – difficult to evidence where publication was for the different purpose of a purported public interest in information about the conduct of wars and diplomacy.[24] Prosecutors may seek to establish that WikiLeaks somehow conspired with Manning by soliciting or inducing him to steal and leak secrets, implicating it in his alleged crimes. That would distinguish WikiLeaks's conduct from routine and lawful publication of secret material given voluntarily to media organisations by their sources. So far the US has not provided any evidence of such conduct by WikiLeaks, and Manning himself denies it.

The First Amendment to the US Constitution may provide strong protection of media publication of even security information in the public interest. In the Pentagon Papers case, the US Supreme Court refused to block publication of leaked defence information about the Vietnam War, with Justice Black stating that 'only a free and unrestrained press can effectively expose deception in government.'[25] However, First Amendment protection will not necessarily preclude a criminal prosecution.

And even the difficulty of establishing a criminal case against WikiLeaks or Assange has not stopped the United States from pressuring financial actors such as Visa, MasterCard, PayPal and Amazon to self-censor and stop processing funding and donations for WikiLeaks.[26]

In Australia, the government also rushed to judgment. Then Prime Minister Julia Gillard called the disclosures 'illegal'.[27] Then Attorney-General Robert McClelland publicly stated that 'there are potentially a number of criminal laws that could have been breached' by the disclosure of US diplomatic cables.[28] Yet an investigation by the Australian Federal Police found no evidence of illegality (and the government had no plans to change the law as a result).[29] That conclusion is not surprising. There is no general legal obligation on ordinary Australians, here or overseas, or on Australian or foreign media organisations, not to disclose foreign government secrets. As the Spycatcher case established, foreign governments also cannot enforce claims of security confidentiality in the Australian courts.[30]

While there are numerous context-specific restrictions on disclosing security information, none of those apply to the WikiLeaks disclosures. For example, under federal statutory and criminal law, and public service employment contracts, Australian officials are prohibited from disclosing protected information (just as Manning was under US law). There is also a crime of divulging official secrets with the intent to harm Australia, which can also cover those who knowingly receive or retain illegally divulged secrets.[31] But no Australian officials are implicated as WikiLeaks sources.

Other security offences are also inapplicable. The crimes of treason and treachery involve assisting those fighting Australian forces or a declared enemy of Australia, but only where the person intends their conduct to so assist.[32] The offence of espionage involves providing information concerning Australia's security, but only where the disclosure is unlawful and the person intends to advantage another country's security.[33] None of these three crimes would apply to WikiLeaks, because it did not appear to release security information with the intention of harming Australia's interests, but rather in the (real or perceived) public interest.

Likewise, publishing the leaks does not meet the fault requirements of Australia's anti-terrorism or sedition crimes, or the offence of harming Australians abroad. There is also no basis in Australian law for declaring WikiLeaks a terrorist organisation or an unlawful association. Also irrelevant are offences relating to ASIO operations, or court orders to suppress security information during judicial or administrative proceedings.[34] While Australia must diligently protect the inviolability of foreign diplomatic communications in Australia under international law, 'Cablegate' leaks involving any embassy communications in Australia were not the result of any Australian failures but were sourced from US personnel.[35]

Under Australian law, as in most countries, the protection of security information is primarily achieved by regulating those entrusted with the information. That means vetting and supervising government personnel, imposing dissuasive penalties for breaches, and ensuring adequate physical security of government records (physical or digital). Prohibiting citizens or the media – as opposed to government officials – from publishing leaked information is often thought to interfere too far with freedom of expression and the public's right to know (though that view may be a little naïve in rare cases, as discussed further below).

Legal freedom of information

A number of troubling legal questions remain. First, some of Australia's existing secrecy offences, which ban any disclosures, are far too wide. In a 2010 inquiry, the Australian Law Reform Commission identified 506 secrecy provisions in 176 statutes.[36] A key recommendation was to replace the federal secrecy offences in the *Crimes Act* 1914 (Cth) with a narrower offence, which would only criminalise disclosures that would harm essential public interests, such as (a) security, defence or international relations, (b) law enforcement activities, (c) the life or safety of a person, or (d) public safety. That recommendation, along with others to narrow security laws, has not been implemented.

Second, penalties for unlawful disclosures by those entrusted with secrets must be balanced against adequate protection of whistle-blowers. The public disclosure of classified information may aim to expose illegal, wrongful or improper conduct by governments and others. As is well known, the WikiLeaks revelations have detailed torture by US forces in Iraq, war crimes by US pilots in Afghanistan, and even proposed espionage by the US against the United Nations Secretary-General. Whistle-blowers should normally exhaust complaints channels within government and law enforcement, but public disclosure may be warranted where there has been no internal action or any investigation has been unsatisfactory.

Australia finally adopted a comprehensive federal whistle-blower protection law in 2013, the *Public Interest Disclosure Act 2013* (Cth), which protects disclosures concerning illegality, maladministration, abuse of public trust and dangers to health, safety or the environment. External (that is, public) disclosures must not be contrary to the public interest. Intelligence information, however, can *never* be publicly disclosed, and complaints must be made within government or to the Inspector-General of Intelligence and Security. This limitation raises the prospect that egregious breaches may not necessarily come to public attention, even if internal processes ultimately work to remedy them. Legal but 'immoral' intelligence activities are also not disclosable.

The leaks reveal that some information over which governments claim confidentiality is genuinely in the public interest. The protection of such information can dangerously cloak state illegality and shield official lawlessness. Whistle-blowers should not be hung out in the wind to take their chances. The law should always recognise defences to crimes of unlawful disclosure where the disclosure was for the purpose of exposing illegality or misconduct.

There will inevitably be many hard cases involving whistle-blowers. There is a spectrum of conscience, from the relatively objective suspicion of crime to subjective moral distaste at government activities or policies. The former is more readily justifiable, the latter less so. Manning sits uncomfortably in between. On one hand, he leaked good evidence of war crimes, was motivated by his concern that the US military 'seemed not to value human life', and did not want to put anyone in danger.[37] On the other hand, he leaked thousands of documents that he could not possibly have read, many of which disclose nothing untoward, and some of which may well endanger others. In most cases, it is not for a strong-headed, moralising citizen to substitute her or his policy judgment for that of democratic parliaments, which ideally represent the collective preferences of all citizens. That an individual believes he or she is acting on conscience does not always mean it is the right thing to do: morality varies sharply.

One's own conscience will not necessarily align with what is in the public interest. There are many grey areas. Jury trials may be the best a citizen of conscience can hope for in hard cases. Ultimately conscience may demand action even if criminal liability is certain.

Third, whistle-blower protections are inevitably connected with the need for adequate media shield laws to protect journalists' confidential sources from compulsory disclosure. Indeed, one of WikiLeaks's brilliant innovations is to create an anonymous online method for sources to disclose material without fear of exposure by journalists under legal threats. A new federal law was passed in 2011, but the availability and quality of shield laws varies among Australian jurisdictions.[38] While there may be rare cases where the law may legitimately require journalists to disclose confidential sources – including in evidencing crime or grave security risks – a more uniform and protective national approach is needed.

Fourth, a cultural shift towards greater openness and information transparency is required in government. Specifically, there must be a greater receptiveness to approving freedom of information (FOI) requests and blunting the instinct to over-classify or refuse disclosure, unless absolutely necessary. The presumption must be in favour of release, not secrecy.

Security restrictions on information

On one hand, WikiLeaks's public interest disclosures indicate a need for laws to ensure greater transparency and less secrecy in government. But there is also a vital question whether the law could better protect security in those exceptional cases where it is truly necessary. The idea naturally alarms anarchists or Tea

Party members opposed to government intervention in free speech or the media. Liberals and human rights advocates too are instinctively squeamish – for well-founded historical and contemporary reasons – about calls for stronger security protections, particularly following the excessive measures taken during the Cold War and after 9/11. It is right to respond with healthy skepticism, and even a little paranoia, to calls for censorship.

But discussion of better security protections should not be taboo or automatically opposed. Security and liberty guarantee and make allowances for each another, including through the modern framework of human rights law. It is well accepted that it is legitimate for governments to protect the confidentiality of a range of information, including personal information (from tax to health records), law enforcement details, legally privileged material, information given in confidence, diplomatic communications, and intelligence. Any restrictions must be necessary in pursuit of a legitimate aim, and proportionate, not excessive.

There are a number of gaps in Australian law which may leave vital security interests exposed. In the first place, it may be necessary for Australian law to protect foreign secrets, which can be as important to our own security as they are to the security of a foreign country. Countries cannot ensure their security by acting alone. Australia has cooperative security and intelligence relationships with numerous countries which enable it to exponentially increase its knowledge of security threats and give it a coordinated capability to respond. If Australia cannot assure foreign partners that their intelligence and diplomatic communications are secure, they may dry up. It may thus be necessary for Australia not only to legally control government officials who handle foreign security information, as is already the case, but also to prevent the publication of it by those to whom it is leaked – subject to all of the critical whistle-blower caveats mentioned earlier.

Vitally, intelligence cooperation concerns not only matters of narrow sovereign self-interest, but a world of shared global threats. Australia has a common interest in safeguarding foreign intelligence about North Korean nuclear proliferation, Syrian war crimes, or global terrorism. Certainly it goes too far for US Secretary of State Hillary Clinton to claim that releasing US diplomatic cables was 'an attack on the international community', but her premise was right: diplomacy is a system of 'alliances and partnerships ... conversations and negotiations that safeguard global security and advance economic prosperity'.[39]

Ironically, in addition to disclosing US abuses, the Wiki-Leaks disclosures also demonstrated that the United States is often true to its word in sincerely promoting human rights in its interactions with foreign governments (or in struggling to address global security problems in the face of inaction by others).[40] Those who bravely inform on human rights abuses in North Korea, Zimbabwe, Syria or a myriad of other places are hardly encouraged to do so by the possibility that WikiLeaks may splash their identity all over the Internet.[41] They do not deserve to live in fear because WikiLeaks may choose to operate unprofessionally, with a cavalier indifference to the safety of others, or on the basis of an unsophisticated commitment to absolute freedom of information, regardless of consequences. One effect of WikiLeaks may well be to chill progressive action by liberal governments, without much affecting the closed authoritarian governments whose secrets WikiLeaks has been less successful at exposing, and who are relatively impervious to foreign criticisms.

It rare cases it is appropriate to use Australian law to prevent intelligence sources and methods, or allied diplomatic communications, from being jeopardised. One implication is that even the media sometimes need to be muzzled in exceptional cases. Media organisations typically express self-righteous indignation at the suggestion, urging governments to trust the Fourth Estate to do the right thing or (unsurprisingly) invoking self-regulation as sufficient. Most of the time there is much to be said for a maximal conception of free speech and a minimal conception of government interference. Much of the time the media does the right thing, such as by not publishing details of sensitive security operations.

But we know that the media can be as untrustworthy as governments and do not always do the right thing: witness Rupert Murdoch's *News of the World* phone hacking scandal, or overreach by WikiLeaks in inadequately filtering sensitive information before publishing it. The media can abuse human rights as well as safeguard them. The media are also not as expert in security matters as governments, and may not understand the security implications of publishing material. The *Washington Post*'s report in 1998 that the United States was monitoring bin Laden's satellite phone led bin Laden to stop using it.[42] Governments also enjoy a particular kind of democratic legitimation which most media does not.

When doing the wrong thing brings risks to security or human rights, the law must have a role to play. Past efforts to do so are discredited because they went too far. Australia's 'D-Notice' system, begun in 1952, fell into practical disuse by the 1970s.[43] (A D-Notice is a request issued to the media and is a self-censorship system. It directs editors to refrain from publishing certain information about sensitive matters related to national security). At the same time, its equivalent voluntary procedure in Britain, the Defence Advisory (DA) Notice, is still used and respected by the media there.[44] Various Australian governments, from Keating to Gillard, have unsuccessfully attempted to revive some version of it. The Australian media most recently opposed a 2010 proposal for reactivating voluntary, cooperative arrangements between it and the government on security reporting.[45] Governments should be entitled to block the publication of the names of intelligence officers or informants who are not breaking the law; the details of intelligence operations the disclosure of which would endanger lives or destroy vital intelligence capabilities in relation to national or global security threats; or sensitive information that is vital in combating human rights violations or negotiating the settlement of conflicts. The defence and perpetuation of freedom and democracy sometimes calls for hardness too – not the iron-fisted toughness favoured by authoritarian rulers or benevolent 'guided' democracies, but one based on a dialogic social agreement (relating to diverse communicative interactions and intellectual openness) that security justifies hard choices in our name.

For this to happen, governments must first rebuild the trust of their peoples. The WikiLeaks disclosures demonstrate that governments routinely overclassify information which should be public, not secret. WikiLeaks is rightly applauded for its tonic or corrective effect. No citizen can trust a government with greater powers to protect security if they are unable to demonstrate that they can responsibly exercise the powers they already have.

Security powers must also be accompanied by stronger safeguards to prevent abuse from occurring and to expose it if it does occur. Independent judicial scrutiny has a vital role to play. Governments alone should never be legally entitled to summarily block the media from publishing domestic or foreign secrets.

Rather, a government should be required to apply to the courts for an order to block publication. In that process, the courts must also be able to weigh security interests against other competing public interests, including the public's right to know as much as is safely possible.

Technical and practical challenges will remain. The law has difficulty dealing with instantaneous global media communications. It takes a second for a person's name to slip off the tongue of a television or radio reporter, or for an Internet or social media post to whizz around the world. Judicial proceedings are slow and jurisdictionally limited: it will often be impossible for the courts of one country to block dangerous security disclosures in another. Media in one country will also not necessarily have the best interests of another country at heart, and their governments may encourage them in this. These are monumental challenges for security and global public safety in the face of collective threats. But they do not warrant abandoning efforts to encourage media responsibility and legal regulation where it is feasible.

Did WikiLeaks endanger lives?

One of the most prominent accusations against WikiLeaks is that it endangered lives by disclosing the names of US informants, including intelligence sources as well as human rights defenders and others.[46] It was reported that the Taliban was soon scouring WikiLeaks to identify targets in Afghanistan.[47] WikiLeaks documents were allegedly found in bin Laden's house in Pakistan.[48] The 'war logs' which disclosed military operational matters were also said to threaten the lives of US personnel. A list of worldwide US critical infrastructure and resources was published, including civilian sites in Australia.[49] Even an Australian ASIO officer was apparently exposed by WikiLeaks's failure to secure its own files.[50]

WikiLeaks responded to the criticisms by variously denying it endangered anyone; claiming to have redacted names; and regretting any harm that occurred.[51] But Assange also declared that informants who were killed deserved it, and consequentially reasoned that the necessity of publishing the information outweighed harm to individuals.[52] As Isaiah Berlin scathingly wrote of revolutionaries, eggs must be broken to make an omelette; an ideologically just end justifies less than savoury means.[53] WikiLeaks supporters further deflected the criticism by claiming that America's killing of civilians was worse; that it was America's fault for not securing its records; or that no-one died.[54] Actually, it is not to the point whether anyone died or not; it was enough that large numbers of people were forced to live in terror of what might happen, and hope that the US or others could reach them before the death squads.

The criticism hurt WikiLeaks because it undermines its undoubtedly sincere human rights aspirations: the goal of freedom of information can hardly justify negligently exposing innocent civilians to real risks of death. It was not only governments but respected human rights organisations and professional media bodies that were critical of WikiLeaks, and they could not be so easily dismissed as part of a global conspiracy of governments.

Thus the Afghan Independent Human Rights Commission stated that '[t]here was no consideration about civilian lives'.[55] Amnesty International, the Open Society Institute, the International Crisis Group, and the Campaign for Innocent Victims in Conflict urged WikiLeaks to redact the names of Afghan civilians, or Afghans working with foreign forces which, incidentally, were authorised by the United Nations Security Council to restore peace and stability in Afghanistan.[56]

The freedom of expression organisation Article 19 also criticised WikiLeaks for flouting the 'do no harm' principle.[57] Reporters without Borders called WikiLeaks's disclosure of names 'highly dangerous' and noted that it may provoke governments to tighten Internet surveillance.[58] It also attacked WikiLeaks's journalism as methodologically indiscriminate and irresponsible, for exposing people to reprisals, and for imprudently threatening the future of the Internet as an information medium.

The indiscriminate or 'incoherent' dump of thousands of documents is hard to justify unless one takes the extremist view that governments must have no secrets.[59] The correlative of media freedom is the responsibility not to abuse it to do harm. It seems that WikiLeaks has taken on board some of these criticisms by developing a 'harm minimisation procedure' to protect 'life and limb'.[60] It remains to be seen whether this will provide effective protection.

Political asylum for Assange?

In August 2012 Ecuador granted 'political asylum' to Assange, who had sought refuge in Ecuador's London Embassy in June 2012. Ecuador's Foreign Minister provided a detailed international legal justification for the decision, claiming that asylum is a 'fundamental human right' owed by all countries.[61] Ecuador believed that Assange was entitled to protection from 'political persecution' because there were 'serious indications' that his 'safety, integrity and even his life' were at risk of 'retaliation' from countries whose information WikiLeaks had disclosed.

In particular, Ecuador believed that Assange was at risk of extradition to the United States, where he would not receive a fair trial, may face a special or military court, be treated cruelly or degradingly, and be condemned to a life sentence or the death penalty. Ecuador further felt that the legal systems of Britain and Sweden would not protect Assange from extradition; that the governments concerned had refused to give Ecuador assurances of his protection; and that Assange's country of nationality, Australia, had not given him 'adequate protection'. Ecuador also stated that the Swedish criminal investigation had not respected his rights.

After granting asylum, Ecuador called on Britain to respect it and grant safe passage to Assange to leave Britain.[62] Ecuador had earlier accused the UK government of threatening to enter its embassy to arrest Assange, which would have breached the absolute inviolability of embassy premises under international law.[63] The only means by which Britain could lawfully enter the embassy are by the consent of Ecuador, or otherwise by drastically terminating its diplomatic status and rupturing diplomatic relations with Ecuador.

The prevailing international legal consensus is that Assange has no legal right to asylum, Ecuador had no power to confer it, and Britain had no duty to respect it.[64] This conclusion actually has little to do with any assessment of whatever dangers Assange may or may not face. Rather, it has everything to do with there being no general right to asylum in embassies under international law, a point confirmed by the International Court of Justice in the Asylum case between Colombia and Peru in 1950.[65] Since a right to asylum in embassies does not exist under international law, Britain has no requirement to respect it when

Ecuador purports to grant it in Britain. Britain is also entitled to refuse Assange safe passage out of Britain and to arrest him once he leaves the embassy, in order to enforce Assange's outstanding European arrest warrant for arrest and questioning in Sweden.

In fact, by granting asylum, Ecuador was unlawfully interfering in Britain's internal affairs and arguably breaching its obligation under the Vienna Convention on Diplomatic Relations not to use the embassy 'in any manner incompatible with the functions of the mission'.[66] Further, by impeding a lawful British arrest of a person in breach of his bail conditions, its diplomats may have breached their obligation to respect the host state's laws.

For practical purposes, in most of the world the older notion of political 'asylum' has given way to the more contemporary international legal concept of 'refugee' status, arising under the 1951 Refugee Convention and 1967 Protocol. That is the context in which the so-called 'right to asylum' mentioned in the (non-binding) Universal Declaration of Human Rights of 1948 is now understood. Assange has not claimed refugee status, as he could have done under British law. He would almost certainly have been refused it because, as an Australian citizen, he has a right to return to live safely in Australia.

Even assuming that there did exist an international right to asylum, it is very unlikely that Assange would be entitled to it on the facts of his case. Asylum aims to give urgent temporary protection to a person under imminent threat of political persecution or violent harm by the host country. This necessarily involves making imprecise probability judgments about what might happen to a person, all the harder in the security field, where the United States may disguise its legal intentions for tactical reasons. Unlike refugee status, the older doctrine of asylum is a less legalistic and more discretionary political grant of protection.

Nonetheless, on balance a range of factors would likely weigh against a legitimate grant of asylum to Assange. The threshold for diplomatic asylum is very high, for example an immediate threat to life, or risk of injury. Yet there is no serious imminent threat to Assange's life or safety from the British authorities. Assange resided safely in Britain for some time. Britain has not laid any 'political' charges against him, and has not threatened to deport him to any country where he faces a risk of persecution or torture, or a risk of political prosecution (including the United States).

Second, there is no imminent prospect of Assange being returned to the United States to face charges carrying the death penalty, whether from Britain, Sweden or Australia. The United States has not laid criminal charges, or sought his extradition, though the outcome of the rumoured secret grand jury investigation is unknown. In fact, the United States could perhaps more easily seek Assange's extradition from the United Kingdom, rather than waiting for his return to Sweden, but has not done so, raising doubts about whether it has identified any secure legal basis on which to proceed against him. Assange's claim instead seems based on the idea that asylum is his 'last opportunity' to avoid extradition to the United States, because return to Sweden would inevitably lead to that result.

But, third, even if the United States did seek Assange's extradition from Sweden or Britain, he would still be entitled to the full protections of domestic and European criminal and human rights law. In fact, extradition would be highly unlikely. For many centuries, democracies have refused extradition for 'political' offences, which are crimes against the political system of another country and, relevantly, include espionage. Such protection is found in the extradition agreement between the European Union and the United States.[67] It is also found in Australia's extradition arrangements with the United States.[68] (Although since 2012 there is a sneaky new power to define new offences as non-political, and thus extraditable, by mere regulation.)[69]

Extradition is refused on the basis that one country should not interfere in the political affairs of another, for instance by helping a government to prosecute political enemies. The law thus recognises that it is not normally the job of Sweden or Britain or Australia to suppress those who leak or publish US secrets. The only exceptions are for violence against government officials or terrorism, which are extraditable, but neither is alleged against Assange. Other protections in extradition law would also apply. The double criminality rule requires that the conduct be an offence in both countries, thus raising a further hurdle for the United States. The specialty rule requires that a person can only be extradited for the offence for which they are requested. Thus Sweden, which has requested Assange only concerning sexual allegations, may be barred from extraditing him to the United States to face other charges (unless the United Kingdom consents).

Swedish and British human rights law, backed up by the binding protection of the European Court of Human Rights, would also not permit Assange to be extradited to the United States to face the death penalty, or if he would face inhumane or degrading treatment or an unfair trial – precisely some of the problems tainting Bradley Manning's trial. Admittedly, the law does not always operate perfectly. After 9/11, Sweden returned a suspected terrorist to Egypt after the Egyptian government promised not to torture him. Egyptian security forces promptly inflicted electric shocks on him. The United Nations found that Sweden violated international law by returning him to torture. While there is always a risk of the law going wrong, the legal systems of Sweden and Britain nonetheless work reasonably well most of the time – Stieg Larsson-style conspiracies notwithstanding. There is really negligible chance of Assange going to the electric chair in the United States.

Fourth, asylum is not available simply to shield a fugitive from facing justice for common crimes according to a fair procedure, in this case the alleged sex crimes in Sweden. Assange had every opportunity – and all the high-powered lawyers necessary – to challenge any procedural or human rights defects in the proceedings against him before the British, Swedish and European regional courts. He was unsuccessful in the challenge he took to the UK Supreme Court, and has not commenced any other proceedings, presumably because his legal advice is that they would be unsuccessful – hence his last resort to asylum.[70]

'Ultra-feminism' in Sweden?

Alleged irregularities or other unfairness in the Swedish proceedings against Assange were part of Ecuador's justification for granting asylum. Swedish prosecutors issued a European arrest warrant on 26 November 2010, requesting that Assange be surrendered in respect of four allegations (but not yet any charges): 'unlawful coercion', two counts of 'sexual molestation', and 'rape'. While Assange must be presumed innocent, the factual allegations are serious: that Assange had sex with a helplessly sleeping woman; that he had sex with another without a condom, against her express wishes; that he violently held down a woman's arms and forcibly spread her legs to have sex; and that he pressed his erect penis against a woman's body without her consent.

Much has been said about the seemingly unusual nature of some of these allegations. Some rusted-on supporters of WikiLeaks have savagely disparaged the Swedish offences as a sign of an 'ultra-feminism' that has 'colonised' Swedish politics[71] – where unprotected sex or even a (presumably blameless) 'morning glory' counts as rape.[72] Such attacks have been coupled with vicious character assassination of the two women who complained. For some, Assange is above reproach and beyond the law: it is always someone else's fault. Again, eggs must be broken. That totalising logic leads fanatics into excusing wrongs done in the name of a good cause; alleged victims of sexual assault are acceptable 'collateral' damage in a larger war.

The campaign to discredit the criminal case against Assange is shocking for its extreme trivialisation of sexual harms and its disregard of women's rights, and for its ignorance about the law. The English courts explicitly accepted that the rape alleged under Swedish law would be rape under English law. And even if Swedish law were more protective of women than that in other countries, one might think that this would be a cause for celebration, not denigration – and an opportunity for the rest of us to get our own sex crime laws in order. If a person's consent to sex is conditional – as where a woman requires a condom to be worn – a refusal to respect that condition vitiates the very basis of her consent. It is, indeed, a fundamental attack on the bodily integrity and personal autonomy of the victim. This is all the more so where the consequences of not wearing a condom may be profoundly harmful – from sexually transmitted diseases (including HIV/AIDS, and thus even death in an extreme case) to unwanted pregnancy and its emotionally difficult consequences (including the contemplation of an abortion, adoption, or becoming a single mother).

In other respects, it may be true that there have been some procedural irregularities in the Swedish prosecutors' case. But there is nothing so gravely irregular as to warrant the dropping of a legitimate criminal investigation and the premature termination of any prospect of justice for the alleged victims. Any irregularities which taint the prospects of a fair trial for Assange should be properly challenged in the courts – Swedish and European human rights – at the point at which any charges are actually laid and a trial commences.

Sweden is acting within its legal rights to compel Assange to return to Sweden to be arrested, questioned, and possibly charged. Even so, much of the present crisis and diplomatic difficulty could have been avoided if various authorities had taken a more pragmatic approach. Sweden could have agreed to question Assange in Britain, or assured Assange that he would not be extradited to the United States on 'political' charges (though the latter promise may be difficult where no US charges have been laid). Britain, in turn, could have promised Ecuador that it would only extradite Assange if Sweden agreed not to send him to the United States, though it is legally doubtful whether the Swedish government could (or should) interfere in the independence of its own courts by prospectively immunising Assange from any future US extradition request.

If Ecuador granted asylum where Assange has no reasonable fear of imminent political persecution, it is an abuse of the rare and precious institution of asylum, which in turn tends to undermine the commitment of governments to protect genuine refugees. Vast numbers of people worldwide face far more serious, imminent risks of harm, yet enjoy nothing like the level of legal protection, celebrity backers, financial guarantors and embassies of refuge that Assange has mobilised. There is also some irony in Assange seeking refuge from Ecuador when that country aggressively suppresses media freedom and targets journalists.

Australia has a limited ability to protect Assange

Assange also claims that the Australian government issued an 'effective declaration of abandonment' by refusing to protect him or make requests on his behalf.[73] That claim is hard to reconcile with the Australian Foreign Minister's statement that Australia had intervened 62 times for Assange between his arrest in December 2010 and August 2012 – more than for any other Australian during the same period.[74]

The support provided has included visits by consular officials, the facilitation of family visits, and contact by consular officials with his lawyers.[75] Attorney General Nicola Roxon also informed Assange's lawyers that Australia had conveyed its expectation to Britain, Sweden and the United States that Assange should receive due process, and received a number of formal assurances from Sweden that due process and procedural fairness will be followed.[76] Assange's denial that he has been assisted by Australia is disingenuous. What he may really mean is that Australia had not acceded to the specific demands he has made of it, including that Australia seek an undertaking that the United States will not prosecute Assange and that the FBI will not target WikiLeaks, and that the United Kingdom undertake not to extradite Assange to the United States.

Australia has the international legal right to make diplomatic protests or inquiries to Britain, Sweden or the United States, but there is no legal duty to do so and Australian citizens have no enforceable legal right to demand it to act. International law leaves it to governments to decide whether they go in to bat for their citizens, and how strongly, and this necessarily brings into play a government's other concerns – for better and often for worse – in maintaining good international relations with other governments.

Politically, many Australians clearly expect their government to do more than it has done for Assange, though there would also appear to be a considerable lack of awareness about precisely what Australia has done already, and what are the limits of its diplomatic rights and capabilities. There is certainly a wide zone of discretion open to the government to take further steps. To give one small example, Australia should have strenuously condemned calls for Assange's assassination. It might have even (cheekily) urged Swedish prosecutors to consider being a little more flexible by agreeing to question Assange in the United Kingdom – though they were within their legal rights to insist he be returned to Sweden.

But there is also a limit to what Australia can do.[77] It cannot interfere in fair foreign court proceedings, including in Europe, where legal safeguards are (comparatively) among the world's best – including in the UK Supreme Court and with the backstop of the European Court of Human Rights. To put it more starkly, Australians would be outraged if, for instance, the Chinese government asked the Australian government to interfere in and override the process or decisions of a (fair) Australian court. So far Assange's case is nothing like the gross miscarriages of foreign justice affecting other Australians in recent years, such as David Hicks's unfair military trial at Guantanamo Bay. (His treatment is certainly better than anything most media organisations can expect under Ecuador's law.)

Australia can hardly ask the United States to politically direct its FBI to cease investigating an organisation suspected of unlawful activities, or to promise not to prosecute WikiLeaks even before independent law enforcement authorities have decided whether to lay charges. Nor should Australia step into the shoes of Assange's lawyers by arguing for his bail conditions in Sweden. Australia should especially do nothing which would thwart justice for the alleged victims of sex crimes by Assange, who have been viciously denigrated by some of Assange's more fanatical supporters. Concern for human rights only extends so far in WikiWorld.

The curious case of Julian Assange

The rhetorical claims and counterclaims surrounding WikiLeaks have generated a deeply confusing and polarised picture, and there are elements of truth on all sides. WikiLeaks must be applauded for putting a much-needed, long-overdue rocket under excessive claims of government secrecy and the galaxy of dangerous abuses and crimes that those claims have concealed. Governments must be condemned for trying to silence or criminalise it – and for failing to become more open and thus to re-establish the trust of their peoples. Contemporary journalism, and government accountability, would be weaker without WikiLeaks. At the same time, some of the WikiLeaks disclosures reveal that there are legitimate reasons why governments and the law should strongly protect security information in exceptional cases.

Equally, WikiLeaks has gone too far in pursuing its intellectually half-baked, quasi-anarchic vision of near-absolute freedom of information, shorn of principled and thoughtful restraint or adequate concern for others. WikiLeaks has engendered an alarming, absolutist belief by some that eggs must be broken; the information utopia justifies any means. Fanaticism is an affliction of the left as much as the right. In the process, WikiLeaks – behind the safety of its computer screens – has not only endangered the lives of those on the frontline fighting human rights violators or terrorists, but has jeopardised global cooperation against shared security threats and hard human rights problems. It has also paradoxically pushed governments to be more secretive and less open – though that can hardly be blamed on WikiLeaks.

The curious character of Julian Assange has played a lead role in all of this, at once courageous, technically innovative, motivated by sincere and noble goals, and hounded by irritated governments. But Assange is hardly the martyr that his more fanatical supporters lionise. For Assange has also led WikiLeaks into overreach and error. He continues to evade justice for alleged sex crimes, and he allows his supporters to systematically denigrate efforts to protect women's rights. While his situation is precarious, he is not entitled to asylum, and he has unreasonable expectations of what Australia can and should do for him.

1   'Julian Assange urges US to end WikiLeaks "witch-hunt"', *BBC News*, 19 August 2012.

2   For example, the *Reducing Over-Classification Act* 2010 (US).

3   See S. Chesterman (2011) *One Nation Under Surveillance: A New Social Contract to Defend Freedom without Sacrificing Liberty*, Oxford University Press, Oxford.

4   L. King, 'Sarah Palin says: target WikiLeaks' Julian Assange like the Taliban', *ComputerWorld UK*, 1 December 2010.

5   S. Chesterman, 'WikiLeaks, secrets, and lies', *Project Syndicate*, 2 December 2010; J. McCarthy (2011) 'WikiLeaks

[SEC=UNCLASSIFIED]', *The Asia Link Essays 2011*, vol. 3, no. 1.

6   E. Farrelly, 'Ambassador's rage doesn't dispel facts', *Sydney Morning Herald*, 29 November 2012.

7   G. Robertson at 'The Media World after WikiLeaks and the *News of the World*', UNESCO Conference, Paris, 16–17 February 2012.

8   'Julian Assange urges US to end WikiLeaks 'witch-hunt''.

9   H. Brooke, 'The WikiFreak: in a new book one author reveals how she got to know Julian Assange and found him a predatory, narcissistic fantasist', *Daily Mail* (UK), 7 August 2011.

10 With 40 per cent of Australians viewing Assange favourably, 30 per cent negatively, and 30 per cent unsure in a UMR Research poll of 1000 people in July 2011: see P. Coorey, 'Most Australians back Assange, poll finds', *Sydney Morning Herald*, 9 August 2012.

11 <WikiLeaks.org/About.html> (last accessed 17 July 2013).

12 <WikiLeaks.org/About.html> (last accessed 17 July 2013).

13 <WikiLeaks.org/About.html> (last accessed 17 July 2013).

14 <www.collateralmurder.com/> (last accessed 17 July 2013).

15 'Australian Federal Police to investigate WikiLeaks "Cablegate"', *Herald Sun*, 29 November 2010; P. Dorling, 'US condemns Rudd', *Sydney Morning Herald*, 8 December 2010.

16 US Vice-President Joe Biden, quoted in Ewen MacAskill, 'Julian Assange like a hi-tech terrorist, says Joe Biden', *Guardian*, 20 December 2010.

17 H. Kennedy, 'WikiLeaks should be designated a "foreign terrorist organization", Rep. Pete King fumes', *New York Daily News*, 28 November 2010.

18 C. Savage, 'U.S. tries to build case for conspiracy by WikiLeaks', *New York Times*, 15 December 2010.

19 G. Greenwald, 'FBI serves grand jury subpoena likely relating to WikiLeaks', *Salon*, 28 April 2011.

20 Uniform Code of Military Justice, Articles 92 and 134; US Code Title 18, Sections 793, 1030(a)(1) and 1030(a)(2); see US Division Headquarters, Camp Liberty Iraq, 'Soldier faces criminal charges', press release, 6 July 2010, last accessed 17 July 2013 <www.cbsnews.com/htdocs/pdf/ManningPreferralofCharges.pdf?tag=contentMain;contentBody>.

21 'Bradley Manning leaked documents to WikiLeaks after finding himself at odds with US army', *The Australian*, 1 March 2013.

22 AFP, 'US must prove Manning helped Al-Qaeda', *Sydney Morning Herald*, 11 April 2013.

23 Juan E. Méndez (2012) *Report of the UN Special Rapporteur on Torture*

and Other Cruel, Inhuman or Degrading Treatment or Punishment,
'Addendum: Observations on Communications Transmitted to
Governments and Replies Received', 29 February, A/HRC/19/61/
Add.4, pp. 74–75; B. Ackerman and Y. Benkler, 'Bradley Manning's
humiliation', *New York Review of Books*, 28 April 2011.

24 *Espionage Act* 1917, 18 United States Code 793.

25 *New York Times Co. v United States* (1971) 403 US 713.

26 E. MacAskill, 'US targets groups with ties to website', *Sydney
Morning Herald*, 9 December 2010.

27 'WikiLeaks acting illegally, says Gillard', *Sydney Morning Herald*,
2 December 2010.

28 'Australian Federal Police to investigate WikiLeaks "Cablegate"'.

29 D. Welch, 'Julian Assange has committed no crime in Australia:
AFP', *Sydney Morning Herald*, 17 December 2010.

30 *Attorney-General (UK) v Heinemann Publishers Australia* (1988) 165
CLR 30.

31 *Crimes Act* 1914 (Cth), s. 79.

32 Commonwealth Criminal Code, s. 80.1AA (treason) and *Crimes Act*
1914 (Cth), s. 24AA (treachery).

33 Commonwealth Criminal Code, s. 91.1.

34 For example, under statutes providing for suppression or non-
publication orders; under the common law doctrine of public
interest immunity; or under the *National Security Information (Civil
and Criminal Proceedings) Act* 2004 (Cth).

35 Vienna Convention on Diplomatic Relations 1961 (adopted
18 April 1961, entered into force 24 April 1964, 500 UN Treaty
Series 95), Articles 24 (archives and documents of a mission) and
27 (correspondence and diplomatic bag); see also B. Saul, 'War
on WikiLeaks reveals need for law reform', *The Drum*, ABC, 7
December 2010.

36 Australian Law Reform Commission (2010) *Secrecy Laws and Open
Government in Australia*, Report 112.

37 Bradley Manning, quoted in 'Bradley Manning leaked documents to
WikiLeaks after finding himself at odds with US army'.

38 *Evidence Amendment (Journalists' Privilege) Act* 2010 (Cth).

39 E. MacAskill, 'Hillary Clinton attacks release of US embassy cables',
Guardian, 29 November 2010, last accessed 17 July 2013 <www.
guardian.co.uk/world/2010/nov/29/clinton-reacts-us-embassy-
cables>.

40 R. Girard (*Le Figaro* reporter), quoted in Steven Erlanger,
'Europeans criticise fierce US response to leaks', *New York Times*,

9 December 2010; Robertson at 'The Media World after WikiLeaks and the *News of the World*', UNESCO Conference.

41   Robertson at 'The Media World after WikiLeaks and the *News of the World*', UNESCO Conference.

42   Chesterman, 'WikiLeaks, Secrets, and Lies'.

43   National Archives of Australia, 'D Notices – fact sheet 49', last accessed 17 July 2013 <www.naa.gov.au/collection/fact-sheets/fs49.aspx>.

44   See N. Grimley, 'D for discretion: can the modern media keep a secret?', *BBC News*, 22 August 2011.

45   C. Stewart, 'Attorney-General Robert McClelland urges media to accept security curbs', *The Australian*, 26 November 2010.

46   'U.S. says WikiLeaks release would endanger lives', *Reuters*, 28 November 2010.

47   'Taliban hunt WikiLeaks-outed Afghan informers', *Channel 4 TV News* (UK), 30 July 2010.

48   AFP, 'US must prove Manning helped Al-Qaeda', *Sydney Morning Herald*, 11 April 2013.

49   D. Welch, 'Leaks offer targets for terrorist attacks', *Sydney Morning Herald*, 7 December 2010.

50   D. Welch and B. Grubb, 'ASIO spy named in global breach of WikiLeaks cables', *Sydney Morning Herald*, 2 September 2011.

51   J. Assange, quoted in David Leigh and Luke Harding (2011) *WikiLeaks: Inside Julian Assange's War on Secrecy*, Guardian Books, London.

52   Julian Assange, quoted in 'Publication of Afghan informant details worth the risk: WikiLeaks founder Julian Assange', *The Australian*, 29 July 2010.

53   I. Berlin (1999) *The First and the Last*, Granta, London, p. 57.

54   Bradley Manning Support Group, 'Did WikiLeaks endanger lives?', last accessed 17 July 2013 <www.bradleymanning.org/commentary/did-WikiLeaks-endanger-lives>.

55   'Human rights groups ask WikiLeaks to censor files', *CTV News*, 10 August 2012.

56   'Human rights groups ask WikiLeaks to censor files'.

57   A. Callamard (Article 19) at 'The Media World after WikiLeaks and the *News of the World*', UNESCO Conference.

58   Reporters without Borders Secretary-General Jean-François Julliard, 'Open letter to WikiLeaks founder Julian Assange: "A bad precedent for the Internet's future"', 12 August 2010.

59   M. Fullilove, 'WikiLeaks: fruit of an unhealthy tree', *The Drum*,

ABC, 16 December 2010.

60 WikiLeaks, 'About WikiLeaks', last accessed 17 July 2013 <WikiLeaks.org/About.html>.

61 Ecuador Ministry of Foreign Affairs, 'Statement of the government of the Republic of Ecuador on the asylum request of Julian Assange', news release no. 42, 16 August 2012, last accessed 23 July 2013 <www.ecuadorembassyuk.org.uk/news/text-of-statement-of-ricardo-patino-foreign-minister-of-ecuador-on-julian-assange%C2%B4s-asylum-application>.

62 'Julian Assange: UK "threat" to arrest WikiLeaks founder', *BBC News*, 16 August 2012. The threat was made pursuant to the *Consular Premises Act* 1987 (UK), s. 1(3) (concerning withdrawal of recognition of diplomatic status of premises).

63 Vienna Convention on Diplomatic Relations 1961, Article 22.

64 M. Happold (2012) 'Julian Assange and Diplomatic Asylum', *European Journal of International Law: Talk!*, June; K. Ambos (2012) 'Diplomatic Asylum for Julian Assange?', *European Journal of International Law: Talk!*, September; A. Duxbury (2013) 'Assange and the Law of Diplomatic Asylum', *American Society of International Law Insights*, vol. 16, no. 32, October.

65 *Asylum Case (Colombia v Peru)* (1950) *International Court of Justice Reports* 395

66 Vienna Convention on Diplomatic Relations 1961, Article 41(3).

67 EU–US Extradition Agreement 2003.

68 Article VII of the bilateral extradition treaty between Australia and the United States requires that extradition 'shall not be granted' where an offence is of a 'political character': Treaty on Extradition between Australia and the United States of America (adopted 14 May 1974, entered into force 8 May 1976, Australian Treaty Series No. 10).

69 *Extradition and Mutual Assistance in Criminal Matters Legislation Amendment Act* 2012 (Cth); see Adam Fletcher, 'Extradition and mutual assistance changes slip in under the radar', Castan Centre for Human Rights Law Blog, 7 March 2012, last accessed 23 July 2013 <castancentre.com/2012/03/07/extradition-and-mutual-assistance-changes-slip-in-under-the-radar/>.

70 In *Assange v Swedish Prosecution Authority* [2011] UKSC 22, on appeal from [2012] EWCH Admin 2849, the UK Supreme Court upheld an earlier court decision dismissing Assange's argument that his European Arrest Warrant was invalid because the Swedish prosecutor who issued it was not a 'judicial authority' (as required

by European Union and domestic law).

71 Farrelly, 'Ambassador's rage doesn't dispel facts'.

72 G. Rundle, 'Did he or didn't he? The murky politics of sex and consent', *Sydney Morning Herald*, 12 December 2010.

73 WikiLeaks, 'Effective declaration of abandonment from Australian government', 19 June 2012, last accessed 17 July 2013 <wikileaks. org/Effective-Declaration-of.html>.

74 'Australia has intervened on behalf of Julian Assange more than 60 times, Bob Carr reveals', *Herald Sun*, 21 August 2012.

75 'Fed Govt defends its consular assistance to Assange', *Lateline*, ABC TV, 31 May 2012, last accessed 17 July 2013 <www.abc.net.au/pm/ content/2012/s3515562.htm>.

76 Attorney General Nicola Roxon, letter to Jennifer Robinson, 11/28972.

77 WikiLeaks, 'Effective Declaration of Abandonment from Australian Government'.

9

SECURITY WITHOUT SECRECY? COUNTER-TERRORISM, ASIO AND ACCESS TO INFORMATION

Mark Rix

> The Foreign Office declined to disclose
> the reasons for deciding that specific files
> should be withheld, with the result that
> the reason for the continuing secrecy is
> itself … a secret.[1]

'With more and more secrecy, there is greater security.'

BOTH MISGUIDED AND NAIVE. The idea that providing ASIO, Australia's domestic intelligence (in other words, spy) agency, with greater powers to prevent disclosure about it and its activities makes Australia and Australians more secure from the threat of terrorism has been repeatedly endorsed by successive governments since the attacks on the World Trade Center and Pentagon in 2001. They have been much more reluctant to explain how secrecy actually adds to security. It's hard to dispute the assertion that some level of secrecy is required by ASIO to enable it to deal effectively with the terrorist threat. It is far more difficult to accept that complete secrecy, and no accountability, equates to water-tight security. Before considering these issues in greater depth, a couple of brief case studies will set the scene.

A couple of preliminary case studies

Intelligence agencies', police forces', public officials', governments' justification for keeping secret the reasons for not disclosing what they regard as secrets captures the central conundrum of this chapter. The reasoning is really quite simple: there can be no security without secrecy. Seldom is evidence adduced to support this line of reasoning because, if the reasoning is accepted as justified, doing so would breach and weaken security. A relevant case, now some years old, illustrates the point that is being made here. The second, more recent case perhaps makes the same point even more resoundingly.

Izhar Ul-Haque, then a Sydney medical student, was charged with training with the Pakistan-based terrorist group Lashkar-e-Taiba in 2003, well before it had been classified as a terrorist organisation by the United Nations. On 5 November 2007 in the NSW Supreme Court, Justice Michael Adams found that all records of interview with Mr Ul-Haque tendered by the Australian Federal Police as evidence were inadmissible, forcing the NSW Director of Public Prosecutions to withdraw the case just before a jury was empanelled.[2] The AFP had also tried to elicit information from Mr Ul-Haque about the terror suspect Faheem Lodhi by questioning him in a maximum security gaol for more than two hours but without first cautioning him or informing his lawyer of the interrogation.[3] Two AFP officers had demanded that Mr Ul-Haque turn informant against Lodhi, who was subsequently convicted and gaoled for twenty years for conspiring to bomb the national electricity grid.[4] When he refused to do so, Mr Ul-Haque was threatened that there would be serious and adverse consequences for him.

While Mr Ul-Haque had briefly trained with Lashkar-e-Taiba in early 2003, the law enforcement authorities had admitted to him that they accepted that his connection to the organisation had nothing to do with Australia, but instead was because of his opposition to the Indian presence in Kashmir. The AFP records of interview were found to be inadmissible because of the improper and oppressive conduct of the AFP (and ASIO) officers involved, and because of the inextricable links between AFP and ASIO, including the disclosure by the AFP to ASIO of what Mr Ul-Haque had said in interview. Justice Adams also found that two ASIO officers (whose identities remain secret) had committed the criminal offences of kidnapping and false imprisonment at common law and another offence under the *Crimes Act*. He also found that the conduct of the ASIO officers amounted to a gross breach of the powers they had been granted under the search warrant which had been issued to them.

Ian Carnell, then Inspector-General of Intelligence and Security, found in his subsequent report of ASIO's actions in the case, contrary to Justice Adams's conclusion, there were insufficient grounds for referring the matter for prosecution. He also concluded that there was insufficient evidence to support compensation to Mr Ul-Haque for false imprisonment.[5]

The recent Ben Zygier, or 'Prisoner X', case in which ASIO was somehow involved, is in its own way even more perplexing than Izhar Ul-Haque's. Trying to figure out exactly what went on is like trying to find your way in the dark in unfamiliar territory without a torch – such is the secrecy surrounding the case that is being maintained by both Israel and Australia. Mr Zygier, a dual Australian–Israeli citizen, was found dead in December 2010 in his 'suicide-proof' prison cell in Israel's maximum-security Ayalon prison. He is believed to have hanged himself with a bed sheet. Evidently, he had been detained by the Israelis for serious breaches of that country's security laws. These breaches allegedly involved passing information to ASIO about Mossad's practice of using Australian passports to enable its agents to spy in countries that are hostile to Israel. The Israeli Prime Minister, Benjamin Netanyahu, has denied that Zygier passed on information to any Australian security agency, specifically ASIO. Australian Attorney-General Mark Dreyfus backed up this claim. Much more seriously for Zygier, he unintentionally sabotaged a highly sensitive and secretive Mossad operation to repatriate the remains of Israeli soldiers killed in the 1982 war in Lebanon. For this, he was evidently charged with treason.[6]

National insecurity

After the 11 September 2001 terrorist attacks in the United States, Australia became a particularly active combatant in the 'war on terror', especially in the field of legislation, with what Professor George Williams referred to on the 10th anniversary of '9/11' as 'an extraordinary burst of law-making'.[7] Its legislative performance has eclipsed the relatively paltry efforts of Great Britain, the United States and Canada, not only in purely quantitative terms but also in the extent to which these efforts have gone in inhibiting the liberties and rights of every Australian. Misuse and abuse of information, inscrutable but far-reaching information classification procedures and downright obfuscation all have become key weapons in the counter-terrorism arsenal of democratically elected governments like Australia's. Indeed, it seems at times to be a war on openness and accountability rather than terror, such are the curbs on transparency and public disclosure that have been introduced since 11 September 2001. Australia has led the field in this particular campaign.

This chapter is primarily concerned with investigating the Australian Security Intelligence Organisation's role in the protection of Australia's national security in what was known around the world officially and unofficially as the global 'war on terror' (at least until 2009, when the phrase was abandoned by the Obama Administration – a decision endorsed in May 2013). In addressing this primary concern, the chapter will consider the powers that ASIO is granted under the *Australian Security Intelligence Organisation (ASIO) Act* 2003, in particular ASIO's sweeping questioning and detention powers and the severe restrictions the Act imposes on suspects, and non-suspects, regarding disclosure of information about their questioning and detention by ASIO.[8] The ASIO Act's restrictions on disclosure of information will be considered with reference to the strict, and complementary, controls on disclosure of 'information' or 'national security information' in Commonwealth criminal and civil trials that are imposed by the *National Security Information (Criminal and Civil Proceedings) Act* 2004. The NSI Act, which, as will be seen, uses the ASIO Act's definition of what Australia's 'security' comprises, puts considerable obstacles in the way of the chances of a terrorism suspect receiving a fair trial. More importantly for this chapter, the NSI Act erects around terrorism cases an almost impenetrable shield of secrecy and lack of transparency, binds the processes for classifying and protecting information in obscure and unfathomable red (more correctly, invisible) tape, and effectively protects the political executive and national security agencies like ASIO from external, independent scrutiny.

In addition to these two acts, the chapter will briefly consider the Public Interest Disclosure Bill that was introduced into the Federal Parliament by Attorney-General Mark Dreyfus in March 2013. This Bill pretends, amongst other things, to make it easier to disclose and investigate wrongdoing and maladministration in the Commonwealth public sector. More simply, it will, according to Mr Dreyfus and its other proponents in the government, legalise public interest whistle-blowing. However, like the ASIO and NSI Acts, the Public Interest Disclosures Bill reverts to the default option of a smug but defensive presumption in favour of not disclosing much, if any, information about defence, security, counter-terrorism or anything else that could conceivably be linked to Australia's 'national security'. As with the ASIO and NSI Acts, the term 'national security' is circularly defined to include 'national security information' (or 'intelligence information') which is in turn defined to include 'national security'.

Together, these three Acts have the effect of creating a sort of three-sided hall of mirrors in which each Act's restrictions on the disclosure, and availability, of information are tightened as one Act reinforces the other in providing fewer and narrower avenues for access to and release of information in the conduct of terrorism investigations and any subsequent trials. Indeed, it seems that the three Acts are all predicated on the assumption that there can be no security without secrecy; in other words that, in effect, secrecy and security are to be equated with each other, and each reducible to the other. This is a very dangerous assumption to proceed on, not only in counter-terrorism cases but also in criminal cases of other sorts, if democracy, human rights and the rule of law are to have real, practical meaning and effect in this country, and especially in the way this country's criminal justice system operates.[9]

Whether or not the three Acts, individually or in conjunction, actually protect and strengthen Australia's national security in the 'war on terror' is also impossible to determine because of the unavailability of the type of information – that is, information which is comprehensive, independent and reliable – required by an average individual to enable them to make a well-informed assessment of the Acts' effectiveness in this area. Because of this troubling dearth of openness, transparency and accountability, it is simply not possible to reach the conclusion that the established legislation – namely, the ASIO and NSI Acts – must be effective because so far as we know Australia has not yet been the victim of a major or even minor terrorist attack.

The absence of evidence in support of the assumption that there is no security without secrecy admittedly does not constitute compelling grounds for rejecting it. More obviously, of course, absence of evidence delivers no compelling grounds for accepting the assumption. In light of this pervasive uncertainty, faith and trust in the integrity of Australia's political and criminal justice system, its traditions, history, the government, or even its politicians, is a possible recourse, but, if adopted, any faith would be blind and the trust largely unfounded. In other words, without accountability and transparency faith and trust are baseless except for the similarly groundless faith and trust that they are in the circumstances the most appropriate or realistic response. And, perhaps more to the point, without openness, transparency and accountability there can be no real security.

In light of the foregoing, it appears that there are a number of alternative ways of framing the chapter's title. Clearly, the most obvious alternative is 'Can there be security without transparency and accountability?' Other obvious contenders are 'Can there be security with transparency and accountability?' and, perhaps the most challenging of the possibilities but too easily dismissed as oxymoronic, 'Can there be security with secrecy but no transparency and accountability?' An affirmative answer to the latter alternative has been, and continues to be, the default option for Australian governments and the defence, intelligence, security and law enforcement departments, agencies and public servants they claim to oversee. This perhaps obscure and cryptic point will become clearer in the course of the following investigation of the counter-terrorism legislation.

The Australian Security Intelligence Organisation Legislation Amendment (Terrorism) Act 2003

The *Australian Security Intelligence Organisation Legislation Amendment (Terrorism) Act* 2003 (Cth) (sometimes referred to as the ASIO Amendment Act 2003, but hereafter simply and generally referred to as the ASIO Act) was introduced into the Commonwealth Parliament during 2003 and enacted later that year. It does not help that the original ASIO Act 1979 (Cth) was amended twice during 2003, but every effort will be made here to keep things as clear and straightforward as possible.[10]

One of the key amendments was the introduction of Part III, Division 3, 'Special powers relating to terrorism offences', which 'created a new system of warrants which, when issued, empower [ASIO] to question and detain individuals for the purposes of gathering intelligence about terrorism offences'.[11] The system of warrants is also referred to as the 'Special Powers Regime'. This regime is regarded as 'one of the most controversial pieces of legislation ever passed by the Commonwealth Parliament' because of the 'vesting of "policing" powers of questioning and detention in a domestic intelligence agency.'[12] Initially, a sunset clause was to have seen ASIO's special powers expire in 2006, but this was subsequently extended out to 2016 (affirmed in the ASIO Legislation Amendment Bill 2006). The amended ASIO Act 2003 extended the questioning period to 48 hours (from 24 hours) if an interpreter is required to be present at any stage of the interrogation of a suspect (or non-suspect). A person requiring an interpreter cannot be questioned for more than a total of 24, 32 or 40 hours 'unless the prescribed authority before whom the person was being questioned just before the duration of that questioning reached that total permits the questioning to continue'.[13] However, under the Special Powers a person can be detained for up to 168 hours (seven days), whether or not they need an interpreter.

It is important to be clear on the circumstances in which under the ASIO Act a person can be taken into custody, detained and questioned. The relevant Minister (that is, the Federal Attorney-General) can consent to a request from the Director General of ASIO for a questioning and detention warrant to be issued if he or she has reasonable grounds for believing that this will 'substantially assist the collection of intelligence that is important in relation to a terrorism offence' and 'that relying on other methods of collecting that intelligence would be ineffective'[14] Thus, a person can be detained without charge, and does not even have to be suspected of having committed any offence (terrorism or other) to be taken into custody and questioned in secret. While being interrogated, a person held in detention has to answer all questions and provide all the information or the 'record' or 'thing' requested of them. A detainee also has to prove that they do not have the information or record or thing requested. If the detainee is unable to do so and does not provide the information, record or thing requested they can be imprisoned for up to five years. A person can also be detained if there are reasonable grounds for believing that if they are not immediately taken into custody they could alert someone who is in the act of committing a terrorism offence that the offence is being investigated; that they might not come before the prescribed authority; or that they could 'destroy, damage or alter a record or thing the person may be requested in accordance with the warrant to produce'.[15]

The secrecy provisions are lengthy and incredibly detailed, but sections of them are worthy of some attention. These provisions are found in the *ASIO Legislation Amendment Act* 2003 (no. 143), Schedule 1, Part 4, 'Secrecy relating to warrants and questioning'. Before the expiry of a warrant, a person (known as the 'discloser') commits an offence if the 'discloser discloses information' and the information is about the issuing of the warrant, the content of the warrant or the questioning or detention of a person under the warrant and/or the information is 'operational information'. Operational information is information that ASIO has or had; a source of information that ASIO has or had (other than the person who is the subject of the warrant); or an ASIO operational capability, method or plan. Even in the two years after the expiry of a warrant, it is an offence for a discloser to disclose information when the information is operational information and/or the information has almost anything else to do with the warrant. In addition to these restrictions and prohibitions, what is known as 'strict liability' applies if the information is operational information, or is about the warrant or the questioning and detention of the person who is the subject of the warrant. It also applies if the discloser is the person who is the subject of the warrant, or is a lawyer acting for that person who was present during questioning or was otherwise involved in representing the person and knew something about the warrant and how they were treated.[16]

The Special Powers Regime has a tightly limited provision for a person who is questioned and/or detained under a warrant to contact a lawyer of his or her own choice but the prescribed authority can impose further strict controls on this contact. If, for example, the prescribed authority is satisfied that contact with the lawyer of the person's choice may lead to the destruction or damaging of a thing or record associated with the warrant, he or she can limit or even prevent contact with the lawyer. And, as the Law Council of Australia points out, the Special Powers enable a person under a warrant to be questioned without a lawyer of the person's choice being present. The prescribed authority can also ask for the removal of the lawyer during questioning if he or she believes the lawyer is being unduly disruptive. In addition, 'Section 34L of the ASIO Act compels a person named in a warrant to give information and items [thing or record] to ASIO regardless of whether doing so might tend to incriminate the person or make them liable to a penalty.'[17]

The *National Security Information Act*, which will be considered further below, also imposes restrictions on a lawyer's access to relevant information. These reinforce and complement the restrictions contained in the ASIO Act. While there is not the scope here to consider the NSI Act's restrictions on a lawyer's access to information in great detail, the restrictions imposed by the Act on a defendant's choice of a legal representative are nevertheless relevant and worthy of some attention. These restrictions are contained in section 39 of the NSI Act, 'Security clearances required in federal criminal proceedings'. This section deals with a situation in which a defendant's legal representative, or person assisting the legal representative, has been notified by the Secretary of the Attorney-General's Department that it is probable that in the proceeding a disclosure of information which is likely to prejudice national security will be made. When thus notified, a person 'may apply' for a security clearance 'at the level considered appropriate by the Secretary in relation to the information [likely to be disclosed in the proceeding]'.[18]

The level of security clearance required by a legal representative is calibrated to match the highest level of classification of the NSI information that is likely to be disclosed. Classifications of NSI information range from 'restricted', followed by 'confidential', up to 'secret' and finally 'top secret'. So if 'secret' is the highest NSI classification for the information likely to be disclosed then a 'secret' level security clearance is required by the legal representative. The process of classifying information, and of determining the level of its classification, is clouded in secrecy and is evidently a completely arbitrary one; no light at all is thrown on the process by the Act itself, including its accompanying Requirements and Regulations or by the Practitioner's Guide. Secrecy and arbitrariness accordingly also surround the process of setting the level of and issuing a security clearance. Nevertheless, as the NSI Act Practitioner's Guide reassuringly points out, 'The security clearance process is conducted at arm's length from the agencies involved in prosecutions.'[19]

But what, after all, is 'information', what is 'national security information', what are 'security' and 'national security', and what is national security information, specifically, that which is 'likely to prejudice national security'? The section below, which considers the NSI Act and its relationship with the ASIO Act, attempts to cast some light on these unnecessarily obscure terms and the phenomena they denote. This is not as easy as it would first seem, because attempting to cast light involves entering another hall of mirrors.

The National Security Information (Criminal and Civil Proceedings) Act 2004

The NSI Act and the ASIO Act together set the conditions under which information in counter-terrorism cases can be accessed and used by lawyers, journalists, members of the public or any other interested parties. The object of the NSI Act is to prevent the disclosure in federal criminal or civil proceedings of information that is likely to prejudice national security 'except to the extent that preventing disclosure would seriously interfere with the administration of justice.'[20] In defining 'information' the NSI Act defers to the Commonwealth Criminal Code. In the Code (subsection 90.1(1)), information is defined as meaning 'information of any kind, whether true or false and whether in material form or not, and includes a) an opinion, and b) a report of a conversation'.[21] The NSI Act supplements this already far-reaching and all-encompassing definition with the phrase 'whether or not in the public domain'.

Thus, in the end, information can be very nearly anything and the term is accordingly vacuous and meaningless. But, the point is of course that the breadth, meaninglessness and vacuousness of the term provide the government, and ASIO, with an almost impenetrable and unfathomable legislative screen for hiding information and tightly controlling its use and disclosure, even in circumstances where this is prejudicial to a terrorism suspect's chance of receiving a fair trial. Indeed, non-disclosure

of any information by anyone seems very much to be the preferred option. Not only does this prejudice the chance of a fair
trial for a suspect, it is also completely prejudicial to democratic
accountability and transparency. The definition of 'national
security information' provided by the Act, which is considered
below, does not improve the situation. Before looking at this
definition, however, the meaning of 'national security' and the
other terms contained in it first have to be considered.

As the Act's Practitioner's Guide redundantly points out,
'The meaning of "national security" is central to the operation of the NSI Act, Regulations and Requirements.'[22] In the
Act (section 8) 'national security means Australia's defence,
security, international relations or law enforcement interests.'
The meanings of these other terms, which are defined in turn,
make national security even broader and more inclusive than
it already is. 'Law enforcement interests' are defined to include
foreign and security intelligence, and the technologies and
methods used in its collection, analysis and security, within its
ambit. These interests have been included in the definition 'to
ensure that law enforcement information which is connected
to national security ... is not excluded from protection under
the NSI Act'.[23] The Act adopts the same definition of 'security'
as that contained in section 4 of the ASIO Act 1979, where
security means the protection of Australia and Australians
from espionage, sabotage, politically motivated violence and
the promotion of communal violence, attacks on the country's 'defence system' and foreign interference, whether these
are 'directed from, or committed within, Australia or not'. To
this sweeping definition is added 'the carrying out of Australia's
responsibilities to any foreign country' in relation to any of
these matters.[24]

Not surprisingly, in addition to defining 'national security' (and the various terms other than 'defence' embedded in it) and 'information', the NSI Act defines 'national security information' to be a sort of supplement to the definitions of these other two terms, ensuring that each is inseparably tied to the other.[25] Building on the object of the Act, 'national security information' is information that either 'relates to national security' or 'the disclosure of which may affect national security.' 'Relates to' and 'may affect' are not further defined or explained. Nevertheless, given the broad meaning of 'national security' and 'information', almost any conceivable information (even that which is inconceivable or non-information) either actually or potentially relates to or affects national security. However, the pièce de résistance in the NSI Act lexicography is 'prejudicial to national security', the definition of which is so utterly circular as to mean almost nothing (and, therefore, nearly everything). The meaning of this term is provided in section 17, where it is defined thus: '1) A disclosure of information is likely to prejudice national security if there is a real, and not merely a remote, possibility that the disclosure will prejudice national security.'[26]

Despite the evident meaninglessness, vacuousness and circularity of these terms they can have very important and very serious effects for a defendant when invoked in terrorism trials. Section 24 of the NSI Act requires the Attorney-General to be notified if the information or its disclosure relates to or may affect national security. Where the Attorney-General determines that disclosure of the information would prejudice national security, he or she issues a non-disclosure certificate to the court (section 26). It is not clear how such a determination is arrived at by the Attorney-General.

In any event, there are different sorts of certificates that can be issued by the Attorney-General if he or she has decided that information prejudicial to national security is likely to be disclosed in criminal (or civil) proceedings. A criminal non-disclosure certificate is issued when the Attorney-General has been notified under section 24 or subsection 25(6) that information relating to, or which could affect, national security will be disclosed by a party to the proceeding or a witness, and he or she believes that the information is likely to prejudice national security. The Attorney-General issues a criminal witness exclusion certificate when he or she has been notified under section 24 or subsection 25(6), or expects 'that a person whom the prosecutor or defendant intends to call as a witness may disclose information by his or her presence' and believes that this information is likely to be prejudicial to national security.[27]

Naturally, a defendant can appeal against the issuing of a criminal non-disclosure or witness exclusion certificate. However, 'the court is required to give greatest weight to the question of "the risk of prejudice to national security" rather than to the needs and rights of the accused.'[28] This is consistent with other aspects of the NSI Act and, as seen above, of the ASIO Act. Worryingly, the new Public Interest Disclosure Bill also shares some of the same aspects.

Public Interest Disclosure Bill

As was noted at the beginning of this chapter, in March 2013 Attorney-General Mark Dreyfus announced that the Public Interest Disclosure Bill, under which public sector whistle-blowers will have more protection, had been introduced to Parliament. According to Mr Dreyfus, the Bill 'reaffirms the

Government's commitment to a culture of disclosure in the Australian public sector'. It includes a framework for the investigation of public interest disclosures, whistle-blower protections and sets out circumstances in which disclosures can be made outside government. The Attorney-General also pointed out that 'Open and transparent government is a key feature of a strong democracy and this bill, along with our reforms to FOI laws, will help build and maintain that culture.'[29]

The objects of the Bill are all highly laudable: promoting the integrity and accountability of the Commonwealth public sector; encouraging and facilitating the making of public interest disclosures by public officials; ensuring that public officials who make such disclosures are supported and protected from adverse consequences that may arise from the disclosures; and ensuring that disclosures are properly investigated and dealt with.[30]

However, these objects have pretty strict limits, which are to be found scattered at various points through the Act. For example, it is noted in Division 2, section 26 in which, among other things, 'public interest disclosures' are defined (this definition runs for several pages) that the limitations which should be taken into account in making disclosures are 'designated publication restrictions' and the need to protect 'intelligence information'. Among the several meanings of 'designated publication restriction' is an order under sections 31 or 38L of the NSI Act dealing respectively with non-disclosure certificate and witness exclusion certificate hearings in federal criminal proceedings and civil non-disclosure certificate and civil witness exclusion certificate hearings in civil proceedings. Included in 'intelligence information' is information identifying 'a person as being, or having been, an agent or member of the staff (however described) of the Australian Secret Intelligence

Service or the Australian Security Intelligence Organisation'.[31]

Intelligence information also includes 'sensitive law enforcement information', which is identical in meaning to that of 'law enforcement interests', included in the NSI Act's definition of national security. Sensitive law enforcement information and law enforcement interests both comprise, among other things, foreign and security intelligence, and the technologies and methods used in its collection. Division 29, section 29 of the Public Interest Disclosure Bill defines and gives examples of different kinds of disclosable conduct (this also runs for several pages). Section 33 deals with 'Conduct connected with intelligence agencies'. There it is stipulated that:

> conduct is not disclosable conduct if it is: a) conduct
> that an intelligence agency engages in in the proper
> performance of its functions or the proper exercise of its
> powers; or b) conduct that a public official who belongs to
> an intelligence agency engages in for the purposes of the
> proper performance of its functions or the proper exercise
> of its powers.[32]

The Public Interest Disclosures Bill does not deal in detail with information or how it is to be protected, because these, as seen above, are already fully covered in the NSI Act, and in the ASIO Act.

The Public Interest Disclosure Bill passed largely unannounced into law in June 2013. It is a potentially important piece of legislation that seeks to protect from dismissal, retaliation or adverse costs decisions Commonwealth public sector whistle-blowers who disclose corruption, fraud and misconduct and other forms of serious wrongdoing. Unfortunately, however, whistle-blowing about federal politicians and intelligence agencies is not included in the Act. In other words, Australian incarnations of the likes of Edward Snowden and Bradley Manning would receive no protection.[33]

Conclusion

The secrecy surrounding information, national security information, security, national security, international relations and law enforcement interests is baffling, all-pervasive and largely impenetrable. Successive Australian governments have successively added to this secrecy and impenetrability. It is far less clear whether this has helped to make Australians more secure from the threat of terrorism. It is clear, however, that it has left them more vulnerable to the secret, clandestine and sometimes illegal activities of ASIO, which, surrounded in secrecy founded on sloppy, all-encompassing and unfathomable legislation, is subject to few if any requirements for openness, transparency and accountability. In the end, this can only lead to one conclusion: there really is no security in secrecy.

1   I. Cobain and R. Norton-Taylor, 'Files that may shed light on colonial crimes still kept secret by UK', *Guardian Weekly*, 26 April 2013, last accessed 23 July 2013 <www.guardian.co.uk/uk/2013/apr/26/national-archives-colonial-documents-secret>. The files relate to events in the final years of the British empire (generally the late 1950s, early 1960s) and deal, among other things, with the Mau Mau insurgency in Kenya.
2   *R v Ul-Haque* [2007] NSWSC 1251, available at <www.lawlink.nsw.gov.au/scjudgments/2007nswsc.nsf/aef73009028d6777ca25673900081e8d/d9a9080227820bddca257389007c91e4?OpenDocument> (last accessed 18 July 2013).
3   N. O'Brien, 'Share intelligence or repeat Ul-Haque debacle', *The*

Australian, 28 February 2008.

4   The NSW Court of Criminal Appeal quashed Lodhi's appeal against his conviction, a ruling subsequently upheld by the High Court of Australia.

5   Inspector General of Intelligence and Security, *Report of Inquiry into Actions taken by ASIO in 2003 in Respect of Mr Izhar Ul-Haque and Related Matters*, available at <www.igis.gov.au/inquiries/docs/ul_haque_asio_2003.pdf> (last accessed 18 July 2013).

6   R. Pollard, 'Israel denies "Prisoner X" Zygier was in contact with ASIO', *Sydney Morning Herald*, 20 February 2013; T. Allard, 'Israeli intelligence told Australia Zygier was in jail', *Sydney Morning Herald*, 23–24 February 2013; T. Bormann, 'Prisoner X sabotaged Mossad operation', *Lateline*, ABC TV, 7 May 2013; M. Nadin, 'Ben Zygier was accused of treason after compromising a Mossad operation', *The Australian*, 8 May 2013.

7   G. Williams, 'The laws that erode who we are', *Sydney Morning Herald*, 10 September 2011.

8   It could be argued that ASIO has been misnamed and that it should have instead been called the Australian Intelligence Security Organisation. Even though this would have more accurately reflected what are evidently ASIO's overriding purposes and objectives, namely the security of intelligence, it would have produced an acronym (AISO) that doesn't roll off the tongue nearly as easily as 'ASIO' does.

9   Some of these issues are considered, from a prosecutor's point of view, in Chris Craigie (former Commonwealth Director of Public Prosecutions), 'Management of Lengthy and Complex Counter Terrorism Trials: An Australian Prosecutor's Perspective', Criminal Justice in Australia and New Zealand: Issues and Challenges for Judicial Administration Conference, 8 September 2011, available at <www.cdpp.gov.au/Director/Speeches/20110908cc-Management-of-lengthy-and-complex-counter-terrorism-trials.aspx> (last accessed 18 July 2013). For a public defender's perspective, see Dina Yehia, '"Being Alert and Alarmed When Acting for Those Accused of Terrorism Offences": Consideration of Areas of Legal and Practical Difficulties', Public Defenders Annual Criminal Law Conference, 27–28 March 2010, available at <www.publicdefenders.lawlink.nsw.gov.au/agdbasev7wr/pdo/documents/pdf/terrorismlaws.pdf> (last accessed 18 July 2013).

10 The first of these is the *ASIO Legislation Amendment (Terrorism) Act* 2003, no. 77 which was assented to on 22 July, available at www.

comlaw.gov.au/Details/C2004A01162/ (last accessed 18 July 2013). The second is the *ASIO Legislation Amendment Act* 2003, no. 143, assented to on 17 December, available at <www.comlaw.gov.au/ Details/C2004A01228> (last accessed 18 July 2013). It is important to realise that acts like the ASIO Act are always subject to further amendment. Thus, on 5 July 2011 then Attorney-General Robert McClelland proudly announced the passage of the Intelligence Services Legislation Amendment Bill through Parliament. Among other things, this Act amended the ASIO Act (it also amended the *Intelligence Services Act* 2001 and the *Criminal Code Act* 1995) to align the meaning of 'foreign intelligence' in the ASIO Act with the meaning in other acts and to clarify that ASIO computer access warrants authorise ASIO to access data held in a target computer at any time during the life of the warrant. The former of these amendments expands the criteria enabling ASIO to collect foreign intelligence to include Australia's national security, foreign relations and national economic well-being. It also redefines 'foreign power' to become the nebulous and wide-ranging 'people, organisations and governments outside Australia': see B. Keane, 'New powers mean ASIO could spy on WikiLeaks', *Crikey*, 20 May 2011, last accessed 23 July 2013 <www.crikey.com.au/2011/05/18/new-powers-mean-asio-could-spy-on-wikileaks/>. In March of the same year, as Keane reports, the smooth passage of the *Telecommunications Interception and Intelligence Services Legislation Amendment Act* through both Houses of the Federal Parliament greatly expanded ASIO's power to share information from wiretaps and computer access with other agencies such as ASIS

11 N. McGarrity, R. Gulati and G. Williams (2012) 'Sunset Clauses in Australian Anti-Terror Laws', *Adelaide Law Review*, vol. 33, p. 309.

12 McGarrity, Gulati and Williams (2012) 'Sunset Clauses in Australian Anti-Terror Laws', pp. 312–313.

13 *ASIO Legislation Amendment Act* 2003 (no. 143), section 34HB, 'Time for questioning through interpreter'.

14 *ASIO Legislation Amendment (Terrorism) Act* 2003 (no. 77), section 34C, 'Requesting warrants'.

15 *ASIO Legislation Amendment (Terrorism) Act* 2003 (no. 77), section 34C. At about 5 pm on 14 May 2013 (the same day that the 2013–14 Federal Budget was brought down), the government tabled the 2011–12 Report of the Independent National Security Legislation Monitor (declassified version) in the Federal Parliament. The Monitor (Mr Brett Walker QC) recommended that ASIO's

detention warrants be repealed, that the process for issuing ASIO questioning warrants be strengthened and that the control order and preventative detention order regime (not considered in this chapter) be scrapped. The Monitor's report is available at <www. dpmc.gov.au/inslm/docs/INSLM_Annual_Report_20121220.pdf> (last accessed 23 July 2013). The Monitor had handed his report to the government in December 2012. Also tabled in Parliament on 14 May was the Council of Australian Governments Review of Counter-Terrorism Legislation. The COAG Review is available at <www.coagctreview.gov.au/Report/Documents/Final Report.PDF> (last accessed 23 July 2013).

16   *ASIO Legislation Amendment Act* 2003 (no. 143), section 34VAA.

17   Law Council of Australia, 'Anti-terrorism reform project: a consolidation of the Law Council of Australia's advocacy in relation to Australia's anti-terrorism measures', June 2012, p. 98, last accessed 23 July 2013 <www1.lawcouncil.asn.au/lawcouncil/images/ LCA-PDF/a-z-docs/Anti-TerrorismReformProjectNov08.pdf>.

18   *National Security Information (Criminal and Civil Proceedings) Act* 2004 (no. 150) as amended (this compilation including amendments up to Act no. 127 of 2010), available at <www.comlaw. gov.au/Details/C2011C00375/> (last accessed 18 July 2013).

19   NSI Act Practitioner's Guide, p. 29. This is a claim which, in the absence of evidence of any sort, is neither verifiable nor falsifiable.

20   NSI Act, section 3, 'Object of this Act'. There is no explanation in the Act itself, or in the Practitioner's Guide, as to exactly what 'seriously interfere with the administration of justice' means. Evidently, it is a secret.

21   This definition of information was inserted into the Criminal Code by the *Criminal Code Amendment (Espionage and Related Matters) Act* 2002 (Act no. 91 of 2002, as amended), available at <www. comlaw.gov.au/Details/C2004A01028/> (last accessed 18 July 2013).

22   NSI Act Practitioner's Guide, p. 10.

23   NSI Act Practitioner's Guide, p. 10

24   ASIO Act 1979, section 4.

25   This is not reflected in the order in which the terms appear and are defined in the Act.

26   NSI Act, s. 17. The second part of the definition is as follows: '2. The contravention of a requirement is likely to prejudice national security if there is a real, not merely a remote, possibility that the contravention will prejudice national security.' In the absence of

any further explanation, either in the Act itself or the Practitioner's Guide, it has to be assumed that 'requirement' refers to something contained in the Requirements for the Protection of National Security Information in Federal Criminal Proceedings and Civil Proceedings (otherwise known as the NSI Requirements).

27 NSI Act Practitioner's Guide, p. 17. For more on the NSI Act, including discussion of equivalent legislation in overseas jurisdictions, its provisions for closed court hearings and the issuing of certificates in civil proceedings, see Mark Rix, 2011, 'Counter-terrorism and Information: The NSI Act, Fair Trials, and Open, Accountable Government', *Continuum: Journal of Media and Cultural Studies*, vol. 25, no. 2, pp. 285–97.

28 International Commission of Jurists (ICJ), *Assessing Damage, Urging Action: Report of the Eminent Jurists Panel on Terrorism, Counter-terrorism and Human Rights*, available at <www.un.org/en/sc/ctc/specialmeetings/2011/docs/icj/icj-2009-ejp-report.pdf> (last accessed 18 July 2013). The EJP cites subsection 31(8) of the NSI Act.

29 Mark Dreyfus, 'Whistleblower protection introduced to Parliament', media release, 21 March 2103, available at <www.attorneygeneral.gov.au/Mediareleases/Pages/2013/First quarter/21March2013-Whistleblowerprotectionintroducedtoparliament.aspx> (last accessed 18 July 2013).

30 Public Interest Disclosure Bill (first reading), 2013, Division 2, 'Objects', available at <parlinfo.aph.gov.au/parlInfo/download/legislation/bills/r5027_first-reps/toc_pdf/13089b01.pdf;fileType=application%2Fpdf - search="legislation/bills/r5027_first-reps/0000">. In Division 3, sections 69 and 70 there is a lengthy list of the office holders who are considered to be public officials, and the agency to which they belong. Curiously, but not surprisingly, the Prime Minister, Speaker of the House of Representatives and ministers, among others, are omitted from the list. This means that 'public servants who blow the whistle on wrongdoing by politicians, including concerns about corruption or bribery, would not be protected under the Bill': see M. Knott, 2013, 'Labor's whistleblower bill just window dressing without change', *Crikey*, 26 March 2013, last accessed 23 July 2013 <www.crikey.com.au/2013/03/26/labors-whistleblower-bill-just-window-dressing-without-an-overhaul/>.

31 Public Interest Disclosure Bill (first reading) 2013, Division 2, 'Objects'. ASIS is Australia's foreign intelligence agency – more

correctly, Australia's overseas secret intelligence collection agency – and is even more secretive and invisible than ASIO.

32 Public Interest Disclosure Bill (first reading) 2013, Division 2, 'Objects'. Besides ASIO and ASIS, 'intelligence agency' means the Defence Imagery and Geospatial Organisation, the Defence Intelligence Organisation, the Defence Signals Directorate and the Office of National Assessments.

33 Suelette Dreyfus, 'Parliament did some work this week: whistleblower bill a milestone', *Crikey*, 28 June 2013, last accessed 23 July 2013 <www.crikey.com.au/2013/06/28/parliament-did-some-work-this-week-whistleblower-bill-a-milestone/>.

10

POWER WITHOUT RESPONSIBILITY?

Jessie Blackbourn

'There is no valid scrutiny of Australia's anti-terrorism laws.'

NOT TRUE. Australia's anti-terrorism laws have been subject to the same types of pre- and post-enactment scrutiny as all other criminal laws; they have been debated in Parliament, though perhaps not always as rigorously as might be hoped or expected.[1] They have been scrutinised by the courts during terrorism trials and reviewed by Parliamentary committees, in particular the Parliamentary Joint Committee on Intelligence and Security ('PJCIS') and the Parliamentary Joint Committee on ASIO, ASIS and DSD ('PJCAAD'), which it replaced. As well as these traditional forms of scrutiny, a number of individuals and organisations have also been asked to review a variety of aspects of Australia's anti-terrorism laws, in order to ensure public confidence in the government.

Certainly, since 9/11, many aspects of Australia's anti-terrorism laws have been criticised. Some opponents claim that longstanding, basic legal rights – such as the presumption of innocence, the right not to be detained without charge and the right to remain silent – have been steadily undermined.[2] As Canadian Professor Kent Roach observed, Australia has 'exceeded the United Kingdom, the United States, and Canada in the sheer number of new anti-terrorism laws that it has enacted since September 11, 2001. Australia's hyper-legislation strained the ability of the parliamentary opposition and civil society to keep up, let alone provide effective opposition to, the relentless legislative output.'[3] At the very least, it is necessary to ensure that legislation is balanced and fair and conforms to democratic values, including through various types of 'checks and balances' and independent oversight mechanisms to evaluate programs and performance.

Background

There have been seven distinctive reviews of Australia's anti-terrorism laws since those laws were enacted. In 2005, the PJCAAD examined the questioning and detention powers of ASIO.[4] Later that year, the Security Legislation Review Committee (the 'Sheller Committee') was established to review the first federal anti-terrorism laws ever enacted in Australia, those introduced after the 9/11 attacks on the United States.[5] This included the *Security Legislation Amendment (Terrorism) Act* 2002; the *Suppression of the Financing of Terrorism Act* 2002; the *Criminal Code Amendment (Suppression of Terrorist Bombings) Act* 2002; the *Border Security Legislation Amendment Act* 2002; the *Telecommunications Interception Legislation Amendment Act* 2002; and the *Criminal Code Amendment (Terrorism) Act* 2003.

In 2006, the PJCIS carried out a review of security and counter-terrorism legislation, in which it assessed a number of the same laws as the Sheller Committee, including those that dealt with the definition of terrorism, terrorism offences, border security, international terrorist activities involving explosive or lethal devices, and the financing of terrorism.[6] In the same year, then Attorney-General Philip Ruddock referred the updated sedition offences introduced into the Australian Criminal Code by the *Anti-Terrorism Act [No. 2]* 2005 to the Australian Law Reform Commission ('ALRC'). Those sedition laws made it an offence for a person to urge another person to overthrow by force or violence the Commonwealth government.[7] In 2007, the PJCIS published its third report, *Inquiry into the Proscription of 'Terrorist Organisations' under the Australian Criminal Code*, which examined a number of anti-terrorism measures relating to the listing of terrorist organisations, where the Attorney-General has a broad discretion to proscribe what is a 'terrorist organisation'.[8]

In 2008, retired New South Wales Supreme Court Judge John Clarke was commissioned by then Attorney-General, Robert McClelland to report on the particular case of Dr Mohamed Haneef (the 'Clarke Inquiry').[9] Dr Haneef was arrested, detained and charged with terrorism offences, but the charges were later withdrawn (see chapter 9). Finally, in 2010, a Counter-Terrorism Review Committee was established within the Council of Australian Governments ('COAG') to report on a number of Australia's federal and state anti-terrorism laws.[10] The Counter-Terrorism Review Committee submitted its review to COAG on 1 March 2013. The report was tabled in Parliament on 14 May 2013 by the Attorney-General.

All of these reviews appeared to provide Australia's anti-terrorism laws with a substantial measure of post-enactment scrutiny. However, they were not without their problems. These involved the comprehensiveness and consistency of the review process; the independence of the reviewers; and the ability to shape the debate and inform the government's counter-terrorism policy agenda. As noted by Professor George Williams:

> problems in the making of anti-terrorism laws can, to an
> extent, be remedied by efficient and effective processes
> of review. However, Australia's record in this regard is
> patchy and inconsistent. Even where reviews have been
> conducted, the level of political commitment to adopting
> their recommendations has been low. Findings of high-level,
> expert panels have been ignored or only implemented years
> later. The common thread of Australia's anti-terrorism laws
> is that they have been enacted in undue haste and reviewed
> and repaired some years down the track, or often not at all.[11]

Were the reviews comprehensive and consistent?

Not really. This outcome can be seen through an analysis of the number of laws that were reviewed, and the range of powers granted to the reviewers to carry out their examination and appraisal.

Overall, a total of 54 anti-terrorism laws have been enacted in Australia since 9/11, many of them highly controversial. Most of this legislative activity 'occurred under the prime ministerial watch of John Howard – on average a new anti-terror statute passed nearly every seven weeks until he was defeated.'[12] These domestic anti-terrorism laws introduced a variety of new terrorism-related offences into the Australian Criminal Code and amended other provisions of the Code, granting new powers to Australia's policing and security and intelligence organisations and altering traditional trial procedures and criminal justice norms. For instance, new legislation enabled ASIO to detain and question people in order to engage in an 'appropriate form of interrogation' for intelligence gathering on terrorist activities.[13] Another example is that of preventative detention, which allowed the Australian Federal Police (AFP) to target suspects who had not committed a crime or had any criminal involvement, take them into custody and detain them for a short period.[14] (Due to constitutional constraints, preventative detention was permissible for only 48 hours at federal level. State and territory legislation, however, enables a detention on the basis of reasonable suspicion to be extended for a period up to 14 days.)

Only a fraction of these expanded national security powers, including unparalleled powers of arrest and detention, have been subject to significant review. ASIO's questioning and detention powers, introduced by the *Australian Security Intelligence Organisation Legislation Amendment (Terrorism) Act* 2003, have been reviewed so far on only one occasion, by the PJCAAD in 2005.[15] In 2006, the Sheller Committee and the PJCIS reported on the *Security Legislation Amendment (Terrorism) Act* 2002; the *Border Security Legislation Amendment Act* 2002; the *Criminal Code Amendment (Suppression of Terrorist Bombings) Act* 2002; and the *Suppression of the Financing of Terrorism Act* 2002.[16] The Sheller Committee examined two further pieces of legislation: the *Telecommunications Interception Legislation Amendment Act* 2002 and the *Criminal Code Amendment (Terrorism) Act* 2003.[17] This last law has also been subject to review by COAG's Counter-Terrorism Review Committee.[18] Finally, both the ALRC and the COAG Counter-Terrorism Review Committee have reviewed different aspects of the *Anti-Terrorism Act [No. 2]* 2005. The ALRC looked at Schedule 7, which created sedition offences, and the COAG Counter-Terrorism Review

Committee examined the new control order and preventative detention order regimes introduced by the Act.[19]

The vast majority of Australia's anti-terrorism laws have, therefore, not been subject to any comprehensive form of post-enactment scrutiny. These include the laws which govern aviation and maritime security, money-laundering for terrorist purposes and national security information. And those laws that have been subject to scrutiny have not been reviewed in a continuing or periodic manner. The Sheller Committee, the ALRC, the Clarke Inquiry and the COAG Counter-Terrorism Review Committee were all established to carry out only one single review, on a particular aspect or a number of aspects of Australia's anti-terrorism laws. Once the reviewer submitted the report, the review process was terminated. Only the PJCIS has the ability to revisit its subject matter and report on more than one occasion, but only if the matter is referred to it by Parliament. So far, Parliament has failed to do so.

On the whole, an overall lack of consistency has been created by the different powers granted to each review under unique terms of reference. The Clarke Inquiry was different to the other reviews. It examined how one aspect of the anti-terrorism laws – the powers of arrest, detention and charge for terrorism offences under the *Crimes Act* 1914 – had been used in one particular case, that of Dr Haneef. Its terms of reference were narrow and unambiguous. It was required to examine 'any deficiencies in the relevant laws or administrative and operational procedures and arrangements of the Commonwealth and its agencies, including agency and interagency communication protocols and guidelines'.[20] All the other reviews have focused on the application of the laws more generally. They therefore contained similar but more open-ended terms of reference.

Reviewers were obliged to examine the 'operation, effectiveness and implications' of the laws.[21] To carry out those terms of reference, the reviewers required access to the relevant information. Unfortunately, not all of the reviewing bodies were granted the same powers of investigation. Access to information was, therefore, not equal amongst the reviewing bodies.

The Australian Law Reform Commission has perhaps the most opaque powers of all the reviewing organisations. The Act which governs the ALRC states it 'has power to do everything necessary or convenient to be done for, or in connection with, the performance of its functions'.[22] However, it does not assert whether this includes coercive information-gathering powers. As a Parliamentary committee, the PJCIS (and its predecessor, the PJCAAD) is granted some powers to obtain information and documents. However, this power is subject to a number of limitations. For instance, agency heads, agency members, the Inspector-General of Intelligence and Security (IGIS) and staff members of IGIS are exempt from being required to produce information or evidence.[23]

Similarly, the Clarke Inquiry had no identifiable powers of access to information. According to the Inquiry's report, witnesses could not be 'compelled to give evidence or produce documents'.[24] Likewise, the Sheller Committee was also absent of coercive information-gathering powers. It obtained its information by calling for and receiving written submissions, holding public hearings, and receiving background briefs from 'a number of Commonwealth and government departments and agencies involved in implementing the legislation under review'.[25] The COAG Counter-Terrorism Review Committee's terms of reference state that 'in conducting the Review, the Committee should provide for public submissions and public hearings'.[26]

Again, this Committee does not appear to hold any special coercive information-gathering powers.

Yet access to the relevant information is crucial to the provision of comprehensive and consistent review, particularly when only some of the anti-terrorism laws are subject to scrutiny. Without such information, the reviewers cannot provide a clear picture of the operation, effectiveness and implications of the Acts. At the same time, not all information gathered for the review may be publicly released. Some of it might be subject to secrecy provisions. It therefore becomes critical that the person appointed to carry out the review is considered credible, particularly in the absence of publicly available evidence supporting their review recommendations. The independence of the reviewer, and their ability to perform the functions of review without being unduly influenced by the government, pertains to that credibility.

How independent were the reviewers?

Some more so than others. The ALRC was perhaps the most independent of all the reviewing organisations. As a federal agency, the ALRC sits within the Attorney-General's department, but is independent from the government. The PJCAAD and the PJCIS were the least independent of all the reviewing bodies. The Committee comprises nine members, five of which must be members of the government. The Committees cannot, therefore, make any claim to be independent from the government. The three other reviewing organisations were substantially independent from the government, even if not legislatively so, like the ALRC.

The Sheller Committee, the Clarke Inquiry and the COAG

Counter-Terrorism Review Committee were all chaired by former judges. Judges, even retired judges, are by their very nature independent from the government. Australia's strict doctrine of the separation of powers ensures that this is the case. Judges were not the only members on the Sheller Committee and COAG Counter-Terrorism Review Committee panels. The majority of the members of the Sheller Committee were members of Australia's integrity branch. This ensured that they were truly independent from the government. The Committee comprised two representatives of the Law Council of Australia, the IGIS, the Privacy Commissioner, the Human Rights Commissioner and the Commonwealth Ombudsman. Only one of the eight committee members was appointed by the government – that was the Attorney-General's nominee.[27]

The COAG Counter-Terrorism Review Committee was chaired by Justice Whealy. The rest of the Committee was constituted of a retired county court judge, a member of the office of the Commonwealth Director of Public Prosecutions, the South Australian Ombudsman and two Assistant Commissioners of the AFP. Like the Sheller Committee, the persons appointed to the COAG Counter-Terrorism Review Committee ensured it maintained a considerable level of independence from the government.

'Independence' can, however, be conceived more broadly than simply whether the person carrying out the review is independent from the government whose laws are subject to review. A further condition of independence is the extent to which the person carrying out the review is influenced by the government in carrying out their reviewing functions, particularly in terms of who the reviewer reports to, and who decides what they can report on. These decisions have been kept very much in the hands of the government. For example, in determining the scope of its review, the Sheller Committee sought guidance from the government on whether only those laws listed in its terms of reference were open to review, or whether subsequent amendments to those laws should also be covered by the review. In this instance, Counsel for the Australian Government Solicitor opted for an expansive review: 'Counsel advised that so long as the review examined the original amendments (in the sense of noting that they had been replaced or amended), it could not be criticised if it took the sensible decision to review the current form of those amendments.'[28] While the Sheller Committee pointed out that 'this approach was obviously a sensible one', it was not one which the government was obliged to take. Concentrating the control of content within the reviewing body might ameliorate potential government restrictions on what can be subject to review.

However, the government retains substantial control over publication of the content of those reviews once they have been completed. All of the reviewers had similar restricted reporting requirements. None of them were allowed to publish their reports prior to submission to the government. Both the Sheller Committee and the Australian Law Reform Commission reported to the Attorney-General, who was then required to table those reports in Parliament within 15 sitting days. The COAG Counter-Terrorism Review Committee reported to COAG. The legislation governing the COAG Counter-Terrorism Review states that if a copy of that report is passed to the Attorney-General, then it must be tabled in Parliament within 15 sitting days.[29] The Clarke Inquiry also reported to the Attorney-General; however, there was no obligatory period within which the Attorney-General should make the report public. As a Parliamentary committee, the PJCIS reports to each House of the Parliament and to the responsible Minister.

This inability to report directly to Parliament or to release the report publicly is important. All of the reviewers were subject to secrecy provisions, which allowed the reports to have information redacted (edited or revised) prior to release. Prior to tabling the Sheller Committee's report in Parliament, the Attorney-General was allowed to

> remove information from the copy of the report if satisfied
> on the advice of the Director-General of Security or
> the Commissioner of the AFP that its inclusion may
> endanger a person's safety, or prejudice an investigation
> or prosecution or compromise the operational activities
> or methodologies of the Australian Security Intelligence
> Organisation (ASIO), Australian Secret Intelligence Service
> (ASIS), the Defence Signals Directorate (DSD) or the
> AFP.[30]

Former Attorney-General Robert McClelland clarified the secrecy provisions relative to the Clarke Inquiry. The inquiry 'will present a public report which, if necessary, may be supplemented by a confidential report'.[31] Finally, the PJCIS is prohibited from presenting a report to Parliament if it contains material which should not be publicly disclosed. This might include material that discloses

(a) the identity of a person who is or has been a staff
    member of ASIO or ASIS or an agent of ASIO, ASIS,
    DIGO or DSD; or

(b) any information from which the identity of such a
    person could reasonably be inferred; or

(c) operationally sensitive information or information that would or might prejudice:

(i) Australia's national security or the conduct of Australia's foreign relations; or

(ii) the performance by an agency of its functions.[32]

Undoubtedly, many of these disclosure restrictions are sensible and reasonable. For example, it would be highly detrimental to the proper functioning of a secret intelligence service to release publicly the names of its agents. However, when these disclosure restrictions are combined with a lack of independence from the government, as was the case with the PJCAAD and is the case with the PJCIS, the credibility of the reviewing body, and therefore the credibility of the review, suffers. The public must be able to trust that when a review makes recommendations – whether they propose winding back or ramping up the anti-terrorism laws – that those recommendations are based on sound evidence and that the person making those recommendations has not been manipulated, influenced, or unduly censored by the government. And while it can be argued that the Sheller Committee, ALRC review, Clarke Inquiry and COAG Counter-Terrorism Review Committee all attempted to establish a level of credibility to gain public trust, their insights and recommendations did not automatically or inevitably translate into a meaningful government response to their findings.

Did the reviews shape the government's counter-terrorism agenda?

Only to a very limited degree. It is worth remembering that, as Professor George Williams has stated, the enactment of a series of restrictive anti-terrorism laws creates

> new precedents, understandings, expectations and
> political conventions when it comes to the proper limits of
> government power and the role of the state in protecting
> human rights. Hence, despite their often exceptional
> nature, anti-terror measures are increasingly seen as normal
> rather than exceptional. This is due both to the passage of
> time and the fact that anti-terror strategies are now being
> copied in other areas of the law.[33]

While the PJCAAD had the most 'success' of all the post-enactment reviews in shaping the government's counter-terrorism
policy, it appears an outlier to all other reviews. The Committee made nineteen recommendations in its report on ASIO's
questioning and detention powers.[34] The Howard Coalition
government (1996–2007) agreed, or agreed in part, with twelve
of those recommendations and rejected only seven.[35] Those
recommendations were incorporated as amendments into the
Australian Security and Intelligence Organisation Act 1979. The
other five major reviews did not fare quite so well as that of the
PJCAAD.

In a combined response to the Sheller Committee's *Report of
the Security Legislation Review Committee* and the PJCIS *Review
of Security and Counter-Terrorism Legislation*, the Coalition
government stated that it supported in whole, in part, or in
principle, nineteen of the twenty-six recommendations made.
It 'noted' one, proposed 'further consideration' of another and
rejected five.[36] The Coalition government did not disagree with
any of the recommendations made a year later by the PJCIS
Inquiry into the Proscription of 'Terrorist Organisations' under the

Australian Criminal Code. The government supported six and 'noted' two of the recommendations.[37] The Coalition government's response to the ALRC's report on the sedition laws was even more positive. It supported all of the recommendations made.[38]

But this 'agreement' and 'support' did not translate into action. Though the Coalition government continued to make some changes to the anti-terrorism laws prior to its electoral defeat in 2007, it did so outside of the review process. It did not further implement any of the recommendations made by the Sheller Committee, the PJCIS or the ALRC.

The current Labor government has improved on the Coalition government's mediocre record of implementing review recommendations since its general election victory in 2007. The Clarke Inquiry into the case of Dr Haneef was the first anti-terrorism review commissioned by the new Labor government. The Inquiry made a number of recommendations, all of which were agreed to by the Labor government.[39] Instead of implementing the proposed reforms immediately, the government instigated a broad consultation on Australia's national security legislation. The outcome of that consultation was the enactment of the *National Security Legislation Amendment Act* 2010. That Act incorporated a number of the reforms proposed by the earlier reviews. But not all the recommendations previously 'agreed' to, or 'supported' by either the Coalition or the Labor governments were implemented.

One academic commentator has described the Labor government's approach to the implementation of anti-terrorism reforms as that of a 'lowest common denominator'.[40] In other words, where different reviews offered a variety of recommendations on a topical issue, the government tended to choose the one that proposed the least radical reform of the anti-terrorism laws. The government's response to recommendations on one aspect of the proscription regime highlights this approach.

The Attorney-General has the discretion to proscribe a terrorist organisation on the basis that it 'praises' a terrorist incident in cases where that praise might encourage a person to carry out a terrorist attack of their own.[41] The Sheller Committee made two recommendations on this issue. In the first instance, it proposed that the 'praise' element should be repealed.[42] As an alternative, it suggested clarifying the law to increase the risk level, so that rather than simply a 'risk' of action, there must be a 'substantial risk' of a person acting after hearing the praise.[43] In its report on the proscription of terrorist organisations, the PJCIS also considered the praise element.[44] Unlike the Sheller Committee, it did not recommend repeal, but it did propose that the government should raise the risk element to 'substantial'.[45] Faced with two options – repeal the measure in its entirety or modify the level of risk – the government opted to implement the lowest common denominator recommendation and amended the level of risk to 'substantial'.

Taken as a whole, both the Coalition and Labor governments have substantially ignored the recommendations of the major reviews of the anti-terrorism laws that they commissioned, despite initially asserting broad support for them. Against this trend, and somewhat surprisingly, in 2010 the Labor government established the office of Independent National Security Legislation Monitor, to provide independent, ongoing and comprehensive review of Australia's anti-terrorism laws.

Does the Independent Monitor offer a better model of anti-terrorism review?

Yes. But it's not perfect. It is too early to tell what role the Independent Monitor will play in the review of anti-terrorism laws. To date, the Monitor has only produced two reports. The first was published in Parliament in March 2012. It steered clear of making any direct recommendations. Instead, the inaugural Monitor, Bret Walker, focused on familiarising himself with the laws subject to review, the academic literature on the subject and the relevant case law. The Independent Monitor's second report was submitted to the Prime Minister in December 2012 and tabled in the Commonwealth Parliament on 14 May 2013. It is only after the government responds to the recommendations in this second report that it will be possible to assess whether the Monitor is able to shape the government's counter-terrorism agenda.

Nonetheless, the Independent Monitor has a number of advantages over the other reviewing bodies. The Monitor is governed by the *Independent National Security Legislation Monitor Act* 2010. This ensures that the Monitor has an official, ongoing mandate that sets out strict structures and guidelines, grants the Monitor a number of powers and provides for the independence of the review. This might make it harder for incumbent governments to ignore recommendations as was the case in earlier reviews. This is particularly relevant for current and future Labor governments, due to the fact that Labor established this additional mechanism to review and report on Australia's national security and anti-terrorism laws, including their compliance with international human rights obligations.

Unlike the earlier reviews, the *Independent National Security*

Legislation Monitor Act 2010 provides for the Monitor to undertake a more comprehensive review, including all of Australia's national security and anti-terrorism laws, as well as all other relevant laws that relate to the national security and anti-terrorism laws.[46] However, the Monitor is not required to review every law, every year. There is broad discretion within the Monitor's remit to choose which laws to subject to review. This could lead to a continued lack of scrutiny of some dimensions of the anti-terrorism laws. The inaugural Monitor has so far used this broad discretion to his advantage – he has examined some of Australia's most contentious and under-reviewed measures, including control orders, preventative detention orders and ASIO's questioning and detention warrants scheme. However, there is no guarantee that the next Monitor will adopt and replicate this same approach.

Interestingly, the Monitor is an office of continuing review. All earlier reviews provided only a snapshot of the operation, effectiveness and implications of the anti-terrorism laws at one period in time. In contrast, the Monitor is not restricted in the number of times that he or she may examine any aspect of the anti-terrorism laws. For example, while a first substantive report examined the ASIO questioning and detention powers and the control order and preventative detention regimes, the Monitor could examine these aspects of the laws all over again next year, in five years, or at any period of time of his (or a subsequent Monitor's) choosing.[47] This might allow the Monitor to identify shifting security trends or unintended legal implications in the employment of sweeping national security and anti-terrorism laws over a longer time period.

As well as reviewing the operation, effectiveness and implications of the anti-terrorism laws, the Monitor must also consider whether the legislation 'contains appropriate safeguards for protecting the rights of individuals; remains proportionate to any threat of terrorism or threat to national security, or both; and remains necessary'.[48] As a result, the Monitor's terms of reference offer a much broader remit for appraisal and evaluation than those of the other reviewing organisations. For instance, his first report stated 'in sum, many more Australians have been and are being killed by people they know at home than have been killed by terrorists. Lives lost by domestic murders are just as valuable as those lost by terrorism. The governmental and social resources deployed to deter, prevent and respond to domestic murders are dwarfed by those devoted to counter-terrorism. We do not sacrifice civil liberties because of the evil of domestic murders. Have they been too much infringed in confronting the scourge of terrorism?'[49]

Further, in order to aid the process of independent review, the Monitor has been granted a number of information-gathering powers not made available to some of the other reviewing bodies. The *Independent National Security Legislation Monitor Act* 2010 stipulates that the Monitor may hold a hearing and summon a person to attend. The Act further provides for a witness at a hearing to be required to take an oath or affirmation. More importantly, the Act states that the Monitor may 'request, by written notice, a person: (a) to give the Monitor the information referred to in the notice; or (b) to produce to the Monitor the documents or things referred to in the notice'.[50] Furthermore, the Act imposes penalties for failing to produce a document or thing or for failing to provide the information requested. The nature of these provisions helps to ensure that the Independent Monitor has access to the information required without being dependent on the goodwill of those from whom the information is requested.

At the same time, the Monitor is subject to the same types of secrecy provisions as the other reporting bodies. The Monitor cannot release a report that contains material which cannot be disclosed to the public. In spite of this, the Monitor does have one advantage over the earlier oversight organisations: the Monitor retains responsibility for censoring reports – such filtering is not externally imposed by the government. If it is necessary for the Monitor to censor some aspects of the report due to, for example, overriding national security concerns, the public can be assured that the declassified report is based on sound and complete evidence.

Finally, the Monitor benefits from being an office of independent oversight. The Monitor is governed by a law that, for the most part, ensures independence. The Monitor is appointed by the Governor-General on the advice of the Prime Minister, who must have consulted with the Leader of the Opposition of the House of Representatives. Though this consultation does not ensure that the Monitor receives total bipartisan support, it does make it difficult for the government to appoint a person who might be overtly sympathetic to the political party in power.

The Monitor has a number of advantages over the past reviewers. However, the office is not perfect. The Prime Minister may interfere with some aspects of the Monitor's review. The Monitor reports to the Prime Minister on an annual basis. The Prime Minister must table that report in Parliament within 15 sitting days of receipt. This year, the fifteenth sitting day was the same day as the federal budget was announced in Parliament. Former Prime Minister Julia Gillard could have chosen to table the Independent Monitor's report earlier; instead, she opted to release it on the last possible day, at a time when the attention of Parliament and the media was focused elsewhere. The Prime Minister may also ask the Monitor to carry out a special report (a 'report on reference') outside of the normal annual review procedure. The Prime Minister may also demand an interim report from the Monitor when carrying out a report on reference. The office of the Independent Monitor might be perceived to be more independent if it was not subject to moderation by the Prime Minister. To achieve this, reports could, for example, be tabled directly in Parliament.

So is there valid scrutiny of Australia's anti-terrorism laws?

Yes and no! A number of Australia's anti-terrorism laws have been the subject of a variety of anti-terrorism reviews. Those reviews have, for the most part, been detailed, considered, measured, and cognisant of the balance that must be found between the pressures of ensuring the security of the state and limiting excessive government overreach into civil liberties. However, the reviews were extremely limited; they were not comprehensive, they lacked consistency, and not all of them were independent from the government whose laws they were tasked to assess and evaluate.

Unfortunately, the government's response to those reviews has been underwhelming. The Coalition government responded meaningfully to only one of the reviews established during its term in office. It mostly agreed with – yet ignored – all the others. The Labor government has to some extent improved on the Coalition government's record of implementing reforms of the anti-terrorism laws. It initiated a major consultation on the anti-terrorism laws, but that resulted in a limited number of minor changes to the laws. It also established the office of Independent National Security Legislation Monitor.

Critically, the Monitor does fill some of the gaps in a number of issues and concerns regarding the operation and implications of Australia's national security and anti-terrorism laws. The Monitor can review every aspect of the legislation. He or she can have access to confidential information not available to Parliament or the public, and can question all relevant persons, including government ministers and members of the police, security and intelligence organisations. The Monitor can hold hearings and require persons to provide them with relevant information. Furthermore, penalties can apply to anyone who does not comply with the Monitor's requests.

Still, it is perhaps too early to ascertain whether the Monitor will be able to shape the government's counter-terrorism agenda. The Monitor's 2012 annual review provided rigorous scrutiny of the anti-terrorism laws. It recommended widespread reform of the laws, including repeal of the control order and preventative detention powers and narrowing of the definition of a 'terrorist act' in the criminal code. It is hoped that the Labor government will not ignore or marginalise the office of independent oversight that it created. However, future elections will likely cause a change in government. A new Liberal government might not feel so compelled to take on board the recommendations of a body that it did not establish and whose major remit is review of anti-terrorism laws enacted by past Liberal Coalition governments. Only time will tell whether the useful foundations and valuable start made in efforts to more effectively review Australia's national security and anti-terrorism laws will gain momentum and achieve credible levels of scrutiny and oversight, or whether such review mechanisms will be sidelined, watered down, obstructed or ignored.

1   See A. Lynch (2006) 'Legislating with Urgency – the Enactment of the Anti-Terrorism Act [No. 1] 2005', *Melbourne University Law Review*, vol. 30, pp. 747–81.

2   See D. Wright-Neville (2005), 'Fear and Loathing: Australia and Counter-Terrorism', *Real Instituto Elcano*, ARI no. 156.

3   K. Roach, cited in G. Williams, 'The laws that erode who we are', *Sydney Morning Herald*, 10 September 2011.

4   Parliamentary Joint Committee on ASIO, ASIS and DSD ('PJCAAD') (2005) *ASIO's Questioning and Detention Powers – Review of the Operation, Effectiveness and Implications of Division 3 of Part III in the Australian Security Intelligence Organisation Act 1979*, Commonwealth of Australia, Canberra.

5   Security Legislation Review Committee ('SLRC') (2006) *Report of the Security Legislation Review Committee*, Commonwealth of Australia, Canberra.

6   PJCIS (2006) *Review of Security and Counter-Terrorism Legislation*, Commonwealth of Australia, Canberra.

7   ALRC (2006) *Fighting Words: A Review of Sedition Laws in Australia* (ALRC Report 104), Commonwealth of Australia, Canberra.

8   PJCIS (2007) *Inquiry into the Proscription of 'Terrorist Organisations' under the Australian Criminal Code*, Commonwealth of Australia, Canberra.

9   J. Clarke QC (2008) *Report of the Clarke Inquiry into the Case of Dr Mohamed Haneef – Vol. I*, Commonwealth of Australia, Canberra.

10 See C. Merritt, and M. Paul, 'Call to rein in ASIO's powers in bid to soften terror tactics', *The Australian*, 15 May 2013, last accessed 23 July 2013 <www.theaustralian.com.au/national-affairs/defence/call-to-rein-in-asios-powers-in-bid-to-soften-terror-tactics/story-e6frg8yo-1226642567202>.

11 Williams, 'The laws that erode who we are'.

12 F. Farouque, 'Australia's terror laws surpass the US', *Sydney Morning Herald*, 23 July 2012.

13 See L. Burton, N. Garrity and G. Williams (2012) 'The Extraordinary Questioning and Detention Powers of the Australian Security Intelligence Organisation', *Melbourne University Law Review*, vol. 36, no. 2.

14 For a full list of the new anti-terrorism laws, see Williams (2011) 'A Decade of Australian Anti-Terror Laws', *Melbourne University Law Review*, vol. 35, pp. 1144–45, note 27.

15 PJCAAD (2005) *ASIO's Questioning and Detention Powers*.

16 SLRC (2006) *Report of the Security Legislation Review Committee*;

PJCIS (2006) *Review of Security and Counter-Terrorism Legislation.*

17 SLRC (2006) *Report of the Security Legislation Review Committee.*

18 COAG, *COAG Review of Counter-terrorism Legislation*, 'Counter-terrorism laws', available at <www.coagctreview.gov.au/ctlaws/Pages/default.aspx> (last accessed 19 July 2013).

19 ALRC (2006) *Fighting Words*; COAG, 'Counter-terrorism laws'.

20 Clarke QC (2008) *Report of the Clarke Inquiry into the Case of Dr Mohamed Haneef – Vol. 1.*

21 PJCAAD (2005) *ASIO's Questioning and Detention Powers*; SLRC (2006) *Report of the Security Legislation Review Committee*; PJCIS (2006) *Review of Security and Counter-Terrorism Legislation*; ALRC (2006) *Fighting Words*; PJCIS (2007) *Inquiry into the Proscription of 'Terrorist Organisations' under the Australian Criminal Code*; COAG (2011) 'Terms of Reference', p. 3.

22 *Australian Law Reform Commission Act* 1996, section 25.

23 *Intelligence Services Act* 2001, Schedule 1, Clause 2(4).

24 Clarke QC (2008) *Report of the Clarke Inquiry into the Case of Dr Mohamed Haneef – Vol. 1.*

25 SLRC (2006) *Report of the Security Legislation Review Committee.*

26 COAG (2011) 'Terms of Reference', p. 2.

27 SLRC (2006) *Report of the Security Legislation Review Committee*, p. 1.

28 SLRC (2006) *Report of the Security Legislation Review Committee*, p. 18.

29 *Australian Law Reform Commission Act* 1996, section 23; SLRC (2006) *Report of the Security Legislation Review Committee*, p. 19; *Anti-Terrorism Act [No. 2]* 2005, section 4.

30 SLRC (2006) *Report of the Security Legislation Review Committee*, p. 19

31 R. McClelland, 'Clarke Inquiry into the Haneef Case', media release, 14 March 2008, last accessed 23 July 2013 <robertmcclelland.com.au/2008/03/14/clarke-inquiry-into-the-haneef-case/>.

32 *Intelligence Services Act* 2001, Schedule 1, Clause 7.

33 G. Williams (2011) 'A Decade of Australian Anti-Terror Laws', p. 1138.

34 PJCAAD (2005) *ASIO's Questioning and Detention Powers*, pp. xiv–xvii.

35 Commonwealth Government (2006) *Government Response to Parliamentary Joint Committee on Intelligence and Security Report on the Operation, Effectiveness and Implications of Division 3 of Part III*

in the Australian Security Intelligence Organisation Act 1979, pp. 1–8.

36 Commonwealth Government (2006) *Government Response to Parliamentary Joint Committee on Intelligence and Security Review of Security and Counter-Terrorism Legislation.*

37 Commonwealth Government (2007) *Government Response to Parliamentary Joint Committee on Intelligence and Security Inquiry into the Proscription of 'Terrorist Organisations' under the Australian Criminal Code.*

38 See Commonwealth Government (2006) *Government Response to Australian Law Reform Commission, Fighting Words: A Review of Sedition Laws in Australia.*

39 Clarke QC (2008) *Report of the Clarke Inquiry into the Case of Dr Mohamed Haneef – Vol. 1.*

40 A. Lynch (2012) 'The Impact of Post-Enactment Review on Anti-Terrorism Laws: Four Jurisdictions Compared', *Journal of Legislative Studies*, vol. 18, p. 66.

41 Commonwealth Government (2008) *Government Response to the Clarke Inquiry into the Case of Dr Mohamed Haneef.*

42 Lynch (2012) 'The Impact of Post-Enactment Review on Anti-Terrorism Laws', p. 66.

43 Lynch (2012) 'The Impact of Post-Enactment Review on Anti-Terrorism Laws', p. 66.

44 Lynch (2012) 'The Impact of Post-Enactment Review on Anti-Terrorism Laws', p. 66.

45 Lynch (2012) 'The Impact of Post-Enactment Review on Anti-Terrorism Laws', p. 66.

46 *Independent National Security Legislation Monitor Act* 2010 (Cth), section 6(1).

47 B. Walker (2012) *Independent National Security Legislation Monitor Annual Report*, Commonwealth of Australia, Canberra.

48 *Independent National Security Legislation Monitor Act* 2010 (Cth), subsection 6(1)(b).

49 B. Walker (2011) *Independent National Security Legislation Monitor Annual Report*, p. 13.

50 *Independent National Security Legislation Monitor Act* 2010 (Cth), section 24(1).

11

POLITICISING INTELLIGENCE: INTELLIGENCE FAILURES AND POLITICS

Robert Imre

'*The Iraq War in 2003 was principally an intelligence failure.*'

IF ONLY IT WERE THAT EASY. In September of 2003 the United States sent in more than 100 000 troops with a 'coalition of the willing', which included Australia, joining over 200 000 further troops and associated private contractors and support people in an invasion of Iraq.[1] The beginning of this conflict was widely disputed, with claims ranging from a 'major intelligence failure' to a politicisation of the data surrounding the weapons capacity of the Iraqi armed forces.

For instance, in 2004, former chief US weapons inspector David Kay had testified to members of the United States Congress that large stocks of weapons – the weapons of mass destruction – in Iraq were unlikely to be found. Intelligence was 'almost all wrong' about Saddam's arsenal.[2] Kay isolated the intelligence sector as the main culprit. Others responded that the real problem was not thin or incomplete intelligence but a selective approach to information, driven by political interference. Politicisation of intelligence is a broad term that can be stripped down to a few core indicators:

> Almost all agree that it involves deliberately distorting analysis or judgements to favour a preferred line of thinking irrespective of evidence. Most consider 'classic' politicisation to be only that which occurs if products are forced to conform to policymakers' views. A number believe politicisation also results from management pressures to define and drive certain lines of analysis and substantive viewpoints. Still others believe that changes in tone or emphasis made during the normal review or coordination process, and limited means for expressing alternative viewpoints, also constitute forms of politicisation.[3]

Other claims and theories included the notion that the United States government had 'threatened' and bullied a number of countries into participation, that Iraq had dangerous levels of 'weapons of mass destruction' and that the 'good' states had stayed away from the war while the 'questionable' democracies had supported the United States endeavors. Examining the facts of the invasion leads us to a number of interesting conclusions and possibilities about how contemporary states use intelligence, and, indeed, what that intelligence is capable of, and quite a different picture emerges.

The failure of intelligence

Intelligence can 'fail' for any number of reasons, and these also depend on the context and interpretation.[4] For example, was it an intelligence failure to convince a number of countries of the necessity for war? Or would it have been considered a failure of intelligence not to convince anyone that the regime of Saddam Hussein needed to be toppled? In either case, people in the extensive bureaucracies of intelligence services are public servants, charged with the duties involved in gathering information about other, sometimes hostile, states. But to picture this as a set of people who are necessarily loyal to one state, competing with others who are necessarily loyal to another state, is quite obviously a simplistic interpretation.

Anyone who has had a job of any kind will know that there are rivalries inside the organisation that will have all sorts of consequences. Organisations do not function on the ability of individuals to all go in one direction. So there will be competition internally; there will be competition among various intelligence communities that seek to do similar work and there will be competition among individual colleagues that can potentially lead to disagreement, rivalry, turf wars and even sabotage. Various competitive possibilities, as well as other factors like clumsy coordination, worst-case thinking and/or shifting priorities, can all combine to limit the usefulness of various kinds of data and information. The human element involved in intelligence as a profession will always make it a murky and muddled practice.

In the case of Iraq, this practice was indeed muddled and murky, and in many cases it was made this way on purpose. Since there was so much riding on the capacity to invade Iraq, and pressure being placed on intelligence workers to come up with a defined argument that showed the necessity for invasion, much of the intelligence regarding Iraq and their military capacity was nuanced in such a way as to ensure that the George W. Bush presidency presented a public case for invasion. It was enough to sow the seeds of doubt in the minds of the international media, as well as the American public; Bush was able to go to war without detrimental effects on his administration's popularity ratings.[5] One way to ensure that an invasion of Iraq remained a viable option was to link the regime of Saddam Hussein with Al-Qaeda.

This also means that much of the data used to support the reasoning behind the invasion was gathered from dubious sources. The Head of the British Army, General Sir Mike Jackson, was famously quoted as saying 'What appeared to be gold in terms of intelligence turned out to be fool's gold, because it looked like gold, but it wasn't.' He was referring to the two Iraqi dissidents, one codenamed 'Curveball'[6] and another a defector named Muhammed Harith. Both sources gave the same story; that was seen as sufficient corroboration; and it was only after the actual war was conducted that both the CIA and MI6 deemed these two sources unreliable. In the rush to prove weapons of mass destruction were part of a large program initiated by Saddam Hussein, the intelligence services chose to believe the stories about 'mobile biological laboratories' used to create some kind of chemical weapon attack.[7] This can be construed as an intelligence failure in terms of believing the stories of unreliable sources, and in privileging one set of claims over another. Here it was clearly haste that caused governments to pick and choose those narratives that supported their preconceived views. Due diligence, and the care needed to assess such complex situations, was lost.

Two high-ranking dissident officials had consistently maintained, in the lead-up to the invasion, that there were no weapons of mass destruction, agreeing with the regular UN assessments and the reports led by the team of Hans Blix. They were Iraqi

Foreign Minister Naji Sabri and 'the jack of diamonds', Tahir Jalil Habbush Al-Tikriti – named as such on the deck of cards the United States intelligence service printed to rate the importance of the people serving in the government of Saddam Hussein.[8] Both sources consistently claimed there were no WMDs and that the reasoning behind the war was false. Who to believe? These conflicting reports and sources are normal in intelligence gathering operations. The only way to assess their validity is to continue gathering intelligence, continue gathering information, and continue to speak with operatives on the ground. Any kind of haste is detrimental to the development of a clear picture of what is happening in any given theatre of information gathering. This does not solve our problem, however, as time could quite simply run out if the wrong group of people were believed to be right!

Intelligence did not fail at all

Hans Blix, former head of the International Atomic Energy Agency (1981–1997), worked as a weapons inspector for the United Nations during the lead-up to the Iraq war, as Executive Chairman of the United Nations Monitoring, Verification and Inspection Commission. Hans Blix knew what was there and what was not there.[9] There was actually a great deal of data collected on Iraq, its military capacity, where it was going with possible future materials, whether or not it had done away with the chemical weapons it was supposed to do away with, and what sort of possible nuclear capacity the country might have. The question was always what to agree upon for a state under such scrutiny. Was it possible to have such chemical weapons using technologies purchased from leading chemical companies and major arms manufacturers? The obvious answer is no. The very presence of chemical weapons, of any kind of weapon of mass destruction, and of everything from small arms such as handguns to military grade weapons such as missiles, tanks, rocket launchers, and so on, meant that British, French, German, Russian and to some extent Chinese weapons manufacturers and chemical companies had to be involved in arms sales directly to the Iraqi government, and directly to Saddam Hussein's regime. This should not have surprised anyone. It was also the case that weapons manufacturers remain in regular contact with their own national bodies; it would be impossible to actually produce the weapons without the explicit knowledge of, for example, the British, French, German, Russian, and United States governments.

In terms of the role of the United Nations and Hans Blix, the Iraqi government made a fatal error, but not the one that the Bush administration commonly sought to convince people of. In Blix's account of the years leading up to the 2003 conflict, he regularly portrayed the Hussein regime as recalcitrant offenders who tried unsuccessfully to hide their weapons capabilities.[10] Blix's accounts have been verified over and over, and eventually led to the sanctions regime being imposed on Iraq, for continually failing to report weaponry, and playing the 'cat and mouse' game that Blix referred to in his book. The Iraqi tactic was designed to convey the possibility of strength to neighbouring countries, rather than hide actual weapons.

Blix repeatedly stated, in reports in the *Guardian* and in official reports to the United Nations during the years of 2002 and 2003, prior to the invasion of Iraq, that the Hussein regime did not have weapons of mass destruction, and had significantly reduced military capacities.[11] This view was borne out by the invading forces in 2003, when they found no such weapons, and saw that the Iraqi military was incapable of mounting any sort of challenge to the invading forces. As later reported:

> Blix has claimed in the past that inspectors had too little time to assess whether Saddam was concealing weapons of mass destruction, as the US and Britain believed. He said that, immediately before the 2003 US-led invasion, his inspectors checked around 30 sites said by British and US intelligence to contain weapons of mass destruction, but discovered little more than some old missile engines and a sheaf of nuclear documents.[12]

Perhaps one of the major problems with Iraq was that it had increasingly become a destabilising force in the region, and was seeking to make decisions independent of consultation with, and manipulation by, the larger powers. When political leaders rely on the support of external governments to prop them up, they will run in to serious difficulties negotiating their stay in power.[13] Furthermore, when Iraq went down this path, it needed to demonstrate that it was still a powerful state with a powerful military, in order to do away with possible challenges to regional authority by Iran or other rival states.[14] Engaging in the cat-and-mouse tactics in dealing with their own weapons, the Iraqi state played a dangerous game and eventually lost, even when Blix repeatedly assured the world that Iraq was simply not capable of the means to engage in such destructive tactics as the Bush regime claimed.

From this point of view, intelligence – if we see intelligence as information to inform decision-making – did not necessarily 'fail'. First, intelligence analysis should be viewed as an imperfect science. Second, a variety of contradictory information about the reality in Iraq was readily available: inspectors were talking to news outlets like CNN and the *Guardian* newspaper, with a great deal of information surrounding Saddam's limited weapons capabilities already quite public. For instance, in 2002 Scott Ritter, a UN weapons inspector in Iraq from 1991 to 1998, was reported as stating:

> I believe the primary problem at this point is one of accounting. Iraq has destroyed 90 to 95% of its weapons of mass destruction …We have to remember that this missing 5 to 10% doesn't necessarily constitute a threat. It doesn't even constitute a weapons programme. It constitutes bits and pieces of a weapons programme which, in its totality, doesn't amount to much, but which is still prohibited. Likewise, just because we can't account for it, doesn't mean Iraq retains it.[15]

The other major contention was that the intelligence about Iraq was heavily politicised, and as such there was a massive push to go to war. As Paul Pillar claimed, the US administration 'used intelligence not to inform decision-making, but to justify a decision already made'.[16] This seems to be the case, as a number of political leaders, including most prominently Tony Blair, Prime Minister of the United Kingdom, and George W. Bush, President of the United States, were able to lead their respective teams of advisors to present the view that it was an international imperative that this invasion occur. The evidence that we have on the push by the United States might tell us two different and conflating reasons that the United States and the George W. Bush administration wanted to see a regime change in Iraq.

First, the Bush regime, along with all of the advisors, including Colin Powell, Condoleezza Rice and Donald Rumsfeld, all believed that a change in regime would trigger further large-scale changes towards democratisation in the region.[17] Destroying a dictatorial regime seemed the right course of action, and was a starting point for the reasoning behind 'shaping' the data that the Bush administration was able to put together. Second, there appeared to be a prevailing view that the regime in Iraq was not only evil, but was also connected to terrorist organisations around the world.[18] The reasoning was that since terrorism was becoming a globalised movement that linked all sorts of tenuous groups and organisations, there needed to be a fundamental shift in how these organisations were dealt with. It was no longer to be dealt with in terms of single movements embedded in some form of national liberation movement, such as the Basque separatists or the IRA, but rather as a global movement that had developed as an anti-Western movement, linking up with various similar groups around the world. If a dictatorial regime such as the one in Iraq was dealing in the global (possibly illicit) weapons trade, then we had a situation in which they needed to be stopped. To complete this reasoning, one way to stop it was to then go to the 'source', take on a head of state and remove that head of state. The resulting 'democratic domino effect' would then ensue in the Middle East.[19]

The truth is somewhere in the middle, of course, and the complexities of all of this are quite difficult to disentangle. It would be impossible for example, to claim that North Korea's isolation allowed it to be part of this nexus of 'global terror', as it has nothing to do with any version of Islam, and always looks to China to bolster its hold on power. Yet North Korea was included in the famous speech by George W. Bush on 29 January 2002, as part of the 'axis of evil' looking to destabilise and eventually destroy the western world.[20] If we take the Bush administration at its word – that it genuinely believed this to be the case, and that Prime Minister Tony Blair also agreed that the western world was under threat from this vast conspiracy – then there is no intelligence failure, but rather an imperative by these world leaders to stop terrorism on a global scale, as well as dictatorial regimes that facilitate these terrorist movements.

What all of this is telling us is that there is a complex interaction between the intelligence community and political decision-makers. Iraq presents us with a particularly interesting, and dangerous, case to examine, since it cost us so much blood and treasure. At the heart of the 2003 Iraq controversy is whether intelligence shaped policy or policy shaped intelligence, or both. From what we have discussed in this chapter so far, it would appear that it is indeed both: it is possible to mount an argument that the Iraqi regime was indeed anti–United States foreign policy, and it is possible to see how world leaders would view the threat posed by Iraq as an existential one – that is to say, a danger to the very existence of the global world order. There were not, however, large stockpiles of weapons in Iraq, and that argument had to be constructed in a different way.[21] Or from another angle, as the Silberman-Robb Report noted, 'in ways both subtle and not-so-subtle, [intelligence] reports seemed to be "selling" intelligence — in order to keep its customers, or at least its first customer, interested.'[22]

The world is a better place without Saddam Hussein

In 2002 former Vice-President of the United States Dick Cheney claimed that Iraq was 'a better place without Saddam Hussein'.[23] This might be the case, as it might generally be better not to have any dictators in the world. But Dick Cheney was not concerned with making the world a better place, and neither were many members of the United States administration at the time. The concern was about a particular power balance and a reworking of the 'world order'.

As scholars of international relations are so fond of saying, states will act in their own best interests to ensure two main things. First, that relative gains are made regarding their own political and economic status in the world. And second, that if that cannot be effected, the status quo is maintained. Regime change in Iraq had long been seen to be an option to shore up the position of the United States in the global world order, not in terms of some grand scheme of exploitation, but rather as a way to mitigate conflicts around the world, and thus stop US involvement in them. Tony Blair has regularly stated that the Iraq war was the right thing to do and even went so far as to suggest that the recent civil war in Syria would have paled in comparison to the inevitable similar catastrophe awaiting Iraq if intervention had not happened in 2003.[24] This is a counterfactual we will never know.

This is why governments around the world can support dictatorships, since a known enemy, or even a predictable semi-stable ally, is far better than a national leader looking to change the status quo. A dictator in their 'own' territory is quite often supported by other nations if that dictator can be relied upon to be predictable. If that predictability starts to become suspect, it is at that point that other nations will have serious problems supporting the regime.[25] At the same time, others such as William Kristol and Robert Kagan have claimed that 'American hegemony is the only reliable defense against a breakdown of peace and international order.'[26]

So was Iraq becoming unpredictable? Was Iraq an imminent

threat? Was the case for military invasion a 'slam dunk'? Interestingly, in February 2001, Colin Powell had stated:

> I think it's important to point out that for the last 10
> years, the policy that the United Nations, the United States
> has been following, has succeeded in keeping Iraq from
> rebuilding to the level that it was before. It's an army that's
> only one-third its original size. And even though they may
> be pursuing weapons of mass destruction of all kinds, it is
> not clear how successful they have been. So to some extent,
> I think we ought to declare this a success. We have kept
> him [Saddam] contained, kept him in his box.[27]

Another interesting question is the exact nature of Saddam's relationship with the US, particularly during the earlier Reagan–Bush Sr. period. The public will never know any closely guarded secrets that Hussein might have had in his control, as he was summarily executed before he could stand trial. It would certainly make some attention-grabbing reading: how the Iraqi regime had dealt with its regional counterparts, and how various Western countries, including the US, had once provided its 'natural enemy' with aid and weapons. 'The Reagan Administration secretly decided to provide highly classified intelligence to Iraq in the spring of 1982 ... while also permitting the sale of American-made arms to Baghdad in a successful effort to help President Saddam Hussein avert imminent defeat in the war with Iran.'[28]

What has emerged is highly selective memory from Western leaders acting in their own self-interest, who then distorted various parts of the intelligence process and cherry-picked data to justify a war decision already made.

We can engage in other counterfactuals and ask if the intelligence was detailed enough to give us a good idea of alternative policy options. For example, if Saddam Hussein was a problem for oil companies and/or major western powers, is there a sum of money that could have been brought to the table to get rid of the entire Hussein family? What sort of intelligence would we have needed to gather to deliver amnesty for the Hussein family, remove them from power, and have them exiled in a neutral country? These are questions that will never be answered, but it bears thinking about when we discuss the value and nature of intelligence in matters of conflict. Intelligence gathering, collating data about hostile regimes, need to be comprehensive as well as flexible enough to accommodate rapidly changing conditions. In hindsight, banishment from Iraq might have been far preferable to the loss of lives and money by the international community.

The fifth estate: why the global media was so uncritical

In US President George W. Bush's famous press conference on 6 March 2003, the President made it a major point to continue to link the invasion of Iraq to the terrorist attacks on the World Trade Center and the Pentagon of 11 September 2001. A mostly scripted press conference in which the President had a set of names to call on, rather than taking spontaneous questions, left the press conference with very little room for criticism.[29] Indeed, the opening question was about his 'faith' and how 'it was guiding him' in his decision to invade Iraq.[30] It is highly relevant to question the actions of the media, especially the large media groups in the United States, since they removed the necessity for accuracy, or questions of nuance, regarding the intelligence gathering in the lead-up to the 2003 invasion of Iraq.

American journalists were wearing red, white and blue

ribbons on their lapels as they reported the news immediately following the 9/11 terrorist attacks, and this patriotism was evident in all of the news reporting for years to come. The George W. Bush presidency was counting on this to act as a kind of 'free pass' from US journalists, giving it the opportunity to achieve a kind of reworking of the global political order in the Middle East that went far beyond the source of the terrorist attacks and the origins of Al-Qaeda as a terrorist network. In fact, virtually immediately after the events of 9/11, private and then public statements from administration officials had begun to target the Hussein regime in Iraq, and regularly began to mention the need to use military force to achieve the objective of removing Hussein from power.

> Declassified documents show that Bush administration officials wanted Saddam Hussein out of Iraq and were ready to start a war in order to achieve it. Just hours after the 9/11 attacks, Secretary of Defense Donald Rumsfeld met in the Pentagon with Air Force General Richard Myers, then vice chairman of the Joint Chiefs of Staff, and other top aides. Notes taken by Rumsfeld aide Steve Cambone (and referred to pages 334 and 335 of the 9/11 Commission Report) show the secretary asked for the 'best info fast ... judge whether good enough [to] hit S.H. [Saddam Hussein] @ same time—not only UBL [Osama bin Laden].'[31]

Building up to the possibility of invasion in Iraq, there needed to be a real and clear set of reasons why it was to be done. Both Richard Perle and James Woolsey, acting as chief advisors to Donald Rumsfeld, were continually calling for invasion, continually stating that the Hussein regime had 'links' to

Al-Qaeda, and that if the Hussein regime had the capacity to garner 'weapons of mass destruction', then the United States was obliged to invade and stop the threat to world peace.[32] About two weeks before the Iraq invasion, Bush was also told by CIA Director George Tenet there 'was a "slam dunk case" that dictator Saddam Hussein had unconventional weapons'.[33] This message was clear, and coupled with the message was the security assessment stating that the Iraqi army was weakened through years of war with Iran as well as heavy sanctions from the international community. The expectation was that overthrowing the regime would be 'easy'.[34] Nonetheless, in reflecting on the ten-year anniversary of the invasion, Hans Blix noted that 'the most important lesson of the Iraq War, I think, has been that an overconfidence in military power has been replaced by an understanding that there are severe limitations on what can be achieved by military means.'[35]

The important point here is not that there was a vast conspiracy to destroy the Iraqi regime. It is twofold: that, first, there is always a broad variety of opinion around what the international order ought to be. And, second, that the intelligence leading up to the invasion of Iraq was presenting a diverse picture, with a number of clear facts that were ignored, and a number of other clear facts that were highlighted to demonstrate the need for invasion. The domestic media in the United States did not critique any of this, and decided to go along with the Bush administration's normative position, designed by Rumsfeld: that Iraq should be invaded because it was an evil regime, and the actual evidence was not so important.

The tipping point was the Colin Powell speech to the United Nations Security Council on 5 February 2003. Powell sought to garner international support for the invasion. He unequivocally stated that Saddam had to be toppled – the dictator had demonstrated non-compliance with Security Council resolutions – that Baghdad had a close working relationship with the Al-Qaeda network, that the immediate danger was based on a growing stockpile of offensive weaponry and that clandestine weapons arsenals were being produced and reproduced in Iraq.

> The issue before us is not how much time we are willing
> to give the inspectors to be frustrated by Iraqi obstruction.
> But how much longer are we willing to put up with Iraq's
> noncompliance before we, as a council, we, as the United
> Nations, say: 'Enough. Enough.' The gravity of this
> moment is matched by the gravity of the threat that Iraq's
> weapons of mass destruction pose to the world.[36]

Powell claimed his conclusions were based on 'solid evidence' and that the Iraq regime had both the capacity and inclination to use these warfare weapon systems. But the reality in 2003 was pointing to a much-weakened Iraqi regime with a declining infrastructure and with no biological (or chemical) weapons production. Iraq also did not have any nuclear weapons. In April 2004, Powell conceded that the intelligence information used to justify regime change in Iraq was inaccurate and 'appears not to be … that solid'.[37]

These allegations, the most serious, and the tipping point for convincing the international community, were found to be exaggerated claims at best. The subsequent Iraq Survey Group, creating what became known as the Duelfer Report, demonstrated that the weapons of mass destruction did not exist.[38] But the salient points remain in the report. There was an ambition in the Hussein regime to replace the destroyed and nullified biological and chemical weapons, as well as stated objectives and ambitions in Iraq for nuclear armaments.[39] As mentioned, David Kay made it clear that there was no arsenal in place in Iraq in 2003. Kay's claim was that intelligence was faulty. He is right to claim it was faulty in terms of the presence of weapons, but many in the Bush administration would say that the ambitions to replace the arsenal was reason enough for the removal of the Hussein regime.

Conclusion

Intelligence systems have not fallen apart, and we are not in danger of having a repeated set of calls to war, or terrorist activities rained down on us, as a result of failed intelligence. As long as governments around the world have people on the ground gathering information, and those people are talking to their respective governments, we will have plenty of information to dissect. And this is precisely why WikiLeaks does not present governments with a huge problem: while WikiLeaks is certainly circulating the specifics of classified information, a vast majority of that information involves work that we already know people are doing. Now we know the particular individuals involved who can present a danger to many operatives on the ground, but, ironically, the presence of Wikileaks as a database does not disrupt the status quo of international relations.

The notion that the Iraq war was premised on a failure of intelligence is a partial reading of the events that led up to the war. It is partly true that intelligence had incorrect information. But intelligence-gathering sources often have incorrect information, since their goal is to first gather information, and sort it out as things progress.

It is also the case that at all levels there is significant competition occurring, including between people acting as sources. Sources can often deliver misleading information, and it is a regular process to question these sources. Similarly, the politicisation of information is a regular occurrence in policy-making circles, and should be taken into account in any decision made about whether or not countries go to war. Intelligence data is not evidence. The two are not mutually exclusive, but they are certainly not the same thing. Data remains data, and facts remain facts, however, and our real question ought to be why citizens so easily followed political leaders into war.

In the case of Iraq, and the invasion in 2003, it was not driven by a failure of intelligence. It was instead driven by a predetermined conclusion that a number of political leaders took to their bureaucracies, demanding that their intelligence services produce enough material to justify an invasion. This is a comparatively easy thing to do, since most states have weapons, and most states will have some form of problematic relationship with other states. The fact that some of the sources lied, and that intelligence agencies as well as the domestic media in the United States were all so eager to believe in the justification for war, provided the perfect set of circumstances for the war to occur.

There is a complex dynamic between policy and intelligence, with both shaping each other in an intertwined relationship. Our problem for the future is how we will manage the policy–intelligence relationship and the machinery of analytical tradecraft as data-gathering abilities increase, secrecy provisions become more pronounced and various forms of politicisation pressure remain likely to continue. One possible solution is to reinforce standards of rigorous objectivity in intelligence judgments, as well as ensuring robust oversight and accountability mechanisms for the security sector, so as not to not rush into decisions to go to war, and to avoid the misuse of intelligence to validate predetermined political options. Thus we would avoid repeating the mistakes that were made in invading Iraq. Simultaneously, poor political decisions should never be allowed to be deflected by blaming intelligence estimates – which are known to be speculative and imperfect – with political leaders manoeuvring to avoid any responsibility by scapegoating the entire intelligence community.

1 There are a number of excellent chronicles of the 2003 invasion. For an easy to read version, see T. Ricks, (2006) *Fiasco: The American Adventure in Iraq*, Penguin, New York.

2 D. Kay, 'Transcript of David Kay testimony before Senate Armed Services Committee', Washington, DC, 28 January 2004.

3 R. Gates (1992) 'Guarding Against Politicization', *Studies in Intelligence*, vol. 36, no. 5, pp. 5–13.

4 A free download straight from the source can be found at <www.gpo.gov/fdsys/search/pagedetails. action?granuleId=&packageId=GPO-WMD&fromBrowse=true> (last accessed 19 July 2013).

5 Much of the media discussion here is taken from the transcript of the excellent PBS documentary *Buying the War*, originally aired 25 April 2007. Transcript available at <www.pbs.org/moyers/journal/ btw/transcript1.html> (last accessed 19 July 2013).

6 The whole story of 'Curveball' and the participation of the German government is documented at <www.spiegel.de/international/world/ the-real-story-of-curveball-how-german-intelligence-helped-justify- the-us-invasion-of-iraq-a-542840.html> (last accessed 19 July 2013).

7 P. Beaumont, A. Barnett and G. Hinsliff, 'Iraqi mobile labs nothing to do with germ warfare, report finds', *Guardian*, 15 June 2003.

8 A. La Guarida, 'US holds the ace but 13 are still wild', *Telegraph*, 15 December 2003.

9 Hans Blix (2004) *Disarming Iraq*, Pantheon Books, London.

10 Blix (2004) *Disarming Iraq*.

11 See 'Hans Blix's briefing to the security council', *Guardian*,

15 February 2003.

12 'Hans Blix: allies used "poor" intelligence ahead of Iraq invasion', *Guardian*, 28 July 2010.

13 R. Rotberg (2010) *When States Fail*, Princeton University Press, Princeton, NJ.

14 For more discussion of whether Iran has been the 'winner' of the 2003 Iraq war, also see H. al-Khoei, 'Did Iran really do so well out of the Iraq war?', *Guardian*, 30 August 2010.

15 'Even if Iraq managed to hide these weapons, what they are now hiding is harmless goo', *Guardian*, 19 September 2002, last accessed 23 July 2013 <www.guardian.co.uk/world/2002/sep/19/iraq. features11>.

16 P. Pillar (2006) 'Intelligence, Policy and the War in Iraq', *Foreign Affairs*, March/April, vol. 85, no. 2, pp. 16–17.

17 Several books have come out supporting this view. The best insight into this is given by Bob Woodward's 2004 *Plan of Attack*, Simon and Schuster, New York, which chronicles the invasion plans and reasons behind it.

18 See T. Karon, 'How close were Iraq and Al-Qaeda?', *Time*, 30 July 2003.

19 See S. Tanenhaus, 'The world: from Vietnam to Iraq; the rise and fall and rise of the domino theory', *New York Times*, 23 March 2003.

20 State of the Union address <georgewbush-whitehouse.archives.gov/news/releases/2002/01/print/20020129-11.html> (last accessed 19 July 2013).

21 The Duelfer Report, referenced here and discussed at the end of the chapter, is available at <www.gpo.gov/fdsys/search/pagedetails.action?granuleId=&packageId=GPO-DUELFERREPORT&fromBrowse=true> (last accessed 23 July 2013).

22 Silberman-Robb Report, also known as the *Report of the Commission on the Intelligence Capabilities of the United States Regarding Weapons of Mass Destruction*, 31 March 2005.

23 Woodward (2004) *Plan of Attack*.

24 Tony Blair has made the statement to BBC News and it can be accessed at <www.bbc.co.uk/news/uk-21841673> (last accessed 19 July 2013).

25 Rotberg (2010) *When States Fail*.

26 W. Kristol and R. Kagan (1996) 'Toward a Neo-Reaganite Foreign Policy', *Foreign Affairs*, vol. 75, July/August.

27 C. Powell, 2001, press briefing aboard aircraft en route to Cairo,

Egypt, 23 February 2001, available at <2001-2009.state.gov/secretary/former/powell/remarks/2001/931.htm> (last accessed 23 July).

28 S. Hersh, 'U.S. secretly gave aid to Iraq early in its war against Iran', *New York Times*, 26 January 1992, last accessed 23 July 2013 <www.nytimes.com/1992/01/26/world/us-secretly-gave-aid-to-iraq-early-in-its-war-against-iran.html?pagewanted=all&src=pm>.

29 George W. Bush at <georgewbush-whitehouse.archives.gov/news/releases/2003/03/20030306-8.html> (last accessed 19 July 2013).

30 'Bush, who became a born-again Christian at 40, is one of the most overtly religious leaders to occupy the White House, a fact which brings him much support in middle America': see E. MacAskill, 'George Bush: "God told me to end the tyranny in Iraq"', *Guardian*, 7 October 2005.

31 M. Isikoff, 'Building momentum for regime change: Rumsfeld's secret memos', *MSNBC News*, 16 February 2013.

32 Woodward (2004) *Plan of Attack*.

33 'Woodward: Tenet told Bush WMD case a "slam dunk"', *CNN*, 19 April 2004.

34 S. Page, 'Confronting Iraq', *USA Today*, 1 April 2003.

35 H. Blix, 'Hans Blix: Iraq War was a terrible mistake and violation of UN charter', *CNN*, 19 March 2013.

36 Full text of Colin Powell's speech, 5 February 2003, last accessed 23 July 2013 <www.guardian.co.uk/world/2003/feb/05/iraq.usa>.

37 Powell, cited in 'Powell admits Iraq evidence mistake', *BBC News*, 2 April 2004, last accessed 23 July 2013 <news.bbc.co.uk/2/hi/middle_east/3596033.stm>.

38 Full report at <www.gpo.gov/fdsys/pkg/GPO-DUELFERREPORT/content-detail.html> (last accessed 19 July 2013).

39 <www.gpo.gov/fdsys/pkg/GPO-DUELFERREPORT/content-detail.html> .

INDEX